The Training Space Ltd
22 Barnwell Court
Mawsley
NN14 1FG
United Kingdom
www.thetrainingspace.co.uk

Ordering Information:
Quantity sales. Special discounts are available on quantity purchases by corporations, associations, schools and others. For details, contact the publisher at the address above. Orders by trade bookstores and wholesalers.

Please contact:

The Training Space Ltd
Tel: (+44) 01536 410078
Email: enquiries@thetrainingspace.co.uk
Web: www.thetrainingspace.co.uk

Every effort has been made to obtain the necessary permissions with reference to copyright materials, both illustrative and quoted. We apologise for any omissions in this respect and will be pleased to make appropriate acknowledgements in any future editions.

Printed in the UK.

First edition.

ISBN 978-1-907581-93-9

Katja Ruge - Photographer
Ellie Hyde - Photographer
Sue Crowther - Editor

Designed by James Hunter, Lee Akers & Toby Stubbs
www.studiokaioti.com

Don't gobblefunk around with words.

The BFG
Roald Dahl

Good writing is clear thinking made visible.

William Wheeler
Journalist and Author

Acknowledgements

My thanks to the children who inspired this book by sharing their secrets of imagination and to the teachers who welcomed me into their classrooms to teach:

Rebecca Payne and Mel Astill – Boothville Primary School
Julia Havlickova, Luke Dix and Annabelle Curran – Pytchley Endowed Primary School
Lynn Newbery – Long Buckby Junior School

- Boothville Primary School
- Weldon C.E. Primary School
- Pytchley Endowed C.E. Primary School
- Kippax Ash Tree Primary School
- South End Junior School
- Lings Primary School
- The Grange School
- Woodford Halse C.E. Primary Academy
- Havelock Junior School
- Ashby Fields Primary School
- Weedon Bec Primary School
- Kilsby C.E. Primary School
- Falconers Hill Academy
- Falconers Hill Infant School
- St James Infant School
- Badby Primary School
- The Abbey C.E. Academy
- Braunston C.E. Primary School
- Danetre and Southbrook Learning Village
- Byfield Primary School
- Welton C.E. Academy
- The Parker E-ACT Academy
- Newnham Primary School
- Staverton CEVA Primary School
- Roade Primary School
- Barby C.E. Primary School
- Wollaston Primary School

Lashings of appreciation to Vicki Masters, Caroline Colledge & Elaine Wagg (Specialist Leaders in Education) for your collective thinking.

Stacks of appreciation to Christy Adetola, who couldn't pronounce a thing, and also to Kate Rawson for her diligent perseverance in the face of an almost impossible task.

A big bow to my own teachers, past and present, the much-loved staff at SS. Mary and John Catholic Primary School and St. Edmund Campion Catholic School, both in Birmingham. A special thank you to my patient mum for her gentle chipping and to my dad for 'knocking it into shape'.

Enormous amounts of gratitude for the challenging questions en route, in particular from Tom Clayton, Tammy Mitchell and Lindsey Smith.

Finally, an especially warm, heartfelt mention for the one who got it 'in the neck' the most...
Ian, my husband - for his honesty, help, but most of all his cuddles.

" You should write because you love the shape of stories and sentences and the creation of different words on a page. Writing comes from reading, and reading is the finest teacher of how to write. "

Annie Proulx

" Words create sentences; sentences create paragraphs; sometimes paragraphs quicken and begin to breathe. "

Stephen King

" All you have to do is write one true sentence. Write the truest sentence that you know. "

Ernest Hemingway

" When we are young, the words are scattered all around us. As they are assembled by experience, so also are we, sentence by sentence, until the story takes shape. "

Louise Erdrich

" This sentence has five words. Here are five more words. Five-word sentences are fine. But several together become monotonous. Listen to what is happening. The writing is getting boring. The sound of it drones. It's like a stuck record. The ear demands some variety. "

Now listen. I vary sentence length, and I create music. Music. The writing sings. It has a pleasant rhythm, a lilt, a harmony. I use short sentences. And I use sentences of medium length.

And sometimes, when I am certain the reader is rested, I will engage him with a sentence of considerable length, a sentence that burns with energy and builds with all the impetus of a crescendo, the roll of the drums, the crash of the cymbals - sounds that say listen to this, it is important.

Gary Provost

The Write Stuff

Transforming the Teaching of Writing

Jane Considine

The Training Space
Transforming teaching and learning

About The Author

Jane Considine is a teacher, author and education consultant. She is passionate about the teaching of reading and writing in primary schools. She has worked with hundreds of schools to help them drive up their standards of writing.

Jane is a very popular presenter and speaks to thousands of teachers in their schools and at conferences each year. Anybody who has witnessed Jane in action finds the experience hard to forget. Her effervescence, combined with her expert knowledge, is "practical, inspiring and motivating".

Creator of the Writing Rainbow, the Reading Rainbow and the EYFS Rainbow, her teaching systems and resources are used in thousands of schools all around the globe.

An avid member of the Twitterati, she is constantly Tweeting her musings. Originally from Birmingham, she now lives in Northamptonshire with her four children, three dogs, two goldfish and one husband.

Jane Considine

PS. She is a proud, active member of the #teachersquad.

Access 'The Write Stuff' online training at www.janeconsidine.com

Jane
Considine
Education

Thank you for your inspiration and challenging my thinking along the way.

- St Mary of Charity CEP School
- Welford, Sibbertoft and Sulby Endowed Primary School
- Swillington Primary School
- Herne CE (Aided) Junior School
- Long Buckby Infant School
- Boothville Primary School
- Great Creaton Primary School
- Weldon C.E. Primary School
- Kippax Ash Tree Primary School
- South End Junior School
- Lings Primary School
- The Grange School
- Woodford Halse C.E. Primary Academy
- Havelock Junior School
- Ashby Fields Primary School
- Weedon Bec Primary School
- Kilsby C.E. Primary School
- Falconers Hill Academy
- Falconers Hill Infant School
- Badby Primary School
- The Abbey C.E. Academy
- Braunston C.E. Primary School
- Danetre and Southbrook Learning Village
- Byfield Primary School
- Welton C.E. Academy
- The Parker E-ACT Academy
- Newnham Primary School
- Staverton CEVA Primary School
- Roade Primary School
- Barby C.E. Primary School
- Pytchley Endowed Primary School
- Lady Elizabeth Hastings C.E. Primary School
- Finedon Mulso C.E. Junior School
- Loddington Primary School
- Ringstead C.E. Primary School
- Wilbarston C.E. Primary School
- Naseby C.E. Primary School
- Chacombe CEVA Primary School
- Wollaston Community Primary School
- Sywell CEVA Primary School
- St Edwards Catholic Primary School
- Syresham St James C.E. Primary School
- Ecton Brook Primary School
- St Luke's CEVA Primary School
- Simon De Senlis Primary School
- Kislingbury CEVA Primary School
- Rothersthorpe C.E. Primary School
- Exton & Greetham C.E. Primary School
- Headlands Primary School
- Woodland View Primary School
- John Hellins Primary School
- Hayfield Cross C.E. School
- Moulton Primary School
- Brigstock Latham's C.E. Primary School
- Great Doddington Primary School
- St James Infant School
- Bugbrooke Primary School
- All Saints Primary School
- Blakesley Primary School
- Alfred Street Primary School
- Caroline Chisholm Primary School
- Kings Cliffe Endowed Primary School
- Long Buckby Junior School
- Irthlingborough Infant School
- Thrapston Primary School
- Husbands Bosworth Primary School

Contents

Introduction

Recently, a head teacher said to me, "Something magical is happening in my school. Who would have thought that magic would happen from something so mathematical?" This system will bring the magic to writing as easily as counting 1, 2, 3.

Do you need your job to be easier? Do the pupils in your class need a clearer message? Want to find out more?

Inside this book is a system for the successful teaching of writing for life. It's effective, exciting and it really works.

What makes good writing? More importantly, what makes a good teacher of writing? This book is for busy teachers and interested parents overwhelmed by curriculum change and inundated with educational initiatives. It has been written to bring clarity to an arena where so much data is available but this data is not transferred to useful information or to effective practice.

The current curriculum provides its own particular pressures around certain competencies in English but does not provide clear pathways for children to improve their skills. Over the years, I have worked with many schools in all sorts of challenging situations with the aim of trying to improve their writing results. What has become clear to me in the fog of information overload is that what is missing is a bold and clear framework that will support all involved to make the necessary improvements.

Writing is very hard to teach effectively. Many teachers fall into the trap of providing a piecemeal collection of experiences, which however stimulating, are not integrated into a clear framework for learning. In my view, writing is far more systematic than a stimulating but unfocused collection of 'bits and bobs'.

This book makes transparent what has been lost in years of political game play and educational interference. The ideas in this book have been ten years in the making. I have been on a long personal journey, pulling schools out of categories, raising expectations and fighting for 'outstanding' judgements.

I know this system works and the many schools I have worked with around the UK know it works too. To be effective, writing should be taught through three zones: the ideas of writing, the tools of writing and the techniques of writing. This book relies on striking imagery to capture the 'shapes' of writing that are then developed through child-friendly hooks. The ideas are called the FANTASTICs, the tools are called the GRAMMARISTICs and the techniques are called the BOOMTASTICs.

The Three Zones Of Writing

1. Ideas ➔  THE FANTASTICs

2. Tools ➔  THE GRAMMARISTICs

3. Techniques ➔  THE BOOMTASTICs

Why is Writing Important?

Why write? Writing crystallises your ideas. It preserves them for others. It reveals the facets of your thinking. Good writing is creating a gem for others to discover.

Chapter 1

Summary

 Research shows that pupils who enjoy writing are good writers.

 Girls enjoy writing more than boys and this is reflected in a correlation between higher attainment and enjoyment.

 Effective writing classrooms have, amongst other things, a positive climate, with teachers who have comprehensive subject knowledge.

 In schools where there are excellent standards in writing, the writing process is taught explicitly and deliberately to pupils by teachers.

THE WRITE STUFF

Why is Writing Important?

I care about writing. I care about the quality of writing in primary schools. There is no research about the correlation between a teacher's sense of caring about writing and the quality of writing produced by pupils. However, as a thinking and critical profession, we are moving in a direction that recognises the need for our teaching to be based on strong evidence-based research – so that we are empowered to engage pupils in valuable learning transactions. Former Ofsted chief Sir Chris Woodhead, who died in 2015, wasn't convinced that educational research was beneficial, declaring:

"We already spend some £50 million to £60 million every year on educational research and I, for one, think we see precious little benefit from it... We need to be constantly on our guard against the self-interest of the expert."

I do not believe Chris Woodhead was right. We need to explore more thoroughly what makes for powerful teaching: that will provide pupils with a lasting sense of how to be skilled writers. This book is a pulling together of where we are at the moment with our understanding of the teaching of writing. It is a reflection on current research into effective schools, action research and teacher feedback about what works in the classroom to improve pupils as writers. There is a precious benefit to considering current evidence into classroom practice and it is the consideration of the commonalities across all these areas that will enlighten our work. Writing is vital for living in the modern world. An understanding of how to glean the most useful teaching approaches will deliver the most precious writing from pupils.

Writing is crucial. Why? Because it is a formal or informal capture of factual information and creative imagination.

It is a means to communicate to an audience the full spectrum of human emotions and intent. Words, if viewed as a commodity, are a powerful exchange of thinking between writer and reader. They drive forward our understanding of one another and ourselves. Ultimately, good writing is carved from clear thinking - and clear writing can further crystallise our thoughts. By the same token, muddled thinking can result in sloppy writing. If, as teachers, we consider our jobs to be fundamentally about learning and fostering enquiring minds, then writing must be deemed as a critical tool to capture, accelerate and sharpen thinking.

Primary school pupils do an enormous amount of writing, not just in their English lessons but across the curriculum. Writing is the trickiest thing that children have to encounter in lessons. It is such a complicated process that relies on pupils coordinating both fine motor skills and cognitive skills. Writing reflects the social and cultural patterns of the writer's time. As they write, children have to orchestrate

appropriate spelling, accurate sentence construction, linguistic choices about content, and textual cohesion. They must even consider the style and shape of their handwriting. (*Myhill and Fisher, 2010; Fisher, 2012*).

Nonetheless, the written word needs celebrating, nurturing and shaping so that it becomes an economic and emotive tool for communication and enables our thinking brains to go beyond the words and make meaning for our own lives.

Even though the focus of this book will be on writing, it is so inextricably linked with reading that it will be difficult at times to discuss writing without making links and references to the interplay between the two aspects. A report to the Scottish Executive Education Department, *Literature Circles, Gender and Reading for Enjoyment (Allan*

Great Creaton Primary School - boys in reading zone, enjoying books with their shoes off and relaxing.

> **The written word needs celebrating, nurturing and shaping so that it becomes an economic and emotive tool for communication**

et al., 2005: 5), captures the way in which reading for pleasure impacts positively on writing attainment and general empathy to the human condition:

"Children who say that they enjoy reading and who read for pleasure in their own time do better at school. Reading for enjoyment is positively associated with reading attainment and with writing ability *(OECD 2002)*. Pupils who read for pleasure also demonstrate a wider general knowledge *(Wells 1986)*, a better understanding of other cultures *(Meek 1991)*, and more complex insights regarding human nature, motivations and decision-making *(Cunningham and Stanovich 1998, Bruner 1996)*."

In primary schools, at Key Stages 1 and 2, writing is currently the subject with the worst performance compared with reading, maths and science. There is also a gender gap in pupils' performance in writing, with girls outperforming boys throughout the Key Stages. Research has attempted to explore the reasons behind boys' underachievement and this can be broadly categorised into two camps. One school of thought hinges on the relationship between male identity and achievement, suggesting that society stereotypes boys as not very good at the written word compared to mathematics. Conversely, other evidence points to wider issues that impact on the gender divide in attainment in writing, such as socio-economic factors *(Ofsted, 2005b)*. Research evidence and inspections find five key causes behind boys' underachievement in writing *(Ofsted, 2005a; 2005b; Younger et al, 2005; Estyn, 2008; Daly, 2003; DfES, 2007)*. This is captured as a summary on page 8 *'Five Factors for the Gender Gap'*.

How boys and girls define a 'good writer'

At Key Stages 3 and 4, there is a correlation between the good writer and reading systematically, regularly and for pleasure. Stephen King, the international best-selling horror writer, makes the link between reading and writing plain:

"The real importance of reading is that it creates an ease and intimacy with the process of writing... Constant reading will pull you into place (a mindset, if you like the phrase) where you write eagerly and without self-consciousness. It also offers you a constantly growing knowledge of what has been done and what hasn't, what is trite and what is fresh, what works and

what lies there dying (or dead) on the page. The more you read, the less apt you are to make a fool of yourself with your pen or word processor."
On Writing: A memoir of the craft - 2000

In 2011, Clark and Douglas suggested that most pupils believed, first and foremost, that the good writer enjoyed writing. This correlates with research across a range of disciplines that enjoyment is a high indicator of success in a particular field. Studies carried out by the *National Literacy Trust (NLT)* found, that in 2009, 45% of puils enjoyed writing across all Key Stages. The figure in 2011 was 47% *(Clark and Dugdale 2009/2011)*. More worrying though were the 14% who did not enjoy it at all. Once again, there were gender differences around the enjoyment of writing, with girls enjoying writing more than boys. Coupled with this, what supported pupils' views of a good writer was the high correlation between enjoyment and attainment. The study revealed that 49% of pupils performing **above** the expected level for their age, and 46% of pupils performing **at** the expected level for their age, enjoyed writing very much. However, writing for pupils was more than just enjoying the process. Aspects cited included: using imagination, using correct punctuation and knowing how to spell. In Key Stage 2 specifically, there was more mention by both genders that neatness and volume of work were indicators of good writing.

As part of a *Teaching Schools*-funded project in 2015/2016, I was commissioned to take a lead within a collaboration of 15 schools in Daventry, Northamptonshire. The key aims of the project were:

- ☑ To develop the impact of English subject leaders across the cluster in raising attainment in writing

- ☑ To raise attainment in writing by engaging reluctant writers

- ☑ To develop, in all teachers of English, the knowledge and skills to weave all aspects of English into the planning and delivery of all literacy lessons

- ☑ To develop teacher skills in identifying next steps across all areas and skills in literacy

- ☑ To build further the use of outstanding texts from which teachers could extract all aspects of English

- ☑ To create, in the Daventry area, a coaching team in direct partnership with three SLEs (Specialist Leaders in Education), offering high quality impact on teaching and learning and with the sustainability to promote further improvement

Five Factors for the Gender Gap

1 Quality of Teaching

Four distinct aspects of weakness were revealed:
i)   Grammar was poorly taught and often not related to pupils' own writing
ii) A mismatch between oral activities and written work
iii) Unhelpful or poorly explained/modelled writing frames
iv) Interventions that were unsuccessful at accelerating standards

2 Writing Environment

In primary schools, time allocated for active and free play to fuel imagination becomes less as pupils mature. The increased constraints of timetabled lessons and restrictive opportunities for movement around the classroom have a more negative impact on boys.

3 Social Issues

Boys were more likely to be affected by negative peer pressure while girls had more positive reinforcement for high attainment and a hard-working attitude. Alongside this, a lack of male primary class teachers had a negative impact on boys' achievement, especially if they were deprived of a male role model at home as well.

4 Classroom Organisation

Setting or misjudged ability grouping had more of a detrimental effect on boys than girls. In general, boys were more likely to experience criticism and a sense of failure at school. Computing hardware and software introduced to motivate boys was sometimes poorly explained and demonstrated and did not fulfil the desired function to impact on the quality of writing.

5 Lesson Emphasis

Within writing-focused lessons, there were particular aspects and strategies that boys disliked compared to girls. Story writing was cited as more favourable to girls than boys, who actually wanted more ownership of their writing and real-life reasons to write. Also, within lessons, there was discrepancy between boys' favourite reads and the genres they were asked to write. Boys disliked time pressure during writing much more than girls. Drafting was deemed by boys as tiresome and they felt much less motivated than girls to undertake it. Girls enjoyed the poetry of language, in particular exploring figurative language and the wealth of possibilities when it came to using similes, metaphors and other poetic devices. Boys felt disconnected from figurative language, disliked it and did not perceive it as an open-ended creative device.

The impact of Specialist Leaders in Education

Specialist Leaders in Education (SLEs) are outstanding school leaders, who are part of a nationwide team which develops local area initiatives. SLEs support and develop the leadership capacity of their peers in other schools. In January 2015, I was lucky enough to work in collaboration with three outstanding SLEs at the Teaching Schools alliance within The Grange School, a primary in Daventry, Northamptonshire:

Elaine Wagg: Director of Teaching and Learning at The Grange School and EYFS lead. Early Years SLE Specialist.

Vicki Masters: Director of Teaching and Learning at The Grange School. Continuous Professional Development SLE Specialist.

Caroline Colledge: English Subject Leader. English SLE Specialist.

The project was funded by a successful bid to the Department for Education (under Teaching Schools allocation budgets) to develop a local process for sharing good practice in the teaching of writing. Seventeen schools were involved in the project and each of the SLEs was assigned schools to mentor within the alliance.

These talented SLEs are not only subject/phase specialists but also have overarching specialisms in teaching and learning in the primary setting, with vast amounts of experience of mobilising change to impact standards in schools in Northamptonshire. Gaynor Yates is Principal at The Grange School and a National Leader of Education. She leads an inspiring school, which facilitates a model of developing school leaders based on recognising personal expertise and growing her senior team's strengths through delegation and trust. Gaynor is a strong, developmental head, who talks about her SLEs with complete respect and has told me personally that they hold her to account and that she is grateful for their diligence and integrity with matters based on teaching and learning. I recommend that this is a school that should be recognised nationally for how people are utilised to their strengths. Any head looking to develop school leadership should try to visit The Grange, to see first-hand their effective people deployment and development.

Elaine, Vicki and Caroline have been tremendous to work with and have contributed significantly to my thinking on issues such as: a clear vision for effective English teaching, and models for planning that are flexible enough to shape a teacher's thinking but robust enough to support engagement for pupils. The ultimate aim of the SLEs within the project was - and continues to be - contributing significantly to improving outcomes for children by growing the capacity of English subject leaders in their settings. The high-quality support that they provide directly to subject leaders is having a positive impact. Informal feedback from head teachers in the alliance is about the benefits on the ground, particularly improving learning experiences for children.

Personal Continuing Professional Development

Caroline Colledge, the English expert on the SLE team, has been notably influential on the development of an effective English vision. During our collaborative meetings, she introduced some crucial concepts, provided shared language and some other guiding principles that helped form the drive behind the project. Caroline is a visual thinker and likes to collate thinking in pictorial form. She is always searching for better ways to understand information, in an era when we are swamped with it, particularly in education. In David McCandless' words:

"In a way, we're all visual now. Every day, every hour, maybe even every minute, we're seeing and absorbing information via the web. We're steeped in it. Maybe even lost in it. So perhaps what we need are well-designed, colourful and - hopefully useful - charts to help us navigate."

With Caroline's determination to summarise our direction visually, and in an approachable format, together as a team the beautiful rainbow analogy was born. From her previous work at The Grange School, the sun in the model, the brightest moments in teaching, represents our duty to inspire children.

Initiate Inspiration: This is the part of teaching where a stimulus is introduced to engage pupils in learning. It is initiated by the teacher to capture children's imaginations and is 'the spark' that ignites their interest in a particular experience, topic, issue, book, piece of art, music, artifact or image.

The raindrops on the model represent that idea of dripping small new concepts over time that will ultimately illuminate a rainbow of learning if all the factors are right within our classrooms.

Enable Empowerment: This is where pupil independence is developed and children have a chance to showcase learning and apply skills within contextualised experiences. It is a time for pupils to orchestrate new skills learnt and rehearse and practise the ongoing development of their English understanding.

This model was returned to time and time again within the project to ensure we never deviated too far from our original intentions. Without the intellectual interchange of ideas with the SLE team, the planning models would not have manifested themselves in the way they did. From my personal perspective, their input, discussions and ideas have been a fundamental part of fashioning my current position on what makes for powerful English teaching and effective learning.

Impact monitoring

The SLEs' hugely positive impact on subject leaders can already be tracked through:

▶ Increased subject knowledge.

▶ Improved quality of teaching and learning.

▶ Improved positivity of subject leaders around managing their subjects.

▶ Prioritised and targeted efforts towards teaching and learning agendas.

All schools are now collating data in order to measure impact, and this will be analysed in spring 2016. The project is expected to have led to increased pupil progress in writing attainment, as well as increased 'good' and 'outstanding' teaching and increased subject knowledge about the national curriculum. Vicki's mathematical mind has supported us all to stay focused on impact monitoring and responding to individual teachers' needs as they arise. Elaine's early years lean has meant we continue to share good practice of what constitutes outstanding English teaching in Foundation Stage settings and she is able to point staff looking for further clarification to excellent practice amongst the schools taking part. Caroline's English understanding has been paramount in challenging my ideas. The succinctness of the concepts 'inspire' and 'empower' have brought clarity to a subject that is at risk from convoluted and vague guidance.

I recommend the SLEs whole-heartedly. They are adept at building strong, trusting relationships and their work to drive up standards is exemplary. To find out more about the project and the final outcomes, or to commission them directly in your school, email: mrs.yates@thegrangeschooldaventry.net

The impact of their work was palpable within the group:

'There is a clear difference in [the] quality [of writing] between classes which have and classes which haven't.'

'It was very supportive and not intimidating! I felt able to be honest about where I was and what I needed support with.'

'[We had the] opportunity to talk things through, clarify understanding of the purpose of the project. We really drilled down into the needs of the school and how to start addressing these.'

It was clear in early meetings with the SLEs that an agreed guiding vision of what effective English teaching constituted needed to be established before more detailed discussions, support and training could be developed as part of the project. This led to an agreed set of seven principles to support effective English teaching.

Some pupils just do not know what to write and get stuck before they begin.

The Seven Guiding Principles for Effective English

 A Happy Place

Children need a learning culture that is based on trust and challenge. The best classrooms foster this culture through a sense of warmth, alongside a focus on high expectations. Teachers in excellent schools excel in their positive classroom climates. *Mortimore et al (1988)* referenced positive climate as one of the main characteristics of an effective school and, since then, researchers have concluded that it has an impact on pupil outcomes:

"Classroom climate (the overall feeling in a classroom, evidenced through teacher-pupil and pupil-pupil relationships) was rated highly in excellent and good schools. For example, in classrooms in both excellent and good schools, children

appeared to be liked and respected by their peers.

"The overall classroom climate in poor schools was less favourable and sometimes unpleasant. Teachers were more likely to display negativity (disapproval, reprimands, expressions of dislike, etc.) and children in poor schools were less sociable and less cooperative than their peers in other schools."
Exploring Effective Pedagogy in Primary Schools (Pearson-Siraj and Taggart 2014)

A happy classroom climate runs deeper than smiles at pupils and pats on the back. A positive learning place is one in which the teacher's enthusiasm for the subject is evident and they respond sensitively to the needs of their pupils. Alongside this,

Designed by Jane Considine and The Daventry Learning Community

an environment is created where children are well-liked and respected.

"...the need to create a classroom that is constantly demanding more, but still recognising students' self-worth. It also involves attributing student success to effort, rather than ability, and valuing resilience to failure."
What Makes Teaching Great (2014 Coe, Aloisi, Higgins and Major)

 Know your Stuff

Teachers need to be experts, with a flair for being able to communicate their skills and knowledge in an illuminating way, so that their pupils are able to think, talk and write clearly, completely, critically and creatively. This is easier said than done. Expert teaching requires a high level of subject knowledge and, in the realm of English, the amount of sub-categories of understanding makes this one of the most challenging areas to teach effectively.

"The most effective teachers have deep knowledge of the subjects they teach, and when teachers' knowledge falls below a certain level, it is a significant impediment to students' learning. As well as a strong understanding of the material being taught, teachers must also understand the ways students think about the content, be able to evaluate the thinking behind students' own methods, and identify students' common misconceptions."
What Makes Great Teaching (2014 Coe, Aloisi, Higgins and Major)

Teachers with good subject knowledge are able to make links outside the specific lesson context, either cross-curricular references or to life beyond the classroom. This expertise, both in the particular subject and others, is critical in the primary school as the class teacher is responsible for delivering a wealth of curriculum content. Research shows a modest relationship between teachers' understanding and pupil gains. During my work in training teachers, I recognise the effectiveness of targeting support around the specifics of English - in particular around the misconceptions related to the subject. This idea is supported by the work of *Timperley et al 2007* and *Blank and de las Alas 2009.*

"This suggests that targeting support for teachers at particular areas where their understanding, or their knowledge of student misconceptions, is weak may be a promising strategy, a claim that is supported by reviews of the impact of teacher professional development in these areas."
Timberley, H (2008) Teacher Professional Learning and Development.

 Make it Clear

Writing is a messy business. A reminder of this can be seen at the Roald Dahl Museum and Story Centre in Great Missenden, Buckinghamshire. The museum displays a vast collection of notes and jottings in pencil that show Dahl's thinking prior to writing. When it came to considering what the BFG would wear on his feet, the author made seventeen separate notes about his character's potential footwear. Circled around one jotting was 'black leather boots', but in the book the BFG wore 'a pair of ridiculous sandals that for some reason had holes cut along each side, with a large hole at the end where his toes stuck out'. Furthermore, the extensive notes Dahl scribbled during the thinking process revealed that, up until the final draft, the 'Oompa-Loompas' were called the 'Whipple-Scrumpets'. This is a sharp testament to the amount of background thinking and consideration required before writing is good enough or creates the effect required. Roald Dahl outlines his seven tips to be a great writer of stories:

1. "You should have a lively imagination."

2. "You should be able to write well. By that I mean you should be able to make a scene come alive in the reader's mind. Not everybody has this ability. It is a gift and you either have it or you don't."

3. "You must have stamina. In other words, you must be able to stick to what you are doing and never give up, for hour after hour, day after day, week after week and month after month."

4. "You must be a perfectionist. That means you must never be satisfied with what you have written until you have rewritten it again and again, making it as good as you possibly can."

5. "You must have strong self-discipline. You are working alone. No one is employing you. No one is around to give you the sack if you don't turn up for work, or tick you off if you start slacking."

6. "It helps a lot if you have a keen sense of humour. This is not essential when writing for grown-ups, but for children, it's vital."

7. "You must have a degree of humility. The writer who thinks that his work is marvellous is heading for trouble."

Roald Dahl books are still popular today. Children enjoy the sense of fun and the cheeky commentary about human flaws.

Peter Lang, a Year 6 teacher at Weldon C.E. Primary School, modelling explicitly the writing process.

In primary schools, we need to enable pupils to be strong writers across a range of genres and non-fiction text types. This challenge is so complicated, particularly as one of the most difficult aspects is finding clarity in your teaching of writing. One of the most striking research outcomes about the effective teaching of writing is that pupils must be explicitly taught about the writing process itself. (*What Works Clearinghouse, 2012; Gillespie and Graham, 2010; Andrews et al, 2009; Graham et al, 2011; Santangelo and Olinghouse, 2009*).

This research identifies the components to achieve effective teaching of the writing process, which requires a strong interaction between teacher and pupil:

☑ Teachers compose and model writing together with their pupils so that it is a lively interactive learning exchange.

☑ Pupils are exposed to modelling of the writer's internal voice as the teacher verbalises aloud word, phrase or clause choices.

☑ Spelling and grammar decisions are noted as ongoing smaller chunks of learning and quick decisions take place en route to a complete sentence.

☑ Sentence combinations and cohesion between them are justified accordingly.

☑ Editing and redrafting of writing is done 'live' so pupils can see the improvements in a transparent way. High value is given to editing, so pupils begin to understand the process of moving from raw to polished versions.

☑ Pupils are guided very clearly with their own writing, with teachers analysing quickly at sentence level for improvement in meaning or intent

Pupils are encouraged to model for one another and memorise strategies to be used in different contexts.

4 Pupils at Heart

When teacher sensitivity is attuned to the needs of pupils in the classroom, there is a direct correlation to their engagement with the task and quality of work produced. I teach an enormous number of children, providing a demonstration lesson service. This work extends from Reception to Year 6 - in a range of socio-economic school situations with a diversity of ethnicity profiles. I always teach using a 'no hands-up' policy, favouring an 'I will talk to your eyes' policy. Children cannot abide detached adults, whether they are in a school, home or other social situation. Amongst the wealth of groundbreaking research in the early years sector, the most fascinating findings of all, in my view, are the studies around eye contact.

"Being looked at is a strong social signal, indicating that the other person is attending to you. In humans, collaborative communication and problem solving is frequently embedded in face-to-face interaction."
Kaplan, Hooper and Gurven (2009)

Teachers can respond more sensitively, challenge appropriately and adjust teaching accordingly when they are watching closely for subtle changes in individuals' responses to tasks. By taking an active role in the learning, we move more like firefighters making judgements in real time. We are able to make a critical difference (and exploit learning time to its greatest potential). There is a powerful link

Pupils respond well to high levels of teacher engagement and interest in their ideas.

here with eye contact, as the *Falck-Ytter, Carlstrom and Johansson (2015)* study shows.

"Being looked at caused the children to perform better...on the cognitive task."

The Pearson report *Exploring Effective Pedagogy*, refers to this aspect of teacher work as personalised learning, defined by the study as:

"Personalised teaching and learning requires a teacher to adapt all the aspects of his or her teaching to the needs of the specific individuals within a classroom group. In order to personalise the learning of the individuals within his or her class, a teacher must be sensitive to the individual needs of each of their pupils and be actively involved with their learning. Teachers need to recognise the individual needs of their pupils by having a good understanding of the individual children within a class, providing teaching and learning materials suitable for the range of children, scaffolding and differentiating the work set and outcomes expected. This strategy captured teacher sensitivity/detachment, the variety and richness of their teaching resources, how they differentiated work and their use of scaffolding to aid learning."

Ultimately, the mark of a good teacher is being able to respond to pupils 'live' in the moment. The best teachers are those who are responsive, sensitive and engaged with the teaching matter in hand. As Daniel Levitin teaches us in his book *The Organized Mind (2014)*, multi-tasking is a bad way to do nearly everything. A classroom and a teacher's life are at high risk of being pulled into a multi-tasking mess as the weight of our daily jobs bears down on us.

 Links and Layers

"There are three ways we can learn information - we can absorb it implicitly, we can be told it explicitly, or we can discover it for ourselves. Implicit learning, such as when we learn a new language through immersion, is usually the most efficient. In classroom settings and at work, most information is conveyed in one of the two latter ways - being told explicitly or discovering ourselves."
Daniel Levitin (2014)

Levitin endorses the power of discovery and believes that the last two decades of research on the science of learning has shown conclusively that we remember things 'better, and longer, if we discover them ourselves rather than being told them explicitly'. This is tricky in my view. Children need certain aspects of learning to be provided 'on a plate', while other aspects can be explored more openly. *Bjork and Bjork, 2011* discuss less the power of self-teaching and more the power of forgetting. This challenges our long-held view that pupils reasoning their own way to answers is productive. Research leads us to understand that more explicit teaching, that is closely directed, is more productive. This, coupled with leaving time for pupils to lose detail, allows them to return to the subject matter whilst taking control of the areas where retention is weak. It is through identifying 'the forgotten' that pupils' understanding is strengthened when they personally 'fill in the gaps'.

The Pearson report, *Exploring Effective Pedagogy in Primary Schools*, found that teachers who made cross-curricular links were much rarer in their sample but were far more likely to be the excellent teachers. Children's brains are crying out for connections and they are constantly seeking patterns and similarities in other areas of their learning in order to better understand the world.

"Teachers in excellent schools were better able to, and more consistent at, making links with areas outside the specific lesson. In classrooms in excellent schools, teachers made cross-subject and extracurricular links explicit for their pupils. They specifically pointed out the links between what children were doing in a particular lesson and what they were learning in other subjects."

The *What Makes Great Teaching* report goes one stage further and refers to 'interleaving'. This is a concept that refers to smaller chunks of learning that are then applied to other tasks and topics, leading to 'better long-term retention and transfer of skills'.

6 Talk as a Tool

Talk is a multi-faceted tool in the classroom. It serves many functions and can be set up in many different group dynamics e.g. teacher to pupil, pupil to pupil, as well as between larger groups of pupils.

Talk can be used by the teacher to emphasise, magnify and make links in learning. Speaking whilst showing a graphic is useful if the talk explains

Pupils who talk about matters of interest are more engaged and engrossed in conversation.

> **Talk can be used by the teacher to emphasise, magnify and make links in learning**

James Britton (1983) put it so eloquently when he said:

"Reading and writing float on a sea of talk."

Talk allows ideas to be shared and manifested from inner thoughts and classrooms need to be buzzing with productive 'idea growing' talk. Talk is paramount to help pupils understand the impact of reading on our thinking minds and the power of writing to influence a reader.

Review, Reflect, Respond

the graphic further and draws out specific information related to it. Careful modelling and explanation by the teacher makes explicit what is often assumed or less obvious. Talk is critical for all subject areas but is specifically more important for the subject of English, as language is the backbone of the subject and pupils need to understand its malleability and choices of language available. The function of talk in our classrooms is not just social but cognitive and cultural as well. Talking through ideas enables pupils to shape and reshape their thinking as they go along. High quality talk is vital to strengthening teaching and learning. Pupils need guidance to build their ideas and part of this process involves feeding off others' spoken input and being suitably challenged as they communicate and deepen their thinking.

Time is the most precious commodity in a primary classroom. Teachers are always crying out for more time, feeling under pressure to fit all curriculum requirements into an already overstretched timetable. Equally, pupils feel rushed and are sometimes submerged in a swamp of unfinished work. They also yearn for more time to complete tasks and produce pieces of work they are proud of, presented to a high standard. Making time to review the quality of work, respond to it specifically (and provide enough reflection space for pupils to consider the smaller steps required to improve their writing skills) is difficult. Without review, pupils may lose their way in terms of how they can continually improve. Talk that is targeted to individuals, and differentiated to their needs, is the most effective means of achieving speedy impact when it comes to writing standards.

Teaching Effective English

Teacher Self-Evaluation

Not Confident

	Not Confident	
A Happy Place		
Know your Stuff		
Make it Clear		
Pupils at Heart		
Links and Layers		
Talk as a Tool		
Review, Reflect, Respond		

Struggling with this!

Designed by Jane Considine and
The Daventry Learning Community

eveloping Confidence   Confident   Very Confident

Getting there!   Got this sorted!   Can do this with
my eyes closed!

Consider

Self-evaluate your personal and whole-school positions on the seven areas of effective English teaching. Use the teacher self-evaluation grid (see previous page) to grade your current position.

Identify strengths and weaknesses and use it as a discussion point with colleagues to strengthen practice further.

School Impact Points

Be a school that prioritises discussions about teaching and learning:

① Share current research (see bibliography as a starting point) and the impact of these findings, both on your teaching and the school's approach.

② Talk to colleagues in a real and honest way about aspects of the job they find challenging and share strategies most likely to have a high impact on standards.

Maisie, Year 3

What Do We Know about Writing?

Learning to write requires careful, deliberate and systematic teaching. This is essential but alone will not guarantee success. Good teaching of writing must enthuse and inspire children by developing their love of language.

Chapter 2
Summary

☑ The commonalities between schools that have excellent writing outcomes can be organised into four areas: reading, teaching and learning, detailed language exposition and clear expectation.

☑ Schools with great results typically prioritise reading. Their reading curriculum is rich and varied. Teachers enjoy modelling expert reading and use quality texts for children to interrogate.

☑ Teaching and learning for writing is often characterised by whole-class, mixed ability teaching with differentiated aspects. A hallmark of outstanding writing teaching is excellent demonstration writing.

☑ Detailed language exposition should be threaded through English teaching sequences so that pupils build up a rich repertoire of language and sentence constructions.

THE WRITE STUFF

What Do We Know About Writing?

Children in our schools are our 'writing apprentices' and our teaching needs to take a highly attentive stance to both the mechanics and the emotive 'magic' of the writing they produce. The differences between schools that do well with writing and those that are less effective are often difficult to pinpoint and sometimes seem to be very subtle. Even though the following checklist might elicit the tired comment that 'we already do that', it's important to consider consistency across the school, depth of understanding and teachers' enthusiasm for the craft of writing.

The nine 'we do that' success strategies

Reading

"I think I see good reading as the best way of encouraging, and making possible, good writing." **A.S. Byatt**

Writing comes first. By that, I mean very young children meet writing in their everyday lives – on signs, in shops, on the web and in books. Reading is the crucial moment when a writer and a reader meet, even though the writer is often unaware of who the reader is or when their work is read. This is the power of writing. It has a life of its own beyond the author and can communicate ideas to a wealth of people across long time frames. Learning to write is a slower process than learning to read. Proficient writers don't just happen. They grow over time as they read the work of talented writers and, as children's skills improve, they become more aware of

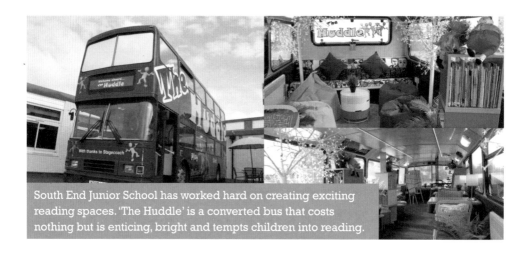

South End Junior School has worked hard on creating exciting reading spaces. 'The Huddle' is a converted bus that costs nothing but is enticing, bright and tempts children into reading.

the effect of their writing on an unseen audience. An ever-increasing knowledge of reading material directly impacts the quality of writing produced by pupils. Learning to be a good writer is difficult because it relies on the mastery of a range of styles, Standard English and the beauty and power of literary devices.

Supporting our writing apprentices

 ## Reading aloud

Reading aloud to a class with the right book is spellbinding. As teachers, we can accelerate and accentuate the plot for those children who find it difficult to immerse themselves into a story. We can take on the voices of the characters and we can create intrigue with the pitch and pace of our delivery. We can take children on a shared experience, where communally, as

a class, we go beyond the words to build an imaginary reading world which all children can share. Moments like these should never be downgraded as 'just reading to them', nor should they be perceived as activities just for the benefit of Foundation Stage and Key Stage 1. Most of us recognise the important interplay between good readers and good writers and this should mitigate against these activities being taken for granted. *Tierney and Pearson (1983)* explain their inseparableness is due to the fact that they are:

"similar processes of meaning construction."

They added that:

"This social act of bringing the text alive and lifting it off the page, with the pupils, at first, as listeners, meant that the language and the 'voice' of the author or poet was strongly present in the classroom. It provided an important background for children's own reading of the text."

Pupils are seen to be spellbound by the teacher's dramatic reading of the story.

Unfortunately, many school activities related to reading are rigidly over-aligned to the reading testing system in England. They tend to be comprehension-based and focused around deconstructing at a text, word, phrase and sentence level. SATs require children to analyse reading to a great depth and construct written answers using inferences and deductions made from within texts. There is an enormous amount at stake in our current testing system for reading and it can sway class teachers towards simply 'prepping' their pupils to pass end-of-year papers.

There are other ways of reading that need nurturing at the chalkface of the classroom. High value needs to be put on reading for its own sake – to let words wash over children's minds and ferment in their imaginations. There needs to be 'ring-fenced' time for pupils to experience the rhythm of language, the tune of words and the crescendos of great plots. Reading all sorts of text types and genres helps children

to acquire the structures of language, so they can be stored inside their memories and manipulated down the line in their own writing. The author and writing coach Roz Morris believes that:

"Reading—the good and the bad—inspires you. It develops your palate for all the tricks that writers have invented over the years. You can learn from textbooks about the writing craft, but there's no substitute for discovering for yourself how a writer pulls off a trick. Then that becomes part of your experience."

William Faulkner likens writing to carpentry, and just as an apprentice carpenter would watch the master, an apprentice writer must read the masters of the written word.

"Read, read, read. Read everything—trash, classics, good and bad, and see how they do it. Just like a carpenter who works as an apprentice and studies the master. Read! You'll absorb it. Then write. If it is good, you'll find out. If it's not, throw it out the window."

As H.P. Lovecraft wrote in his essay *Literary Composition*, merely learning rules for writing is not enough. We must all become better readers as well:

"No aspiring author should content himself with a mere acquisition of technical rules. …All attempts at gaining literary polish must begin with judicious reading, and the learner must never cease to hold this phase uppermost."

The ten minutes a day pledge

The 'sentence focus' approach works on the principle that for every child, every day in primary school, there will be a ten-minute period of time dedicated to reading a story, non-fiction or poetry. Those ten minutes should be over and above any reading that occurs in timetabled English lessons. The reading should be of a particular type, outlined below:

▶ The class teacher will read aloud in an engaging way, changing voice and style to match the text. The teacher should act as a performer.

▶ The period should be a non-pressurised time in the school day, based around enjoyment rather than a deconstruction exercise built around tight questioning.

▶ It is important that time is available during the school day to allow children to get 'lost in a book'.

▶ Pupils might lie down with their eyes shut, the lighting in the room might be changed or you might even consider inviting pupils to bring in 'reading slippers' from home.

The ten minutes a day arrangement should be a relaxed, calm and positive time in the school day to promote the enjoyment of reading. The arrangement comes with one condition – that it is matched by another ten minutes of home reading. Home reading is defined as 'adult reading to child' or 'child reading to adult', both having value in the reading and writing process.

It is interesting to note that *Cunningham and Stanovich (1988)* isolated the benefits of the reading experience from the effects of other factors on academic development. They found that even among pupils with poor attainment and weaker reading skills, extensive reading was linked to higher progress rates in general knowledge, vocabulary, verbal fluency and comprehension. This will be of little surprise to most practising teachers.

Reducing the reading gap

In another study, *Anderson, Wilson and Fielding (1988)* found that time spent reading books was the best predictor of a pupil's future proficiency.

We know as teachers that the readers in our class grow richer in terms of language, general knowledge and cultural understanding, amongst other things, whereas the poor readers are associated with less effective learning trajectories. A poor reader in primary really does need exposure to hundreds of thousands of words each year. This can sound daunting but as *Adams (2006)* observed, just ten minutes a day will expose a child to around 700,000 words a year. This will propel a student from the 30th percentile to the 70th percentile for exposure to the written word.

Percentile Rank	Minutes of Reading Per Day	Baseline - Words Read Per Year	Plus 10 Minutes – Words Read Per Year	Percentage Increase In Word Exposure
98	65	4,358,000	5,028,462	15%
90	21.1	1,823,000	2,686,981	47%
80	14.2	1,146,000	1,953,042	70%
70	9.6	622,000	1,269,917	104%
60	6.5	432,000	1,096,615	154%
50	4.6	282,000	895,043	217%
40	3.2	200,000	825,000	313%
30	1.8	106,000	694,889	556%
20	0.7	21,000	321,000	1429%
10	0.1	8,000		**Based on reading level, ~300,000 words**
2	0	0		

Distribution of time spent reading books outside of school, with estimated words read per year and projection of increased words per year if each child's average daily time spent reading were increased by ten minutes. Adapted from *Adams (2006)*, with baseline data from *Anderson, Wilson and Fielding (1988)*.

Ten minutes a day is a good aim but children need to be guided towards rich and varied texts of different types.

"Now and then there are readings which make the hairs on the neck, the non-existent pelt, stand on end and tremble, when every word burns and shines hard and clear and infinite and exact, like stones of fire, like points of stars in the dark..." **A.S. Byatt (1990)**

 No sets for English

The case against ability grouping

Recent evidence on the effects of grouping by ability, either by allocating students to different classes, or to within-class groups, suggests that it makes very little difference to learning outcomes *(Higgins et al, 2014)*. Although ability grouping may allow teachers to target a narrower range of pace and content of lessons, it can also create an exaggerated sense of within-group homogeneity and between-group heterogeneity in the teacher's mind *(Stipek, 2010)*. This can result in teachers failing to make necessary accommodations for the range of different needs within a supposedly homogenous ability group, and over-doing their accommodations for different groups, going too fast with the high-ability groups and too slow with the low-ability groups.

The *Organisation for Economic Co-operation and Development (OECD)*, a Paris-based think-tank, analysed successes and failures of education systems in 39 of the world's most developed nations.

It found that countries that divided pupils into ability groups at an early age tended to have higher numbers of school drop-outs and lower levels of achievement.

In the UK, one in six pupils is divided according to their academic ability by the age of seven, according to a study conducted last year by the UCL Institute of Education, University College London.

Beatriz Pont, an education analyst and one of the authors of the OECD study, said streaming by ability at an early age 'fuelled a vicious cycle' in which teachers had low expectations of students in the lowest sets. These students were often 'locked into a lower educational environment before they had a chance to develop...their potential', she said.

Her study – *Equity and Quality in Education: Supporting Disadvantaged Students and Schools* – found the most experienced and capable teachers often taught pupils in the highest sets.

Ability streaming 'exacerbates inequities' because immigrants and pupils from low-income families are more likely to be placed in low-ability groups, she said. The UK and the US had the joint highest proportions of pupils in schools that divided according to ability, at 99% each. Countries such as Finland, that are well-known for their high-performing education systems, had a far lower proportion – 58%.

Dividing pupils into ability groups was commonplace in the UK in the 1940s and early 1950s. By the early 1990s,

> **The gap in reading skills is considerably more narrow in the UK than France, Germany and Finland**

it had virtually disappeared because studies had shown it had no effect on overall attainment. It is gradually being reintroduced into UK schools.

The OECD study also shows the UK has a higher proportion of pupils with poor reading skills than its rival nations. In the UK, 18% of 15-year-olds do not have basic reading skills. This is average for OECD countries, but several countries have considerably lower proportions than this. Finland, Norway and Sweden have 8%, 15% and 17% respectively, while Shanghai-China – grouped together for the purpose of the study – only had 4%.

Almost a fifth – 18% – of 25 to 34-year-olds in the UK did not complete the last years of secondary school. In Canada, the US and Germany, the figures were 8%, 12% and 14% respectively.

The researchers showed that the UK is better than most of its rivals at managing to reduce the gap between pupils who are new to the country and those who are born here. The gap in reading skills is considerably more narrow in the UK than France, Germany and Finland.

Of the rich nations, the UK has a far higher proportion of pupils opting for academic subjects (as opposed to vocational ones). More than two-thirds (69.5%) of older secondary students are on academic courses, while 30.5% are on vocational courses. This is the eighth lowest proportion of pupils taking vocational courses of all countries. Across the OECD, the split between the two types of courses is almost equal, while in Germany, Austria and Finland a higher proportion of pupils are enrolled on vocational courses than academic ones.

Pont said that countries should strive to make academic and vocational courses equivalent. To further improve their education systems, she recommended countries should prevent pupils from retaking a year, eliminate setting by ability and allocate funding according to students' needs.

A spokesman from the Department for Education said it was for schools to decide how and when to group and set pupils by ability. "Research shows that when setting is done well, it can be an effective way to personalise teaching and learning to the differing needs of groups of pupils," he said.

"When setting is not based on accurate assessment of ability, or isn't used to adapt teaching to the needs of the group, then it can be divisive and limit pupils' aspirations."

(3) Whole-class teaching

Allow learners to discover key ideas for themselves

Enthusiasm for 'discovery learning' is not supported by research evidence, which broadly favours direct instruction *(Kirschner et al, 2006)*. Although learners do need to build on what they already know, if teachers want them to learn new ideas, knowledge or methods they need to teach them directly.

I like to think of this as 'holding the writing hand' of our pupils. Pupils need to have high expectations about writing but also a clear sense of aspects to be included at various points in the process. Sentence stacking is a very explicit way to share writing criteria or rules with pupils but it's important to let them have a go at applying the skills and shaping their personal sentences. Our teaching of writing needs to be bolder and slower. Pat Thomson coined the phrase 'slow knowing' in a report she wrote entitled *Whole School Change: A review of the literature (2007)*.

This 'slowness' is critical. We need to teach in smaller sentence-based chunks with accurate intent and where every word is deliberated over for its deserved place within the text. Pupils need to see what a tricky and messy business writing is and yes, sometimes it will quicken, but largely it will be quite a slow and painful commitment.

"The children were able to see that the words don't just come straight to me and that I have silent moments when I need to think. This really helped them to see me as a writer." **Teacher involved in the 'Writing is Primary' project.**

Anderson (2001:25) reminds us that: "...as teachers of writing we need to be familiar with the writing process so that we can pass it on."

Boothville Primary School has moved to mixed ability grouping to provide excellent learning models for all in the class.

Teachers need to provide a running commentary of the writing process. We can equate this to 'a window to the mind' so that pupils can see a teacher's internalising process explicitly.

I believe that we need to go even further than passing it on. We need to provide a clarity of commentary that moves children through a daily pathway of sentence stacking. When they look back at a 14-lesson unit of work (e.g. on a non-chronological report), they should be able to see that every sentence they have worked hard to shape over a period of time has value and a well-earned place in the final piece.

 ## More writing space

As part of my consultancy work, I teach demonstration lessons and what always strikes me is the lack of space given to model writing. If a lesson is going to be chunked into three or four parts, and a sentence is demonstrated at each point, then it would be much handier and clearer if there were three or four wipe boards that didn't get wiped off too quickly because the pacy lesson was moving the learning on. Writing needs time to breathe. Everyone needs time to think. Sentence stacking needs to be built up chronologically in a measured way and defined by personal thoughts, tools and techniques to make ideas gather weight and quicken on the page.

Space really makes a difference — not the aesthetic quality of a classroom but the actual space to capture writing in real time. Modelling is powerful and provides a forum for our writing apprentices to see us as experts at sentence construction, exemplifying the internal process of the writing craft as an external 'viewable' experience. Pupils are privy to a sneak peek of the possibilities at the point of writing. As teachers, if we keep building sentence by sentence, carving each component little by little, over time a longer text will be created to an extremely high standard.

Show children, with clear parameters, words that will be effective and not so effective.

Many teachers fall into the trap of modelling well at the beginning of a unit, or sporadically during a unit, but lose touch with the power of modelling to build the bigger shape of the text over time. Every sentence needs to be purposeful, modelled with a short-burst commentary and left to infuse in the minds of the apprentice writer. If three sentences are demonstrated, then these need to be on show throughout the lesson (ideally even longer) and captured on a working wall. A great writing classroom is one with designated spaces for the modelled moments that support chunked teaching and exemplary demonstration.

5 More rejection of not-quite-right writing

Maths is easier to teach as there are right and wrong answers, whereas in English the possibilities are enormous at any point of writing.

Nonetheless, it is important for benchmarking reasons that pupils get a sense of quality and learn which constructions are working and why. Editing is crucial but pupils feel loathe to do it. From their perspective, once there has been an investment of time, they regard most of what they do as good enough or better. If we take a position of being supercritical of the 'good enough' parts, rejecting them wholesale (while giving reasons why and insisting on a rewrite at sentence level), then pupils will begin to shape their own high expectations for their writing.

A Year 5 pupil once wrote the following sentence:

"The sudden storm stabbed wildly at the strong trees."

Whilst teaching, I called 'strong' ridiculously rubbish – to a palpable communal class gasp. Despite their initial shock, pupils can handle it more if the feedback is clear, if a bit dramatic, and doesn't confuse them about the message. For example, 'good try' is particularly difficult for pupils to respond to. I explained that 'strong' didn't support the force and damage the storm was capable of and asked them to replace it with a different adjective that would evoke a sense of the overpowering storm. 'Strong' was replaced with 'trembling' and so the sentence then read:

"The sudden storm stabbed wildly at the trembling trees."

Suddenly, this sentence gained momentum and the impact of 'trembling' was twofold: firstly, it added to the storm's destructive nature and secondly, it now personified the trees and used alliteration to create more reading appeal.

 Best books as models

"Read, read, read, read, read, read and then read some more."

Children need to be exposed to good, significant and classic authors. It is our duty as teachers to assure these authors that we invest time in their work and care about their craft, their artistry and the importance of their themes.

The *Centre for Literacy in Primary Education* works hard to collate and source age-related, quality texts that can support the nuts and bolts of the writing process.

Texts must form the basis of our teaching. It is from texts that pupils can begin to understand the complicated, multi-faceted business of writing. Authors' work acts as a direct model for pupils to imitate. That imitation can be guided through one of the three zones of writing or through a combination of them. The three zones of

This head teacher promotes reading through her 'Book of the Week'.

writing are ideas, tools and techniques. These will be discussed in detail in Chapters 7, 8 and 9 respectively.

Texts offer a wealth of shapes of writing, enabling pupils to begin to categorise, visualise and assess the commonalities between narratives and non-fictions. They provide a store of ideas, techniques and tools that can be explicitly drawn out and used as a basis for pupils' own writing. Teachers need to alternate between using whole texts and extracts to exemplify specific points and build pupils' repertoires of successful writing.

7 Detailed construction

Outstanding teaching is the art of authoritatively imparting knowledge to ensure that students are learning.

As teachers, we need to showcase expertise in writing. One of the most effective ways to do this is to provide a running commentary of writers' decisions, choices, changes and edits at the point of writing. We need to show pupils the invisible, so they can begin to know the challenges a writer faces at the point of composition. Where teaching is outstanding, the teacher is highly adept at articulating the inner decision-making of a writer.

The notable features of demonstration writing are:

▶ Rereading to ensure that sentences flow,

sound right and have a pleasing rhythm.

▶ Including deliberate errors to generate discussions about more effective alternatives e.g. precise verbs, evocative adjectives.

▶ Taking responsibility for spelling and punctuation and noticing times when aspects might need checking.

▶ Demonstrating explicitly through the three zones of writing: ideas, tools and techniques.

▶ Discussing writing choices with pupils so they understand why one way was more effective than another. This includes justifying choices in relation to the intended purpose of a piece.

8 Language hoarding "Finders, keepers, hoarders, writers"

Seeking language out, and collecting it in categories, will help pupils to group together words with similar meanings and functions. The FANTASTICs, discussed in more detail in Chapter 7, can act as a nine-part thesaurus system for gathering words, phrases, clauses and sentences. Most of the FANTASTICs are tools to gather ideas that are externally experienced, e.g. action, noticing, hearing. However, feelings and thoughts support pupils to get into the heads of their characters and explore what is happening inside. Organising collections of words and phrases in terms of their functionality within sentences will strengthen and support choices for children. Banks of words can be collected through the ideas, tools and techniques of writing.

⑨ Big displays of pupil writing

Successful pupils' writing needs to be valued. Sentence-stacking displays are a capture of exemplary children's work. They are a space to showcase the very best written contributions. These are not the modelled pieces of writing that the teacher has produced. The sentences that are celebrated on the display are a combination of pupils' work across the classroom. The focal point of the sentences will be clear. For instance, a feeling sentence might include a fronted adverbial to describe Little Red Riding Hood's journey in the forest. Any sentence

from any member of the class can be chosen for the display board as long as it meets the writing criteria. The sentences are banked and displayed on a large display board and individual pupils are credited for their contributions.

Improvements in pupils' self-esteem were noted as one of the outcomes from the sample schools involved in our action research project (*Daventry Writing Project: 15 schools – 2015*).

Sentence stacking showed pupils the importance of constructing writing carefully and concentrating on the artistry and craft of writing. It was also satisfying to find classes were kept on task in terms of bigger, whole-picture genre outcomes.

The sentences are stacked over time, but by the end of the unit they can be read as a completed piece of work.

Consider

What are the features of your school's writing curriculum and delivery that are particularly successful? Interview the pupils and find out what aspects of the writing environment, curriculum content and teaching and learning they like or dislike.

School Impact Points

Take part in a learning walk in your school and gather evidence of strengths in practice across the nine successful commonalities. Use the findings to consider ways to bolster improvements in weak areas.

1. Reading aloud
2. No sets for English
3. Whole class teaching
4. More writing space
5. More rejection of not-quite-right writing
6. Best books as models
7. Detailed construction
8. Language hoarding
9. Big displays of pupil writing

(on further investigation, Linda confirmed that she meant flushed as in *crowded)

What is Effective Planning and Teaching of Writing?

Children respond to the excitement of a passionate unfolding of ideas. The trick is to skilfully link learning from one day to the next, so a complete piece builds effortlessly over time.

Chapter 3

Summary

☑ A common shortcoming in the writing produced by primary-aged children is quantity (in other words, their failure to complete texts they have started).

☑ Frequently, the internal structure and semantic cohesion of children's written work leaves the reader in a state of confusion.

☑ Typically, teachers' expectations are too short-term and this leads to piecemeal writing activities, which don't allow children to construct their texts fully and coherently.

☑ Many teachers adopt a strategy that does not facilitate the systematic building of writing skills. More careful analysis - and controlled presentation and demonstration of what is required from children - is necessary.

☑ It is essential that children learn about the components of great writing and how they can use the 'sentence stacking' technique to achieve finished pieces, which are both coherent and of high quality. This strong, explicit modelling procedure has been shown to be highly effective.

What is Effective Planning and Teaching of Writing?

In my experience, there are two main weaknesses with writing in the primary school. Firstly, pupils rarely seem to finish or complete an extended piece of writing, which has then been edited to a good standard. Secondly, pupils lack the skills to navigate the reader through their writing in a logical way. Essentially, this weakness stems from a narrow understanding of conjunctions and the functions of different sentence types.

Completing texts

The first dilemma is the elusive finished piece. Whether teaching Year 1 pupils or a Year 6 class, teachers must train children to have the stamina to produce a completed story or non-fiction piece. Children cannot be taught new skills and knowledge as well as being expected to write a completed piece in one lesson. The biggest challenge is to build their writing up over time so that it hangs together as a complete body of work.

Internal structure

Teachers often focus their teaching around the big idea or event. This means many snippets of writing are grouped around high interest points in a story or key information in non-fiction. Michael Rosen calls us the teacher generation of 'extraxitis'. In other words, our work is littered with lots of bits and bobs but we rarely have time to tie it together cohesively in order to enhance pupils' understanding or the quality of their work.

"Coherence, one of the influential features in judging the quality of writing, has been considered to be a subjunctive and hazy concept which is hard to teach and learn."
Crewe, (1990); Lee, (2002)

The sequence of teaching a unit with a

clear genre or text type outcome is often talked about, explained or illustrated with exemplar planning models. However, on closer inspection, this is often littered with an array of related activities that send us off course when we should be focusing on the important, bigger job of building a completed story or text type.

The 'bits and bobs' trap

Most teachers have good intent and a sense of clarity around what they are trying to achieve by the end of a two to three-week unit. Primary school teachers spend a lot of time (so much time) gathering engaging texts – picture books, novels or films – to captivate pupils' thinking. Most teaching in primary schools is lively (if a bit chaotic), interspliced with paired talk and differentiated tasks that are related to a text. However, what is not obvious through quick lesson observation or learning walks is how these learning experiences link over time to ultimately form a completed piece.

Once planning is scrutinised in this way, it soon reveals that many of us fall into the 'Little Red Riding Hood' persona of teaching. Imagine as teachers that we are Little Red Riding Hood, basket in hand. On Monday, we are having an experience day and walking in the woods. On Tuesday, we are gathering flowery words. On Wednesday, we are thinking about what Grandma looks like. In our teaching and learning baskets, there are loads of bits and bobs. Some of the prompts will help us enormously when it comes to writing

but down the line the children have to select which prompts to use and in which order. Essentially, these are all useful activities to help us write a story, but en route there is not enough emphasis on the chronological carving up of sentences, running one after another, to tell the story precisely. This is why the teaching of maths is so different to the teaching of English, mainly because it relies on the skill of the teacher to teach over a period of days. It requires the teacher and the pupil never to lose sight of the larger goal in place. Far too often I see planning that features a string of wonderful learning exchanges under a theme or text, followed by a chasm of silent writing where too much pressure is put on pupils to produce excellent, complete genre/text-types.

Sentence stacking

In the classroom, English teachers always need to keep their sights on sentence making. The business of sentence building is a crucial aspect of our work and during learning episodes we mustn't stray too far from this goal. Sentences are vital. They are the building blocks of larger texts and pupils need support to make sentences that match the correct audience and purpose of the writing. During individual lessons, time needs to be chunked to provide opportunities to sentence-build. Not only that, sentences need to be stacked together to guarantee a completed piece. Working in this way sharpens up how we tackle a unit of work. It forces us to think about what is realistically achievable over a unit while we 'hold the writing hand' of each child and enable them to be capable writers.

A sentence-stacked lesson

If a lesson is focused on sentence making, and sentences are modelled for children exemplifying particular features, it is vital to work out how many sentences to demonstrate using new aspects or revised aspects that we have experienced before.

Most English lessons in primary schools last between 50 and 60 minutes. With this in mind, there are probably three models that can be explored:

Two or three sentences stacked within a lesson

Four or five sentences stacked within a lesson

Six sentences stacked within a lesson (any more than this might be too challenging to model clearly enough).

The stacking refers to the fact that we are going to gather sentences together chronologically (unless we are building in a flashback) or organisationally (non-fiction structures) and according to what we are attempting to build. I will explain this further once I have outlined learning-chunked teaching. Pupils, like adults, engage more with short, intensive moments of learning that they can apply immediately and come back to at a later

date in order to check what has been remembered or forgotten. Alan Pritchard discusses pupil concentration span in his book, *Ways of Learning*:

"The average concentration of an American adult is thought to be seven minutes, which purportedly accounts for the time between adverts in American television programmes, while the British adult concentration span is supposed to be slightly longer, at 11 minutes; however, elsewhere it is suggested that the "average adult" has a concentration span of 20 minutes. All of the easily traceable reports on concentration span seem to neglect to cite their sources. Irrespective of this, the observation that children seem to have very short concentration spans is of importance to teachers. Long introductory phases to lessons will fall on deaf ears after a few minutes of concentration have elapsed."

Learning 'chunks'

The number of learning chunks will be associated with the number of sentences being built in a lesson. For instance, three sentences corresponds to three learning chunks.

Teaching in smaller components is a notion that challenges our current mode of teaching English. Sometimes, the teaching of English is at high risk of being a lesson of two halves. The first half is a bubbly collection of stimulating talk, that is perhaps coupled with drama, while during the second half of the lesson the pupils settle down to their independent activities, with the teacher's attention targeting one small group.

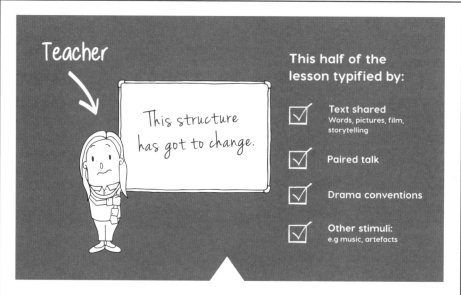

Typical English Lesson Structure
A lesson of two halves

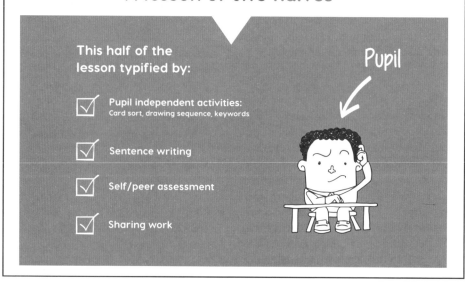

Systematic teaching works in a different way and facilitates short-burst interventions, with an emphasis on the crafting and construction of sentences. A lesson is typified by a learning conversation between teacher and pupils, with both parties actively participating in a session.

This approach avoids a 'lesson of two halves', where teacher and pupils risk losing direction or where pupils are unclear of what they have to do because they have been left to rely too heavily on their own devices. In primary schools, despite the focus of a lesson often being intriguing and engaging; (a dusty diary in a suitcase, a film clip with an unusual opening or a retelling of a story with artifacts), the intent of what will be drawn from these experiences often gets lost in a tangle of choices and a cacophony of voiced opinions. Since the alternative approach works by keeping sentence building at its core, this tethers creative ideas to a practical building of sequences of words that communicate meaning.

Lesson planning

This model works on the principle that both inspiration and empowerment are required to develop a learning climate that works. Inspiration is a necessary aspect of our daily teaching in English, to ensure that pupils are engaged and excited about the texts we are building together. In *What is the Research Evidence of Writing? (2014)*, evidence is gathered about pupils' attitudes to writing, including enjoyment and confidence. The evidence suggests that enjoyment of writing is related to attainment *(Clark, 2012)*. This way of planning will ensure more writing successes for pupils, improve attainment and, in turn, feed their confidence in the subject.

Initiate phase

This is the part of the lesson where the teacher initiates pupil interest and engagement. The core purpose is to inspire and captivate pupils' attention.

▶ Drama conventions: hot-seating characters, real or imagined, freeze-framing scenes, the role of an important object in a story, the conscience alley of a troubled person, thought-tapping of central character or communal voice to share an important conversation, to name but a few.

▶ Artifacts relating to story or non-fiction text e.g. a letter from a story character, items in a character's coat pocket, a suitcase/bag belonging to a character, map of an explorer featured in information text, medal of an Olympian linked to autobiography, dig up a time capsule for a history story retrieved.

▶ Music to enhance mood or as a backdrop to storytelling.

▶ Film – short animation to be used as context for writing (footage related to non-fiction text).

▶ A powerful piece of written text, loaded with textual features to explore.

Proposed English Lesson Structure
A learning chunks model

LEARNING CHUNK ONE

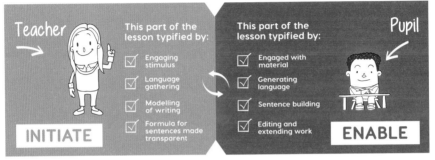

LEARNING CHUNK TWO

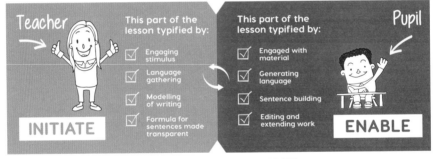

LEARNING CHUNK THREE

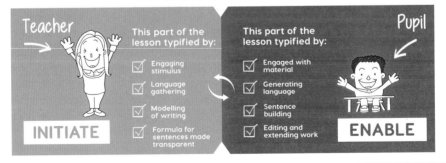

▶ Pictures from books that can be explored together.

▶ Newspaper article of a real event to inspire other types of writing.

▶ An imaginary artifact, e.g. a dragon's egg or a complaint letter from a person in the community.

▶ An experience in the community, e.g. a walk in the woods, an experience within school (a picnic in the school grounds) or a visit from a special visitor (a Roman soldier or Oscar's grandma).

Through the stimuli, resources and experiences, the intent of the inspiration part of the lesson is to entice pupils into learning and awaken intrigue and interest about what is to come. The hallmarks of the inspire section of a lesson are:

▶ **Imagination** – focus on developing ideas and unusual lines of enquiry.

▶ **Creativity** – encourage new and unique thoughts connected to the ideas you are exploring.

▶ **Memories** – make ordinary moments extraordinary so that pupils remember them forever.

▶ **Excitement** – build excitement through slow reveals of information, cliffhangers and tales from strange characters.

▶ **Possibilities** – explore a range of 'what ifs', 'what nexts' and different directions.

▶ **Magic** – add a bit of sparkle and unusual happenings to a story or real-life mystery.

The possibilities are as wide as your imagination will allow and will most certainly brighten up English sessions. That's why they are captured as the sun's rays on the *Effective English* graphic on page 13. In my experience, we are very good at the inspirational and creative aspects of teaching. The more challenging part is trying to break learning down into bite-sized chunks, not just within the lesson but over a series of lessons, so that good quality outcomes can be achieved.

Enable phase

Children need clear performance expectations for any given piece of work. They need to know that this is their opportunity to apply skills that you, as the teacher, have specifically taught, either during that session or over a period of time. The contextualised application of basic skills is the most effective way to strengthen learning and memory and to ensure that these are consolidated effectively. The enable phase not only facilitates the teaching of the sentence features of the task at hand, but also showcases previous learning from a range of precisely acquired skills. On the following page, are the elements that should be woven through a unit, so that pupils have numerous opportunities to practise these skills through a range of texts:

▶ Decoding ▶ Sentences

▶ Phonics ▶ Grammar

▶ Spelling ▶ Comprehension

▶ Vocabulary ▶ Punctuation

▶ Text Structure ▶ Cohesion

These elements are captured on the *Effective English* figure as raindrops. They can be drip-fed over time as skills and techniques that need to be used and applied in a vast array of writing and reading learning situations (see page 13).

The English teaching sequence

An overall unit of work needs to be a mix of structured provision and memorable experiences. Once pupils are intrigued and interested, the business of teaching particular competencies comes into play. As teachers in this modern age, we can be encouraged, inspired and validated by many different sources. Social media, in particular the verbose and opinionated educators on Twitter, both challenge and corroborate my personal views. One of the stand out edubloggers is Tom Sherrington *@headguruteacher*. His blog *Principles of Effective Teaching* caught my eye, in particular principle 11.

"**11. Get some balance 1.** *Over time, a series of lessons, you need a mix of Mode A teaching (straight, rigorous cycle of explain, model, practice, feedback) and Mode B teaching (awe and wonder inputs, open-ended explorations, hands-on practicals, off-piste spontaneity). I'd suggest no less than 80% Mode A for most subjects but you need some Mode B for you and for your students to enjoy and embrace the whole process. Now, obviously, I've completely made this up without any evidence. It's my gut feeling. Take that for what it is. Or leave it! Or adjust the percentages.*"

Essentially, Mode A and Mode B teaching are the guiding principles underpinning the English teaching sequence model. The sentence-stacking sessions (Mode A) are a time to explain, model, structure writing and provide differentiated tasks and feedback. Experience sessions (Mode B) are the awe and wonder inputs, open-ended explorations, hands-on practicals and rich immersion time that could be planned for (or occur spontaneously).

Like most things in life, when it comes to planning a unit of work you have to start with the end in mind.

To help you, the following *Teacher Sequence For Writing* outline will enable you to start your planning with the end in mind, so you can map sentence-stacking sessions and experience sessions.

Teacher Sequence For Writing

Three Week Unit

MONDAY

TUESDAY

WEDNESDAY

THURSDAY

FRIDAY

MONDAY

TUESDAY

WEDNESDAY

THURSDAY

FRIDAY

MONDAY

TUESDAY

WEDNESDAY

THURSDAY

FRIDAY

By the end of the unit there needs to be a genre outcome, e.g. an adventure strory or holiday brochure

Teaching Sequence

with **Experience** sessions mapped in

MONDAY   TUESDAY   WEDNESDAY   THURSDAY

FRIDAY   MONDAY   TUESDAY   WEDNESDAY

THURSDAY   FRIDAY   MONDAY   TUESDAY

WEDNESDAY   THURSDAY   FRIDAY

☆ = Experience

N.B. Experience defines a session with a free-feel immersion in a topic or book through a visit, or interviewing an expert. The lesson could be brought to life through an extended drama session or replicating an associated experience of a character. When - and how often - to include experience sessions will be a matter of professional judgement.

Are you planning a story unit? Which genre?

▶ Adventure

▶ Story with familiar setting

▶ Spooky

▶ Science Fiction

▶ Suspense

▶ Detective

Are you planning non-fiction?

▶ Recount

▶ Non-chronological report

▶ Biography/autobiography

▶ Instructions

▶ Balanced argument

▶ Explanation

▶ Letter

▶ Persuasion

Unit of work on Pinocchio - rich in drama conventions and exploring and gathering ideas through the FANTASTICs.

Next comes the decision about how long the unit of work will last.

For example: Adventure story = three weeks = 15 hours of lessons with 5 hours of lessons a week. This is illustrated overleaf.

Teaching Sequence

with **Experience** sessions and **Sentence Stacking** mapped in

Unit Outcome = Adventure Story

MONDAY — S^3

TUESDAY — S^3

WEDNESDAY — S^3

THURSDAY — ☆

FRIDAY — S^3

MONDAY — S^2

TUESDAY — S^3

WEDNESDAY — ☆

THURSDAY — S^3

FRIDAY — S^3

MONDAY — S^2

TUESDAY — ☆

WEDNESDAY — S^2

THURSDAY — S^4

FRIDAY — S^3

☆ ▪ Experience

Ⓢ ▪ Sentence Stacking lesson

③ ▪ Amount of sentences exemplified and written in lessons by pupils

N.B. During this unit, 34 sentences will be modelled by teacher and written by the pupil to complete the specified genre outcome.

It is worth planning for some experience sessions (i.e. open-ended immersion time), enabling you to explore any aspect of the unit of work in detail. For example, an extra long drama session, a debate listening to different views of the villagers in role, or a chance to go outside and explore the environment for ideas. These sessions give the opportunity to take the pressure off and develop ideas more deeply and slowly. Think carefully about how many of these more open-ended sessions you want and map them into your plan using 'E' as a code to represent experiences to enhance writing.

I have mapped in three experience sessions within an adventure story unit. I am going to reference *The Lion, the Witch and the Wardrobe* by C.S. Lewis so we have a shared frame of reference as I explain the idea of experiences.

Experience 1: Explore playing hide and seek in the school grounds to collect feelings and perspectives. Walk through an imaginary wardrobe with real old coats and re-enact the scene using conscience alley as a device to 'thought shower' Lucy's initial feelings and thoughts.

Experience 2: Watch nature programmes about cold areas, e.g. *The Arctic*. Listen to film scores with icy environments, e.g. *Happy Feet*, *Ice Age* and the instrumental music in *Frozen*. Watch film clips with snowy environments to gather words and phrases.

Experience 3: Set up a drama where pupils meet an animal character that can talk. This animal knows something that you don't and

is prepared to reveal it to you. Research and discuss stories with characters that talk in human voices, e.g. *Pinocchio*, *Fantastic Mr. Fox* and *Alice in Wonderland*.

These experiences are related and relevant but separate from the more directed sentence-stacking sessions. All other sessions become sentence-stacking sessions.

The teaching sequence plan outlines a suggested three-week teaching unit, comprising three experience sessions and twelve sentence-stacking sessions. If the provisional number of sentences are outlined in each session, then over time a complete adventure story can be exemplified using 34 sentences. The diagram shown previously details the number of sentences built within each session. The complete adventure story can be seen to be exemplified using 34 sentences in all. This level of prescription is necessary to tackle the issues of uncompleted pieces of work, teachers disappointed by the writing outcomes and a collection of themed bits and bobs in books.

To explain the process in more detail, let's imagine that this planning is for my Year 5 class. The pupils want to feel successful at writing an adventure story based on *The Lion, the Witch and the Wardrobe* so, as their teacher, I need to plan for a complete story. My three specific, strategic choices might well be:

1. **An alternative chapter** — we have already read Chapter 5 and we are going to change and alter it.

2. **A predictive chapter** — we haven't read Chapter 5 and we are going to write our own version without knowing what actually happens.

3. **A complete story** with some aspects of *The Lion, the Witch and the Wardrobe* used as a model.

Considering that this is only a fifteen-day unit, and three days have already been mapped in for open-ended activities, one of the chapter options seems the most likely choice. I think one of the biggest undiagnosed problems of teaching English in Key Stage 2 is the fact that we will be reading larger novels as our models and we will have to build writing outcomes from these. In primary schools, we are traditionally relying on creating short stories and this can be troublesome when our aims are more encompassing. As teachers, we need to think more closely about how we are going to integrate individual lessons in ways that, over time, make a complete whole.

In this case, having 34 sentences mapped out on the plan, I need to ask myself…

▶ Can I write an alternative chapter in 34 sentences?

▶ Can I write a whole short story in 34 sentences, with aspects of the book reflected in my story?

Holding their writing hand through a unit

If we don't find time to deliberately teach at sentence level, then children are at risk of producing poor quality writing. Equally, if we don't pare our teaching back to this level, then children may have unclear expectations and may either write too much (with a tendency to write drivel) or 'get stuck' and be unable to complete the writing task. Once we outline our writing goal in terms of specific sentences, we must ask ourselves if what we are asking is a reasonable request. I believe that it is.

Lesson by lesson

In this adventure story unit, I am going to look at planning a whole story with the idea of a magical wardrobe being a doorway to another world. It will include one central character and use some of the language features deployed by C.S. Lewis.

Take a look at the teaching sequence plan and now take a look at the first Tuesday. We have a target of three sentences. These are easily achievable by the majority of Year 5 pupils in a lesson, but this is not the issue. Sentence stacking is a model that requires every sentence to be defined by particular writing rules that will be demonstrated. Some aspects of what we want the children to write will be a generic hook and therefore open to 'writerly' choices and interpretation. Other aspects will be set or clearly outlined.

Learning Chunk
in English lesson

Initiate	Model	Enable

☑ How is the teacher inspiring learning?

☑ Is engagement capitalised on for writing?

☑ What stimulus is being shared?

☑ Following inspiration, what sentence or sentences is/are being modelled?

☑ What writing rules are being shared?

☑ What aspects can be adapted or need including?

☑ Are the pupils clear about the sentence they need to construct?

☑ What zone of writing are they writing through?

An English Lesson
divided into three learning chunks

	Initiate	Model	Enable
Learning Chunk 1	Initiate	Model	Enable
Learning Chunk 2	Initiate	Model	Enable
Learning Chunk 3	Initiate	Model	Enable

Monday

Based on 'La Luna' a short film by Pixar Animation Studios.

LO: To be able to use a double adjective in the story setting.

· I can use the word bank to write a describing sentence.
· I can write a setting sentence with a double adjective.
· I can use alliteration in my setting sentence.

Initiate

Story-tell

Show the first still from "La Luna" (empty sea). Story-tell for 5 mins to establish where the story is set. Model in talk double adjectives to describe the sea: "The soft, warm sea", "The indigo, still sea" etc.

Story-tell

Continue to story-tell with the next still from the film (the sea and the bow of the boat showing), using double adjectives to describe the weather: "The soft, gentle wind", "The warm, silent breeze" etc.

Story-tell

Show the still of the three characters in the boat. Story-tell: "Across the sea came a small wooden boat. Inside the boat were three very important people." Tell the children they are from the same family. **Who do you think they are?** Put children in 3 groups, one for each character. Each group writes adjectives for their character around a photo on large sugar paper.

Model

Phrase/Sentence Building

Peg up the phrase "indigo, still sea".
Discuss: **What special name do we give to these describing words? How many adjectives do we have here? Are they in the best order?** Move them around and discuss which one sounds the best. Ask children to offer other adjectives to describe the sea. Teacher scribes them on cards for a word bank, testing a few out on the washing line.

Phrase/Sentence Building

Peg on the washing line the phrase "warm, silent breeze." Move the adjectives around and discuss which one sounds the best. Ask children to offer other adjectives to describe the breeze. Teacher scribes them on cards for a word bank, testing a few out on the washing line.

Teacher Writing

Teacher writing:
Model writing descriptive phrases of the 3 characters using a double adjective each time. Pick words from the children's word banks:
"a ...., ...grandad, a ...., ... dad and a ...., ... boy."
Model with ambitious language.

Enable

Teacher/Children Writing

Teacher models writing a setting sentence with the double adjective.
"It was a magical night. A very magical night. On this night there was a ...., ...sea."
Children write their own setting sentence as above.
Are your adjectives in the best order?

> **Challenge**
> Can you use alliteration? Can you begin your adjectives with the same sound?

Teacher/Children Writing

Teacher models writing a setting sentence using the double adjective about the breeze. Children continue to write their own setting sentence with the double order? adjective:
"On this night there was a ...., ...breeze."
Are your two adjectives in the best order?

> **Challenge**
> Can you think of any other words for 'big'? Write them on the chart.

Children Writing

Children write the rest of the sentence using double adjectives: "Across the sea came a small wooden boat. Inside the boat were three very important people, "a ...., ...grandad, a ...., ... dad and a ...., ... boy."

> **Challenge**
> Can you use alliteration? Can you begin your adjectives with the same sound?

KS1

Devised by Annabelle Curran of Pytchley Endowed Primary School.

Tuesday

Based on 'La Luna' a short film by Pixar Animation Studios.

LO: To be able to use repetition to grip the reader.

· I can write a simple sentence.
· I can write sentences with repetition.
· I can open this sentence with my own words.

Initiate

Film Clip
Show the film up to the 3 men 'waiting'.

Brief discussion: What do you do when you are waiting around? What does it feel like when you have to wait?

Drama
Label each child wih a sticker, 'Grandad', 'Dad' or 'Boy'. Tell them we are going to use drama to think about what the characters did as they waited.

Film Clip
Show the next film clip up to the scene with the big moon.

Story-tell
Story-tell with repeated phrases. "Suddenly, the moon rose over the horizon. It was a huge moon. It was a huge silvery moon. It was a huge, silvery dazzling moon."

Model

Spect-acting (Drama convention)

Teacher models and set rules

Teacher story tells 'waiting' with repeated phrases while the children mime how G, D and the B spend their time. Children watch each other while in role. 'Grandad crossed his arms'. Repeat for each group's actions.

Degrees of Meaning
Teacher and children read word cards about:
"Bright/Light" together.
Teacher models how we decide if the word is a 'high' word, 'middle' or 'low'. Discuss what this means. Children tell teacher the best places for the remaining words.

Model
Teacher writes the repeating sentences. Teacher in role as writer decides (and rejects) certain words.

Enable

Teacher/ Children Writing
Teacher models writing a sentence with repetition.
"Waiting was hard to do Grandad...... Dad......... The boy........"
Children choose what the characters do as they wait and repeat it throughout their sentence.

Challenge
Can you change the beginning of this sentence? Make sure it is about waiting.

Degrees of Meaning
Children sort words for "Big". Give children a pack of 9 words. Ask them to sort into 'high', 'middle' and 'low'.

Challenge
Can you think of any other words for 'big'? Write them on the chart.

Children Writing
Children write the next part of the story describing the moon using repetition.
"Suddenly, the moon rose over the horizon. It was a huge moon. It was a huge, silvery, dazzling moon".
Children change words.

Challenge
Can you change the beginning of this sentence? Make sure it is about the moon rising.

KS1

Wednesday

Based on 'La Luna' a short film by Pixar Animation Studios.

LO: To be able to write a sentence saying "how" something moved, using words ending in "ly".

· I can write a simple sentence about how things moved.
· I can use a "ly" word from the wordbank.
· I can make up my own 'ly' words.

Initiate

Film Clip

Show the film from the beginning to recap. Stop film when the boy is at the top of the ladder. Story-tell with adverbial "ly" words.
"The boy climbed carefully...He held on tightly....He let go and floated gently....He threw the rope quickly..." etc.

Story-tell

Show the still of the boy climbing the ladder.
"The moon shone brightly in the sky and the boy knew it was time. He looked at Dad and Grandad. Wordlessly, they handed him the rope. Placing it carefully over his shoulder, the boy climbed slowly up the ladder".

Story-tell

Show the still of the boy floating. **How did the boy feel? Do you think he had done this before? How do you know?**
"As he reached the top of the ladder the world slipped away from him. He drifted softly into space and floated gently in the darkness. Below him, Dad and Grandad seemed as small as ..."

Model

Teach

Teach children that we often use "'ly'" at the end of a word to show how the thing or person is moving. Mime and feedback to practice using "ly" words.
Teacher holds up a word card "climb." Children mime then class feedback how they did it; "quickly", "slowly", "carefully", etc. Repeat for 'floated', 'flew', 'walked', 'stepped', 'talked'.

Model Word Order

On washing line, build adverbial phrase 'The boy climbed slowly up the ladder'. Discuss and model how we can move the "ly" word to say 'The boy slowly climbed up the ladder'. **Is there anywhere else that the "ly" word can go?** Tell children that as writers, they have to decide the best place for the "ly" word.

Model Word Order

On washing line, collect adverbs, "gently", "beautifully". Move the words around. Discuss which arrangement sounds the best, Is there anywhere else that the "ly" word can go?

Enable

Make a Class Word Bank

Challenge: Can you think of other actions in this story? What "ly" words would go with them?

Have A4 pages ready around the tables with pics and words taken from the film so far, (rowed, sat, climbed, floated, talked). Children go around tables and write "ly" words that go with these words on Post-its. Attach to word bank page.

Teacher/ Children Writing

Challenge: Can you change the action on the ladder? What is the best "ly" word now?

Teacher models writing the action sentence "The boy climbed the ladder" with the adverbial "ly". Children write the ladder sentence choosing an "ly" word. Refer to word banks.

Teacher/ Children Writing

Challenge Can you use alliteration? Can you begin your adjectives with the same sound?

Teacher in role as writer, model writing the action sentence "The boy floated" with an "ly" word. Choose/reject words from word bank. Children write their own "floating" sentence choosing an "ly" word.

KS1

Devised by Annabelle Curran of Pytchley Endowed Primary School.

Thursday

Based on 'Le Luna' a short film by Pixar Animation Studios.

LO: To be able to think of 'noisy' words about work and jobs (onomatopoeia).

· I can sing the song with noisy words.
· I can make up some noisy words for the song.
· I can carefully select the best noisy word for certain jobs.

Initiate

Film clip

Show the film the whole way through, up to Dad and Grandad arguing.
So why have they gone to the moon? What is their job? What tools do they use for their job?

Experience day
Take the children outside with a variety of cleaning tools (brushes, spades, dustpans, dusters, rakes). Allow children to 'clean' the moon with their tools.

Story-tell

"It was hard work getting the moon shipshape and tidy. Shooting stars fell like raindrops and the moon continued to glow brightly. 'Goodness me,' thought the boy. 'This is hard work.'"

Model

Generating Onomatopoeic Words

Teacher sings an echo song as the children clean the moon. Sing to the tune of Old Macdonald. Use noisy words: bang, clatter, screech, thud, thump, scrape, clink, clank, clunk, rattle, whoosh. "We are cleaning up the moon, e-i-e-i-o. With a swish swish here and a swish swish there…"

Drama and Story-tell

Teacher models/sets out rules for the drama.
Working with a partner, teacher freeze frames as Grandad, Dad or the boy busy working. Teacher and partner think of a 'thought'. Model to children how partner speaks as actor comes alive when tapped. Show how to freeze when tapped again.

Enable

Sound-scape

Put children into small groups. Give them a few mins to rehearse the echo song with their choice of noisy word. Work around groups, rest of class echo the new lyrics as we clean the moon.
Making a word bank of 'noisy' words. Give out Post-its for children to write the noisy words from the song. Stick the Post-its on the tools that made that noise. Save the words for the working wall.

Challenge:
Can you find two noisy words that rhyme for the song? Can you sing these instead of repeating one word?

Thought Tap

Rehearse one another's thought tap.
Whole class mime working on the moon, then freeze on command. Teacher story-tells: "It was hard work getting the moon shipshape and tidy. Shooting stars fell like raindrops and the moon continued to glow brightly." Teacher taps groups in turn to speak.

Challenge:
Can you change the action on the ladder? What is the best "ly" word now?

KS1

Devised by Annabelle Curran of Pytchley Endowed Primary School.

Friday

Based on 'La Luna' a short film by Pixar Animation Studios.

LO: To be able to use 'noisy' words in my sentences. (onomatopoeia).

· I can say some noisy words to go with the story.
· I can write a sentence with 'noisy' words.
· I can use alliteration or rhyming words in my noisy sentence.

Initiate

Story-tell

Show a still of the boy sweeping up stars.
"Unfortunately, the stars kept coming. Clink. Another star fell. Splat. There fell another one. Swish. Another star landed at his feet. 'Will we ever finish this job?' thought the boy."

Film

Show short time lapse of shooting stars at

www.youtube.com/watch?v=S_jd fyp8pL0 (1 min)

Music
Give out 'twinkly' instruments. A few children at a time create background music as we watch the shooting stars on screen.

Model

Making a Word Bank

Have large sugar paper ready with a picture from the film in the middle (the stars on the moon). Model adding noisy words for the stars landing on the moon. Teacher models 'jingle', 'clank', 'swish', 'thud'.

Teacher Writing:

Teacher models the repeating sentences with onomatopoeia:
"Clink. Another star fell. Crash. Another star fell. Swish. Another star fell."

Enable

Making a Word Bank

Children make a word bank with the rest of their table on large sugar paper.
("whizz", "clang", "bang", "splat", "whoosh", "swoosh", etc).

Challenge:
Can you use alliteration or rhyming words?

Teacher/ Children Writing

Children write three sentences that include the noise of the falling stars
Choose your favourite three noisy words. Use the word banks to help.

Challenge:
Can you change the action on the ladder? What is the best "ly" word now?

KS1

Devised by Annabelle Curran of Pytchley Endowed Primary School.

Lesson Plan

Based on 'Let's get a Pup' by Bob Graham.

LO: To write three effective sentences for our story.

Steps to Success:
· I can include an alliterative sentence.
· I can describe what can be seen and use adverbs.
· I can write a simile.

Initiate

Story-tell

Story-tell the beginning of the story. Explain Lucy's excitement at getting a new puppy. Generate a bank of names as examples for children. Collect some suggestions.

Degree of Meaning

Discuss which words are 'look' words from the following list: smell, stare, glimpse, skip, run, glance, run, jump
Sort into strong/weak or big/little look words e.g. stare/glare, glance/glimpse.

Comparative Word Bank

Comparison with brown; negative words/ phrases e.g. rotten banana skin, pile of rubbish.
Positive words: chocolate bar, chocolate milkshake, teddybear, woolly jumper.

Model

Collect Word bank

As the family walked next to the kennels:
Names: Scrumpy, Rex, Barney, Lola, Danny, Wibble.
Actions: scratched, wriggled, barked, leapt, danced, wagged.
Action quiz with teacher.

Model Using Adverb

Bobby bounced. They fell in love. Then they noticed Rosie. With many a backward _____ they walked away _____ly.
e.g. with many a backward stare they walked away slowly.

Build a Simile

Rosie is brown like a
_____ (adjective)
_____ (simile)
Simile = Similar/same

Enable

Children Talking/ Writing

Talk pairs can you talk 4 possibilities together.
Write three names in these short sentences.

_____ barked.
_____ jumped.
_____ raced.

Challenge:
Can you invent dog names and actions for your snappy sentences?

Children Writing

Gather a range of alternative words for 'look', choose most appropriate and pair with adverb.

Challenge:
Can you add in extra information that shows family feelings?

Children Writing

Write a simile using positive ideas of things that are brown in colour.

Challenge:
Can you add extra information to make simile more interesting? e.g. Rosie is brown like fizzy coco-cola being gulped by a thirsty boy.

KS1

Lesson Plan

Based on 'Heart in the Bottle' by Oliver Jeffers

LO: To write powerful sentences for our story.

Steps to Success:
· I can include action and a subordinating conjunction in a sentence.
· I can write a complex sentence.
· I can include personification.

Initiate

Story-tell

Story-tell Jessica and Grandad's relationship up until the beach scene.

Predict what is happening at the beach. Paired talk. Share ideas and reveal.

Verb Bank

Story-tell up until the whale drawing. Gather 'ing' action words to fit the picture e.g. running, racing, leaping, pelting, skipping etc

Personification

Story-tell to the empty chair. Gather ideas through the FANTASTICs

1. Noticing
2. Feeling
3. Thinking

Model

Include Conjunction

Establish writing rules: 1. cannot use fly, flew or flying. Talk about alternative action verbs.2. cannot use colour as an adjective for Grandad description. Introduce conjunctions – as, while, whilst. Gather verb bank for Jessica. 1. Cannot use colour as adjective.

Complex Sentence

_____ ing to see Grandad, Jessica _____ .
Skipping to see Grandad, Jessica was bursting with excitement to ask him more questions.

Build a Character Description

Jessica verb at the adjective chair.
A adjective tear _____ .
She thought about _____ .
Show how if a character is changed to something inanimate then feeling applied to that object it will then personify it.

Enable

Children Talking/Writing

Complete following rules Grandad verb
_____

adjective kite as Jessica verb _____ adjective _____ .
e.g. Grandad struggled to control the wild kite as Jessica paddled in the glistening sea.

> **Challenge:** Can you include alliteration to describe sea? e.g. frothy foam/ salty sea/wild waves.

Children Writing

Follow 3 writing rules–

1. ing verb,
2. comma,
3. Ending that makes sense.

e.g. Rushing to show Grandad, Jessica clutched her made drawing.

> **Challenge:** Can you include an adverb to show Jessica's feelings? e.g. excitedly, happily, joyfully.

Children Writing

Follow 3 writing rules–

Demonstrate through the model how to flip to personification using a flower.
e.g. The flower stared at the empty chair. A lonely tear trickled down its petal face. She thought about the time they had together.

> **Challenge:** Can you use personification strategy for another object? e.g. table, picture, lamp, etc.

KS2

Lesson Plan

Based on 'Wolves in the Walls' by Neil Gaiman

LO: To write three effective suspense sentences.

Steps to Success:
· I can use rhyme and repetition to set scene.
· I can use pathetic fallacy.
· I can include a double adjective into a complex sentence.

Initiate

Share Text

"Lucy heard noises. The noises were coming from inside the walls. They were hustling noises and bustling noises. They were crinkling noises and crackling noises. They were sneaking, creeping, crumpling noises." Find patterns.

Writerly Techniques

Progress pitstop: can you tell me what pathetic fallacy is? Explain it is a match between character feelings and weather/nature. On a washing line, model a sentence that begins with determiner (the). Collect frightening weather.

Word Banks

Collect a range of words to capture the movement of the wolves.
Verbs: Leaping, bursting, jumping, lunging, pouncing, darting
Adjectives: (to describe wolf) hungry, skinny, matted, smelly, angry, enraged, ferocious.

Model

Explore Patterns

Patterns: rhyme, alliteration, group of three.
Demo for birds: scratching, gnawing, clawing, flapping, scraping, flipping. Distribute focus. e.g cats, rats and bats.

Pupils have to follow model provided.

Model Two Banks of Ideas:

Frightening weather: storm, rain, gale, thunder, hail, fog.
Violent Verbs: strangled, stabbed, throttled, punched.

Complex Sentence

Explain model:
1. Start with a verb
2. 'through the walls' added next
3. Adjective before wolf
4. Finish the job (can't have wolves touch Lucy)
e.g. Bursting through the walls, the hungry, skinny wolves circled Lucy's bed.

Enable

Children Writing

Pupils work in pairs to generate sounds related to their animal and group with rhyme, alliteration and group of three. Share effective examples.

Challenge: Can you add a deepen the moment sentence to reveal how frightened Lucy is?

Children Writing

Complete sentence and follow model: The weather verb keep action outside, Lucy

e.g. The fog suffocated the terrified trees, Lucy shivered in her bed.

Challenge: Can you add a deepen the moment sentence? Can you continue to build personification of nature?

Children Writing

Build a complex sentence starting with an 'ing' verb. Next include a noun phrase with a double adjective.

Challenge: Can you create extra tension and add a further sentence? Remember to ensure the wolves don't touch Lucy.

KS2

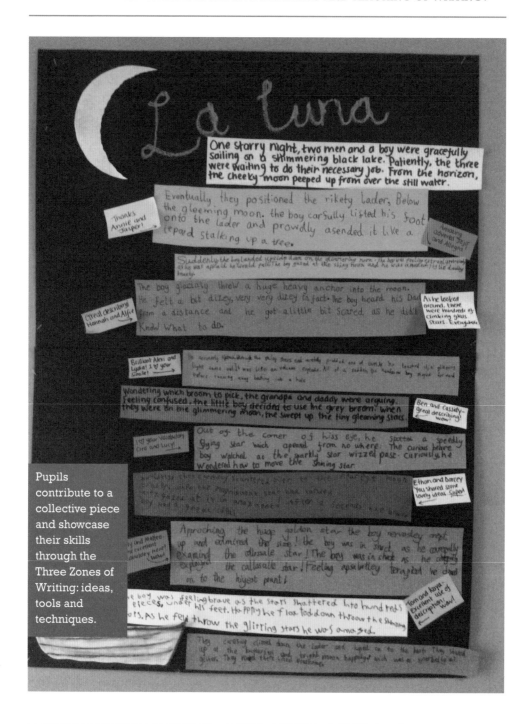

Pupils contribute to a collective piece and showcase their skills through the Three Zones of Writing: ideas, tools and techniques.

Lesson planning

An individual lesson is based on a sentence model, broken into separate chunks. The focus areas are drawn down from the *Effective English* model and provide a framework for teaching.

Initiate section: a stimulus to capture the pupils' imaginations and set up a sentence.

Model section: Close modelling a sentence that outlines clear writing features and techniques.

Enable section: Pupils write their sentence following the model.

In a lesson with a target of three sentences, there will be three learning chunks.

Going back now to my Year 5 class and the first sentence-stacked lesson. I need to build three sentences in the allocated lesson time and the features of the sentences will be:

Sentence one: use a repeated word or phrase for effect.

Sentence two: include a simile using the word 'like'.

Sentence three: use a question to draw the reader.

The model I will be using with the pupils:

Sentence 1: Repetition for effect - The summer holidays spent at Grandma's house: what a long, extremely long so-called holiday this will be.

Sentence 2: Simile using 'like' - Grandma's house was like a dusty patchwork quilt and every square on the quilt was her chance to tell a laborious story about people I didn't know.

Sentence 3: Question to the reader - How was I going to make it to the end?

Choose plot points from the following list to build a story journey for the following character.

Outlined below is the complete story that will be modelled over the sequence.

Adventure Story
Narrative Plot Points

1	2	3	4	5	6	7	8	9
Initial Problem	Contrasting Two Events	Meet a Friend	Building Suspense	Intriguing Discovery	Find a New World	New Character	Secret from the Past	Home Safely

Each narrative plot point is broken down into a teaching sequence over time. Please note: sometimes one plot point will serve as a focus over more than one day.

Outlined below is a chronological teaching sequence that exemplifies how each plot point is developed into sentences.

Week 1: Monday – Three sentences

Narrative Plot Point

1.

Sentence 1: Repetition for effect - The summer holidays spent at Grandma's house, what a long, extremely long so-called holiday this will be.

Sentence 2: Simile using 'like' - Grandma's house was like a dusty patchwork quilt and every square on the quilt was her chance to tell a laborious story about people I didn't know.

Sentence 3: Question to the reader - How was I going to make it to the end?

Week 1: Tuesday – Three sentences

Narrative Plot Point

2.

Sentence 1: Pathetic Fallacy – The first few days were dismal and the dark rain mirrored my mood.

Sentence 2: Simile using 'as' – On Thursday, I woke as the warm yellow fingertips of the sun stroked my face and Grandma told me Gladys was arriving with her niece.

Sentence 3: Focus on character's sense of smell – Grandma was polished and pristine, smelling of lavender soap and chemically-infused hairspray.

Week 1: Wednesday – Three sentences

Narrative Plot Point

3.

Sentence 1: Short sentence – Grace was naughty.

Sentence 2: Short sentence – I could just tell.

Sentence 3: Fronted adverbial (how) – With a burst of excitement, she yelped "Hide and seek!" and ran deep into the back part of the house.

Week 1: Thursday

Experience day 1: Re-enact hide and seek and walking through a wardrobe full of coats.

Week 1: Friday - Three sentences

Narrative Plot Point

4.

Sentence one: Rhyme – My heart was thumping and jumping in my chest.

Sentence two: Double adjective – Suddenly, the ornate, imposing wardrobe caught my eye and I had a hunch this could be her hiding place.

Sentence three: Complex sentence – Creeping across the creaking floorboards, I reached up expectantly to undo the latch.

Week 2: Monday – Two sentences

Narrative Plot Point

5.

Sentence one: Alliteration – Inside the wardrobe, coats crushed my ribs, my face felt fur and a musty aroma mingled with mothballs.

Sentence two: Three adverbs/adverbial phrases (how, where, when) – I waited for Grace's face to pop out wildly amongst the fabric and fur when she saw my shoes.

Week 2: Tuesday – Three sentences

Narrative Plot Point

5.

Sentence one: One word (I know it is not technically a sentence) – Nothing.

Sentence two: Dialogue – "Grace! Where are you? I can't see you!" I said, my voice shaking but thankfully muffled by the coats.

Sentence three: Ellipsis – I couldn't see her and I just kept walking…how strange!

Week 2: Wednesday

Experience day 2: Watch information and story clips of cold landscapes. Take guided tours of icy scenes from books and films. Gather ideas and language.

Week 2: Thursday – Three sentences

Narrative Plot Point

6.

Find a New World

Sentence one: Metaphor – Grace was an illusion.

Sentence two: Inner thoughts - This house was sending me mad.

Sentence three: Onomatopoeia - Thud! My body tumbled onto the crisp white bed of snow.

Week 2: Friday – Three sentences

Narrative Plot Point

6.

Find a New World

Sentence one: Question – Where was I?

Sentence two: Adjectives – This was a cold and brightly illuminated place that froze your brain to attention.

Sentence three: Personification – The trees trembled with every descending

snowflake and the snowbells shivered at the sight of my appearance.

Week 3: Monday – Two sentences

Narrative Plot Point

7.

New Character

Sentence one: Dialogue – "Hello, Mr. Chambers?"

Sentence two: Action – I turned quickly on my heels and there under the glare of the wintery sun was a fox, smartly dressed and wearing a hat at a jaunty angle and spectacles on the end of his nose.

Week 3: Tuesday

Experience Day 3: Explore stories that include talking animals. Use drama conventions to find out more about why authors use them in stories.

Week 3: Wednesday – Two sentences

Narrative Plot Point

7.

Sentence 1: Conditional – I should have run away but his eyes were trustworthy, not shy.

Sentence 2: Complex sentence – As I followed him through the woodland, he mumbled to himself about secrets of the past.

Week 3: Thursday – Four sentences

Narrative Plot Point

8.

Sentence 1: Double adverb (how) – At his lair, the fox made tea in china cups suspiciously slowly.

Sentence 2: Simile – The fox took a while to warm up like his kettle and told me a long story about Grandma as a girl when she borrowed one of his polka-dot scarves.

Sentence 3: Focus on feelings – The fox twisted a handkerchief as he spoke, too embarrassed to ask for it back.

Sentence 4: Onomatopoeia – I left in a hurry, raced back through the wardrobe and fell into the arms of Grace with a thud!

Week 3: Friday – Three Sentences

Narrative Plot Point

9.

Sentence 1: Precise verb – Grandma called us for tea; a knowing smirk was exchanged between Grace and I.

Sentence 2: Focus on what the character can see – As Grandma poured the tea into floral china cups, I noticed she was wearing a polka-dot silk scarf.

Sentence 3: List of three – She had borrowed, taken, stolen the scarf after all: maybe this was going to be the best summer of my life.

At first, many teachers worry about this being an over-prescriptive approach. In actual fact, the model acts as a support hook for the weakest writers whilst the highest-attaining writers can write to the brief yet still showcase their full competencies.

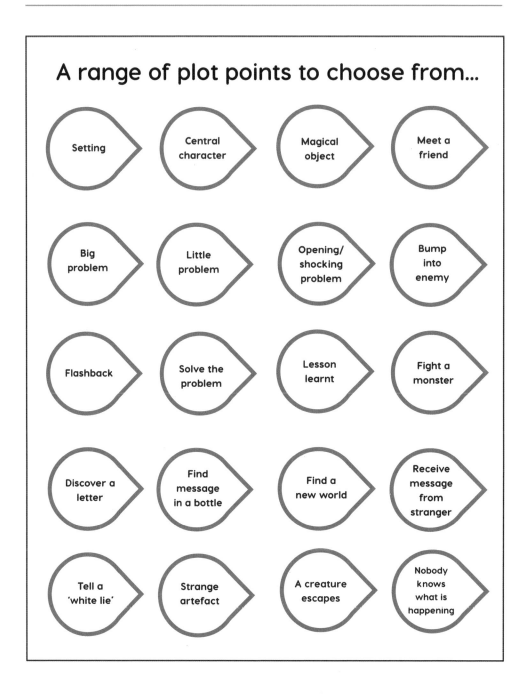

A range of plot points to choose from...

Setting

Central character

Magical object

Meet a friend

Big problem

Little problem

Opening/ shocking problem

Bump into enemy

Flashback

Solve the problem

Lesson learnt

Fight a monster

Discover a letter

Find message in a bottle

Find a new world

Receive message from stranger

Tell a 'white lie'

Strange artefact

A creature escapes

Nobody knows what is happening

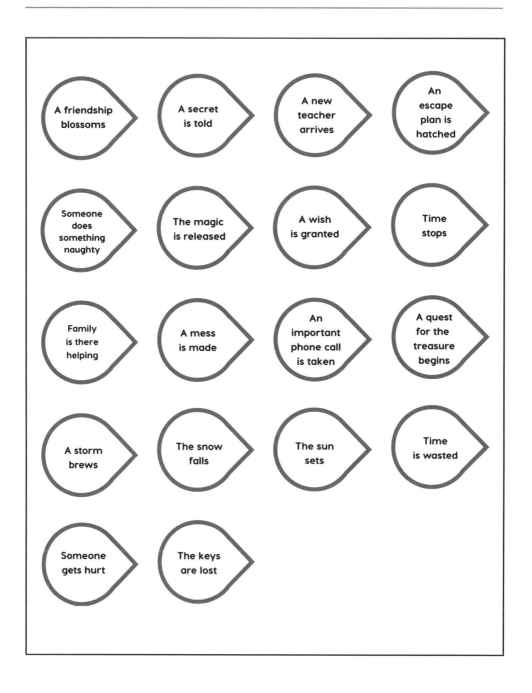

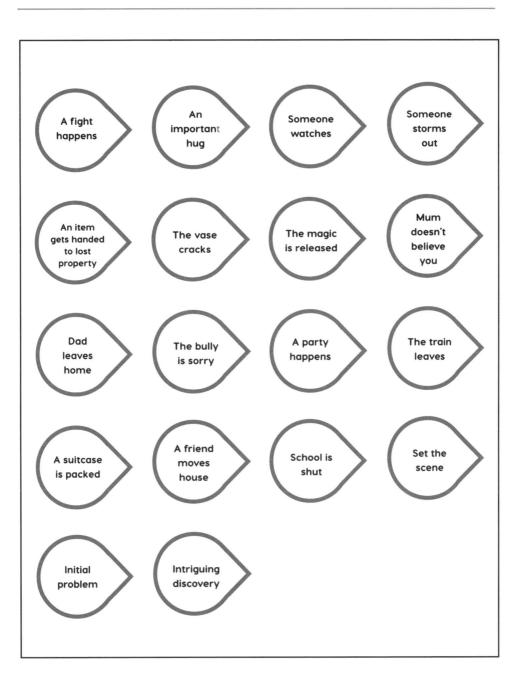

Working wall

During any teaching unit, the shape of the story, or non-fiction, will be either slowly revealed with the class or set in place before the more detailed sentence stacking takes place. The overall maps for writing will be explored in more detail in later chapters. This particular story follows the map opposite.

Each of the narrative plot points needs to be fleshed out through the ongoing teaching, with a sentence-stacking approach. They build up chronologically over time in the story (unless a flashback is built in) and enable both the pupil and teacher to ensure that work is finished in the designated time.

Massive 'sentence stacked' model

The display of the narrative journey, or non-fiction shape, in the classroom enables children to see the 'shape' and complete structure of the text at hand. To supplement this, schools have found particular success with highly visible

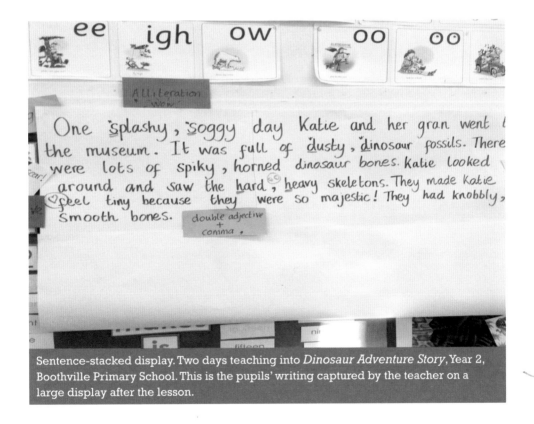

Sentence-stacked display. Two days teaching into *Dinosaur Adventure Story*, Year 2, Boothville Primary School. This is the pupils' writing captured by the teacher on a large display after the lesson.

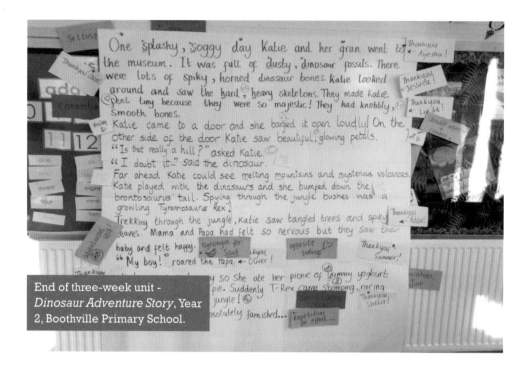

End of three-week unit - *Dinosaur Adventure Story*, Year 2, Boothville Primary School.

An enormous sentence-stacked display in a Year 1 classroom at Pytchley Primary School. Pupils' contributions are celebrated day by day as the genre builds.

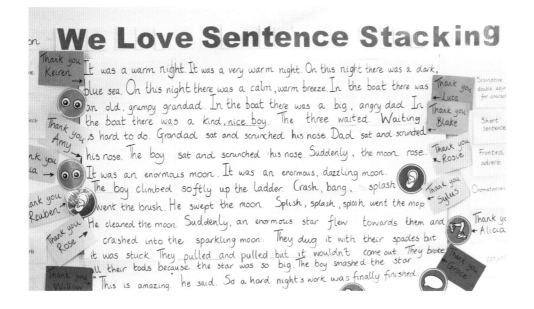

text models, comprising the children's own sentences. As part of the high value given to writing, this model is labelled so the pupils can see who has provided a sentence for the larger communal piece of writing. For example, if we look back on the model provided for children on their first lesson, not only will each pupil have their own version of this in their books, but they will have the sense that sentences can be spliced from anyone in the class and 'jigsawed' together as you work towards a completed piece over time. The sentences included in the communal model are selected by the teacher and may take the following forms:

Sentence 1: Repetition for effect - The summer holidays spent at Grandma's house, what a long, extremely long so-called holiday this will be.

Sentence 2: Simile using 'like' - Grandma's house was like a dusty patchwork quilt and every square on the quilt was her chance to tell a laborious story about people I didn't know.

Sentence 3: Question to the reader - How was I going to make it to the end?

Alternative version of the three sentences

Spending six weeks at Grandma's: six long weeks; six long, boring weeks; six long, boring and monotonous weeks. Grandma's house was like a second-hand shop where no one bought anything and Grandma had forgotten why she had bought it herself. What could I possibly do to entertain myself for the whole summer holidays?

This 'sentence-focus' approach increases the value of the individual sentence, not only from the perspective that every sentence contributes towards the meaning of the text, but also the selection of individual sentences highlights the importance of choice and precision in the construction of a piece of writing. Pupils are genuinely thrilled when they see their names chosen for the collective model and, as teachers, we are able to keep a close eye on sentences produced daily. Every day, the model is added to after the lesson and the best examples are sifted through to make final choices for the wall.

Provided part or paragraph

when it's not working try

Time is of the essence in classrooms and, even with a sentence-stacking approach, teachers can feel hard-pushed to ensure that a genre or text type is finished. This is where the provided part or paragraph is so effective. Essentially, when we need to adapt our plans in response to where the pupils are, or we want to delve deeper at certain points into a story or non-fiction piece, a part can be provided. This is powerful in narrative writing, particularly if we need to show the passing of time in a plot, if we want to replicate a tricky

Look closely at this Year 6 piece of work from Pytchley Primary School - based on Jim Henson's *The Storyteller (The Soldier and Death)*. Notice how the teacher has provided a paragraph to move on a pedestrian part of the story.

aspect of a written model or if we worry pupils might get too lost in fighting the dragon and not finish.

Sentences provided by the teacher to show the passing of time or a repeated event for an adventure story:

Night after night, James fought the dragon in his dreams. Every morning, his duvet was in a tangled heap on the floor and his hair wet with sweat.

This approach is also helpful in non-fiction. If, for instance, we only have time to explore three sets of opposing views in a balanced argument (and we want to provide one more) or we want to give the ingredients of the recipe or we want to describe two of the less interesting events of our recount to the zoo.

Here is an example of sentences, provided by the teacher, to quickly explain lunchtime events on a class trip to the zoo.

At 12 o'clock, we all stopped for lunch. Mrs. Gibb distributed chocolate bars to those who had finished. The sun shone and every one was chatting about the sea-lion show.

Cohesion

Think back to the beginning of the chapter, when I mentioned the other national weakness in pupils' writing – namely understanding the integral structure of text. Navigating a reader through a piece of text relies on more than the use of conjunctions. We have to open our minds to the broader aspects of cohesion and that can sometimes mean referring back to an earlier point or using whole sentences that bridge one idea to the next.

Halliday and Hasan (1976, 1986) believed that cohesion and coherence were the two most important textual elements of good writing. As a profession, we have taken an over-simplistic view of cohesion and the importance of exemplifying cohesion for children. The images of footprints are used through the book. These footprints feature on our narrative maps and non-fiction shapes, placed between templates of jigsawed shapes to highlight when

Footstep visuals (as used by this Year 2 pupil) encourage children to talk through their writing, stepping from one idea to the next.

steps are required to guide the reader through the textual landscape. Cohesion is important not only within sentences but also across ideas, paragraphs and sections too. Future chapters will include more references to the importance of textual cohesion, showing how we should teach children to signpost readers through pieces of writing.

Differentiation

Lower attaining writers feel completely supported every step of the way with this process and the small chunks enable them to have absolute clarity around expectations at any point in the sequence. The expectations are made transparent through a sentence focus. If, at any point, individuals or groups are unsure (or need extra support with sentence building), words, phrases and clauses can be provided - in envelopes or on word cards/strips - to give pupils banks of ideas. These banks need to be tailored to specific sentence points.

For example:

Sentence three: Personification – The trees trembled with every descending snowflake and the snowbells shivered at the sight of my appearance.

The lowest attaining group might need an envelope containing human actions and emotions that could be applied to environmental features. For example:

Human attributes – quivered, screamed, cried, huddled, wept, sobbed, sang, whistled, hummed.

Items in nature – grass, petals, bluebells, bushes, swallows, finches, clouds.

Deepening the moment sentence

The highest attaining writers have a chance to excel using this model. Within a learning chunk, they will initially be required to follow the writing rule of the sentence, but after that they will be able to write extra, as long as they stay within the narrative plot point. Training pupils to write 'deepening the moment' sentences for the chronological part of the story that is the focus of the session will sharpen their expertise at staying on the point. This enables the unit to remain cohesive from lesson to lesson. It means that when a new lesson begins, everyone is in the same place and the class can pick up the story from where you left off. In many ways, we want to discourage our high attainers from simply writing more. It's helpful instead to provide challenges at sentence-stacking points, so pupils can reflect back on previous skills learned in English lessons or include vocabulary for specific effects.

Across the UK, there are currently two main types of systems in place for capturing pupils' work while they are writing.

Way 1: A free use of wipe board while pupils are at the composition stage and are considering ideas for writing. Other ideas include: a class book to stick in 'bits and bobs', work done on paper, smaller activities or ideas around photographs or pictures. Sustained independent writing to be assessed is captured elsewhere.

Way 2: A more pristine record of the learning journey – to be recorded with an emphasis on presentation, with a reduced written load on wipe boards and a heavier capture of evidence in books. Sustained independent writing of complete pieces is often captured in this book too.

You might recognise one of your school's approaches here, or perhaps it is a mix of both. I suggest a sentence-stacking approach that it is somewhere in between. I want to make it clear at this point that I'm not averse to wipe boards (I really enjoy teaching with them) but one thing that is critical about sentence stacking is that every sentence produced by this approach is precious and crucial to the finished product.

There have been many times during my teaching when a child has written a striking metaphor and, in the blink of an eye, wiped it off their wipe board since they'd considered it to be silly/inappropriate. I could cry when this happens. Writing is so difficult, and when children get it right, it has a quality that is so fresh and open and untainted by tired clichés and haggard phrases. It is essential that children are taught to value English and recognise good writing, whether it is other people's or their own.

Classroom books, to facilitate sentence-stacking, work best if they are A4 double-sided books, with a blank page on one side to make jottings, note down ideas and practise. The other side is lined - for pupils' completed sentences. If, as teachers, we know there are going to be three sentences stacked in the lesson, then the blank side can be marked into three sections. We work on the principle of a new page for a new day. If pupils need more jotting space, an extra white sheet can be added as a hinged overlay.

Pupil's English Writing Book

'Inspiration Page'

(Functioning like a wipe board for notes, jottings, vocabulary, ideas)

Blank Side ▶

Learning Chunk 1

Learning Chunk 2

Learning Chunk 3

▲ **Marked to allocate space for ideas at learning chunk**

'Writing Page'

Lined
Side

Pupils' English books - working with sentence stacking

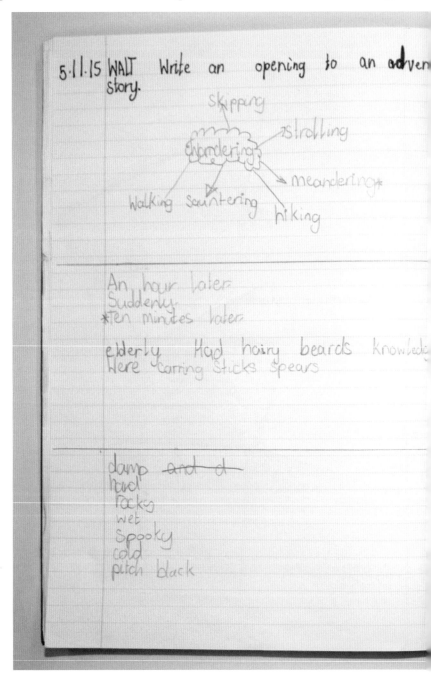

An amazing thing once happend to me.
I was meandering in the woods when
suddenly I stumbled and found myself
falling deeper, deeper, deeper! My limbs
went stiff.
Ten minutes later I woke up in a
pitch black damp place. I could see
day light in the distance, far far in
the distance. I was determined to escape.

Then to my relief, I saw someone - a girl. She was about my age but
she didn't look like any of the girls I knew. And I don't think I looked
like any of the boys she knew. She took me home to meet her family —
and what a family it was!

The men had hairy beards and
wore torn clothes, the women were
carrying rocks, and had dirty faces,
and the children were pointing at me!
I could see a roaring fire, a tiny
baby sleeping, and a lady scooping meat
for the children. I felt absolutey heart
broken. because I didn't know these
people.

A fabulous start Charlie.
Keep up the hard work.

A Year 3 example. Notice on the left side, it is used as an ideas-gathering page for collecting words and practising ideas.

4/11/15   WALT: Build Suspense which ends with a Cliffhanger

Dark, cold, Inky darkness, Vale of darkness, unlit, dim.

- All of a Sudden.
- At that moment.
- In the blink of an eye.
- As quick as a flash.

- Wriggle out of the hands grasp.
- Kick.
- grab the hand.
- walk the other way.

- Pummel the hand desperately.
- pierce the hand.
- spear it.
- Slice.
- Slash.

- Maliciously.

- Acting in defence.
- Acting as if it was a knife.
- Eager to defeat.
- Desperate to stab.
- Acting like a knife
- Acting as his heroes.

·Outside, he stood on the hard. concrete playground,
covered by the blanket of darkness. Tired from
her the events that had happened. he ~~gazed~~ watched
back into the mysterious darkness of the
classroom~as a feeling of anticipation
crawled into ~~his~~ body.
         Charlie's

In the blink of an eye, as charlie swivveled to
check his eerie surroundings, a chilled, pale
hand ~~clenched his throat~~ x ~~the a hand was~~
~~protrudiged from the cold window~~ protruded from
the   open window, clenching him mercilessly
by the throat. The sheer .strength of the
hand shook ~~the~~ him viciously, towards the window
As ~~this~~ life was in danger ~~a~~ Charlie pummeled the
              his
hand maliciously with ~~her~~ ~~the~~ the scissors, punching deep
within the skin. The scissors, acting in charlie's defence,
near enough skinned the villanous hand to the bone
~~x~~ which produced a blood-curdling scream...

A Year 6 example of a writing book. Pupils mark off the left hand side into sections, aware of how many chunks they are going to write. There are no lines on the right hand side, so pupils have a clear view of textual cohesion and the importance of paragraphs.

Consider

① All the strategies that are currently used within teaching and learning that promote genre completed texts.

② Is there a sense that the direction of a unit becomes less clear over time? Do teachers start with clear modelling, but find themselves derailed by pupil choices about content or shape?

School Impact Points

① Analyse planning closely. Does it really facilitate the building up of a whole piece of writing over time?

② Through book scrutinies, follow the coherence of units and check that work isn't a themed collection of related activities.

③ Discuss the impact of 'Sentence Stacking' to support the teaching of completed pieces of work. Designate 'Sentence Stacking' boards so large ongoing models of pupil work can be built over time.

"Reading brilliant stories gets me excited for writing."

Daniel, Year 6

What are the Non-Fiction Shapes for Writing?

Teaching writing is like a jigsaw puzzle. Give children a picture of what is expected so that they know how to fit the pieces together.

Chapter 4

Summary

☑ Non-fiction shapes function as frames that visually represent the structure and organisation of that text type.

☑ The shapes serve as a powerful teaching tool to 'act out' and articulate text-talk sentences that would be effective in a component shape.

☑ The shapes are best enlarged, so pupils can step on and through them and are able to see the whole shape of the writing they are trying to construct.

THE WRITE STUFF

What are the Non-fiction Shapes for Writing?

As explored earlier in the book, we have identified that pupils are weak at completing whole pieces of writing. Non-fiction writing is particularly challenging because there are few similarities across the different text types. Reflect for a moment on the nature and language of a holiday brochure, selling a resort in Italy, compared to a balanced argument exploring the fors and againsts of school uniforms.

The purposes of non-fiction writing are broad and varied. This makes it much more difficult for teachers to extrapolate the key features, the language and the structure. In relation to children finding the completion of work so hard, the non-fiction shapes have been designed to provide a clear visual representation of the structure of each text type.

These maps should be large enough to build like a jigsaw on the hall or classroom floor – so children can see the shape and recognise it as the underlying structure of the non-fiction text type. Many teachers have had great success with laminated versions of the non-fiction shapes, enabling photographs, key words and sentences to be stuck on and/or written within them.

The footprints are crucial. They highlight the importance of helping the reader step to the next big idea. The footprints also serve to support the class teacher. Why? Because they make the need to teach textual cohesion, and joining words, more explicit.

With a large visual shape on the floor, pupils are encouraged to 'walk the walk and talk the talk'. They jump on the map and around the map, talking the text and articulating - in sentences - aspects of writing that should be included within that section. Different pupils can be positioned at different points on the visual shape and asked to represent the sentences that ought to be included in that text type and position.

These shapes start as bold, jigsaw-like representations, but down the line they become a mental image for children when they are trying to construct non-fiction writing independently.

The non-fiction shapes are a backbone in many classrooms. They are used as a clear pathway for children to reference on their working walls. They also enable teachers to break down their demonstration of writing into bite-sized chunks, show children where they are on the map and explain the shapes they are working within.

Children find it very difficult to conceptualise the whole shape of a text type. This is why the completion of work is one of the biggest challenges for teachers. To support children's thinking, 'massive maps' enable them to see the whole piece of writing. Not only do they capture the whole genre in a highly visible way, they also allow oral or written layers of language to be added in key locations.

This is an ideal way to build writing up over time and break it down into a logical teaching sequence. It means that when there is a lesson focus on a particular

Pupils working with the persuasion shape for writing, gathering ideas to sell their chocolate bars.

Working large with a non-fiction shape - a recount shape is captured here so pupils can see the whole shape of this text type.

genre-related objective, pupils are able to 'see' where they are on the map.

A large map enables pupils to talk about the features of non-fiction text types and to plot these in the correct places. It is a highly kinaesthetic approach to engaging the whole class and encouraging teamwork and collaboration. Pupils can work as a whole class, or in groups, to add words, phrases and whole-sentence ideas.

"Walk the walk, talk the talk, write the write."

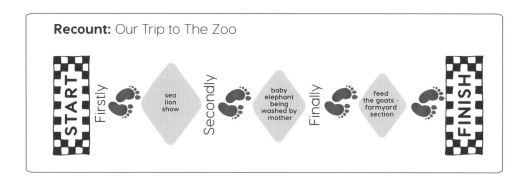

This plotting can be done with pictures or photographs. Later, it can be expanded from note form to demonstrate how genre-driven sentences are developed. For example:

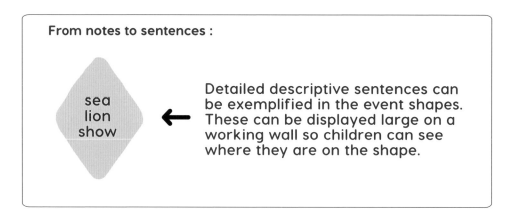

"Firstly, the sea lions somersaulted through the air as we watched in awe during the opening of the spectacular show."

1 **Firstly = adverb**

2 **somersaulted = precise verb**

3 **spectacular = adjective**

Working with a large non-fiction shape. Pupils can see the whole shape of this text type and walk and talk down it.

Pupil making notes about the sounds to be included in the recount, based on *The Stone Age Boy* by Satoshi Kitamura.

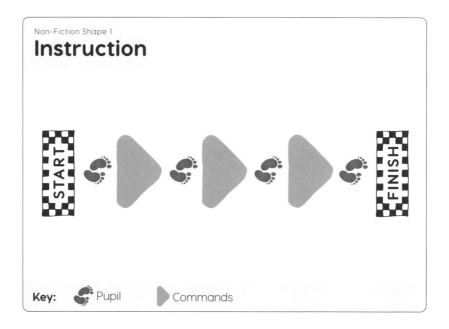

Non-Fiction Shape 1
Instruction

Key: Pupil · Commands

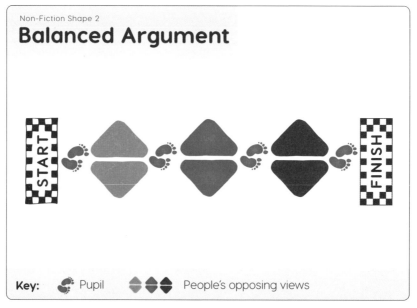

Non-Fiction Shape 2
Balanced Argument

Key: Pupil · People's opposing views

Non-Fiction Shape 3

Explanation

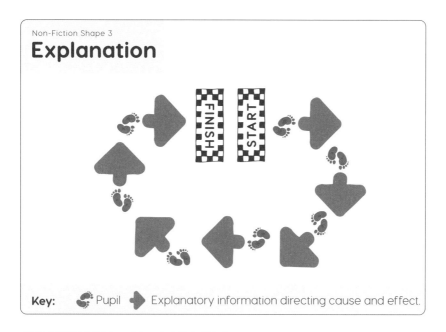

Key: 👣 Pupil ➤ Explanatory information directing cause and effect.

Non-Fiction Shape 4

Persuasion

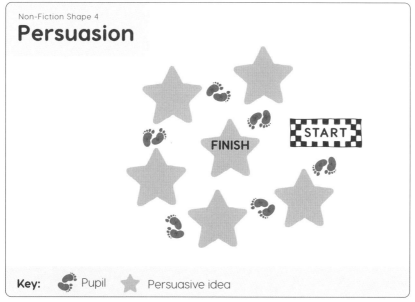

Key: 👣 Pupil ⭐ Persuasive idea

Non-Fiction Shape 5

Non-Chronological Report

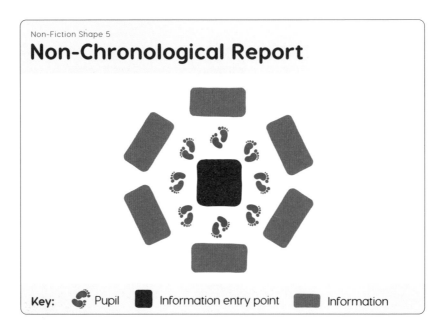

Key: Pupil ■ Information entry point ▮ Information

Non-Fiction Shape 6

Recount

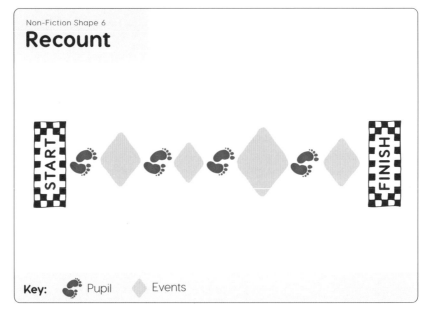

Key: Pupil ◆ Events

Non-Fiction Shape 7
Biography

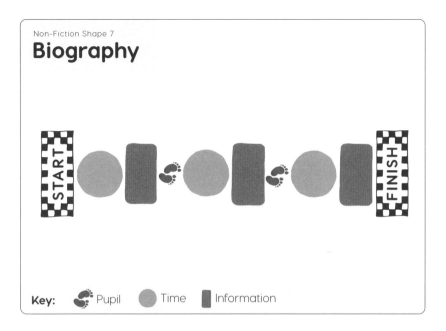

Key: Pupil · Time · Information

Non-Fiction Shape 8
Letter: Complaint/Persuasion

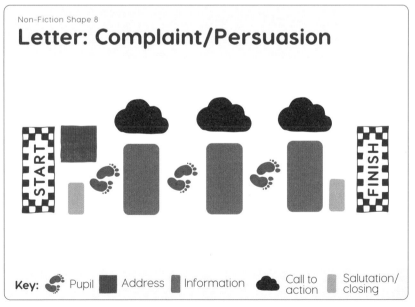

Key: Pupil · Address · Information · Call to action · Salutation/closing

NEWSPAPER

Model Newspaper text based on Goldilocks and the Three Bears organised onto a newspaper shape.

START

Bear Necessities... Nicked!

Goldi – Locked Up!

Early yesterday morning, a disturbing incident took place in a cottage located deep within the Dark Woods. It is thought that a smallish girl with incredibly curly hair may be responsible for this invasion of privacy and damage to property suffered by the well-respected Bear family. Although it is as yet unclear why this vandalism occurred, locals suspect that naughtiness and boredom may have played a significant part in the unfortunate events that have left a whole family inconsolable and traumatised.

"My chair is ruined," Baby Bear (4 years) told us between tears.

Shock Discovery

Bear Family returned home yesterday morning following a mid-morning search for honey to discover that their home security had been breached. They went on to discover further devastation such as half-eaten food and vandalised furniture, in what appears to have been a mindless criminal act.
The intruder was said to be disturbed from what police describe as an extremely deep sleep in their only child's bed. She managed to skilfully escape and is still at large. Police warn she may be desperate and dangerous.

Traumatised Baby

As a result of the shocking discovery of Goldilocks in their house, the impact on Baby Bear has been devastating. The little bear has developed deep psychological problems since the incident such as: bedwetting, nightmares and sleepwalking. Mummy Bear and Daddy Bear have reported an increased financial strain due to having to purchase new furniture to replace the broken chair.

Baby Bear traumatised by nightmares after an accomplished break-in by girl.

"It was horrible, really horrible. I just wish that she hadn't broken into our house!" a distressed Mummy Bear (42) told us.

Ongoing Investigation

Police have apprehended a possible suspect and investigations are continuing. The identity of the accused cannot be revealed for legal reasons; however, eye witnesses have reported seeing a blonde, arrogant girl. Forensic investigation continues.

FINISH

Key: Headline ■ Subheading ■ Information Photograph □ Caption

Pupils build their newspaper based on the Anthony Horowitz-Alex Rider series, *Skeleton Key*. Pupils fill in the shapes with the appropriate text.

Once pupils understand the non-fiction shapes of writing, they are able to analyse texts they meet and organise them into their separate component parts. As you can see on the adjacent page, the newspaper article based on Goldilocks and the Three Bears has been distributed into the separate sections that make the complete newspaper text. This helps children see the similarities and differences between the functions of the various aspects of the writing.

Pupils provide 'for and against' viewpoints on a balanced argument shape.

Consider

Making large laminated shapes that are stored in a central area in the school (marked up instructions, non-chronological report, newspaper etc.).

Organise resources so they can be shared across the whole school and re-used with wipe board pens.

School Impact Points

In light of the national curriculum, discuss the long-term view for each class's coverage of non-fiction text types.

1. Is there a good balance between story and non-fiction?

2. Is there clear progression from Key Stage 1 to Key Stage 2?

3. Do Key Stage 2 children meet challenging text types such as balanced argument and newspaper?

Draw up a non-fiction long-term plan to ensure coverage and progression across the school.

Amrit, Year 2

What are Narrative Journeys for Writing?

Learning to write should never be a journey without maps. The pathways to success are many and varied but all need to be signposted.

Chapter 5

Summary

☑ Pupils need help to 'see' the whole picture of what they are trying to create in their writing. In other words, they need help in moving from visualising to communicating.

☑ Stories can be categorised into nine broad story journeys. The central character moves through each one, experiencing both positive and negative incidents.

☑ Pupils produce completed pieces of work - with more control over what happens to their central character - if they build a personal journey for their protagonist, marking the highs and lows.

THE WRITE STUFF

What are Narrative Journeys for Writing?

Narrative journeys are a way of conceptualising and grouping stories. A hallmark of the journeys is sharpening children's perception of the impact of key events on the central character. The Nine Story Journeys allow readers and writers to consider more closely the central character's pathway through a story. Ultimately, having this knowledge of a central character's journey, and an effective method to analyse and plan stories, will improve the standard of pupils' narrative writing.

Pupils' talk is an integral part of learning. The centrality of speaking and listening is borne out through the necessity for pupils to discuss all parts of the writing process.

After experiencing a story, talk is vital for understanding the key elements.

In order to facilitate pupil engagement, talk should be used as a strategy to share ideas, to speculate and to reflect on what is important. This approach to teaching writing encourages oral rehearsal of informal and formal structures that can eventually form the basis of pupils' own stories.

Ways in which this is particularly important in the Nine Story Journeys system are:

▶ Articulating parts of 'known stories' and how they can be mapped on journey planners.

▶ Identifying and discussing evidence found in stories that fits particular story models.

▶ Talking about textual features in pairs and groups.

▶ Verbalising thoughts on the main character's perspective as he/she moves through the journey of a story.

Pupils follow in the central character's footsteps to plot point the key parts of a story.

▶ Telling others about their story ideas and the sequence their story follows – and why.

▶ Using formal sentence structures prior to writing.

▶ Listening to their peers' ideas about story structure.

▶ Using their talk to help them construct notes on the visual story symbols to ensure their writing comes alive.

▶ Extending their language as they manipulate known structures and make them their own.

Reading and writing for a range of purposes

The Nine Story Journeys enables pupils to engage with a range of story types and to understand their individual structures. This vital and valuable knowledge will support pupils in the analysis of stories encountered and the construction of their own original stories. Once pupils can commit the system to memory, it will be a powerful means for them to be able to interpret and understand texts. Ultimately, it will be a way of seeing stories as different shapes, and following these patterns will assist them in creating and designing stories that emulate the story journeys.

The approach is particularly valuable in the following ways:

▶ Retrieving information and evidence from known stories and applying these to the Nine Story Journeys system.

▶ Commenting on the textual features used by writers and beginning the sorting process to define a journey type.

▶ Responding to texts and applying narrative structures in a way that heightens engagement.

▶ Evaluating the character's perspective, positives and negatives on the journey and critical points of character change.

▶ Building character empathy and considering choices made on the story journey.

▶ Enabling writing that is focused, has direction and shape.

▶ Supporting structural analysis and inclusion of features that will help the construction of text.

▶ Encouraging powerful language choices that will bring the character to life.

A working wall showing a character's return journey, based on *The Way Back Home* by Oliver Jeffers.

What are the Nine Story Journeys?

The nine distinct journeys outlined capture the nature of the central character's exploration as a story unfolds.

1. Happily ever after

A character's journey to find lasting happiness

A central character with humble beginnings has obstacles to overcome in order to achieve success or happiness. Often, there are supportive characters to provide help and guidance.

2. In search of a goal

A character's journey to reach a goal

A central character embarks on a quest for a goal, experiencing highs and lows on the journey before finally achieving what they intended.

3. There and back again

A character's return journey

A central character goes on an unplanned journey. Their destination is strange, curious, exciting or disappointing. They live the experience but find they are pleased to go home.

4. Defeating the enemy

A character's journey to overcome evil

A central character is a hero/heroine on a quest to overcome a monster or bad character. There is a struggle but good triumphs over evil and life is easier for the community.

5. Achieving the impossible

A character's journey to achieve the unthinkable

A central character has a dream or is put in a difficult situation. They are determined to achieve success or overcome the situation. Those around them are unsupportive but a mentor appears and they exceed expectations.

6. Everyday life disrupted

A character's journey where a new person leads to a changed outlook

A central character begins the journey by leading their everyday life. Suddenly, an invited or uninvited guest brings enormous change to their world and they learn from them.

7. Chaos to calm

A character's journey to harmonious union

A central character misunderstands another character and further chaos is caused as communication continues to break down. Calm is restored when characters resume direct communication.

8. Enlightenment

A character's journey of positive inner change

A central character has a negative outlook on life. A significant event or person jolts them into a new, more positive way of living.

9. Misguided

A character's journey of negative inner change

A central character sets their mind on a goal and aims to reach it regardless of the pain and suffering caused to others and themselves on the way.

The Nine Story Journey Maps

Each story journey has a visual story map. These support writing by providing a clear structure and can be used to:

- **Analyse stories (a useful deconstruction tool)**

- **Plan stories (a useful reconstruction tool)**

- **Build ideas and vocabulary into chronological order to be used at varying points in the story**

- **Structure the writing process**

The central character

The central character is always located at the beginning of a journey, with the intention that he/she will move from left to right.

Thematic symbols

On some of the visual maps, images are used to highlight the central character's starting point, finishing point or both. The symbols are self-explanatory when the story definition is read.

e.g. happy

e.g. rise in social status

e.g. 'in love'

Story Journey Pathway

The central character's pathway is marked by small footsteps. Main plot details are briefly noted on the 'track'.

Positive and negative steps

As the character moves through the story, he/she can take positive and negative steps along the way. The positive steps (+) are positioned above the pathway line and the negative steps (-) are positioned below the line.

Consider taking a well-known story with your class, such as Cinderella, and marking in the plot points. Pupils will need to know the story and be able to summarise it effectively. This can be done through:

▶ Pictures (exact illustrations from a book or screen shots from a film).

▶ Diagrammatic representations of key events (e.g. Cinderella with a broom).

▶ Summary sentences.

▶ Key words.

Once the bare bones of the plot line are in place, discussions with the class can take place and the positive and negative aspects of Cinderella's plotline can be marked. With Key Stage 1 children, these can be shown with smiley faces.

With Key Stage 2 children, these can be represented on a number line using positive and negative numbers. These highs and lows are the points of interest in the stories and, as teachers, we need to focus children's writing construction around these aspects.

Targeting writing efforts to these moments of the central character's journey will produce more engaging writing. Otherwise, the story may be at risk of turning into a retelling, which feels very stilted and overuses the phrase 'and then'.

Exemplar Key:

   = Very positive incident

  = Positive incident

 = Slightly positive incident

   = Very negative incident

  = Negative incident

 = Slightly negative incident

Pupils find it hard to write if they are disinterested in the subject or lack knowledge about the subject or context.

Fleckenstein et al (2002), Berne and Wolstencroft (2007) and *Artell* agree with the power of the visual to strengthen thinking. Artell states:

"The ability to think visually and textually bolsters students creatively and helps young writers express themselves more effectively in today's visual culture". **(Artell 2005: vii)**

The means and mechanisms to plot a character's journey will solve two issues:

1. Tackling the whole shape of a story will support the coherence of the piece.

2. Clarity will facilitate the construction of more empathetic writing.

Pupils in a nursery setting re-enact a negative moment for Jack and the Beanstalk. This is the moment the giant sees Jack.

Cinderella - Plot Points

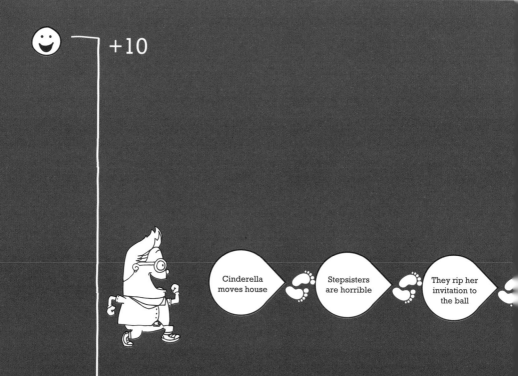

 Fairy Godmother magically gets her to the ball

 She dances with the Prince

 Her glass slipper is left behind

 The Prince finds her when the shoe fits

They live happily ever after

Cinderella - Plot Points

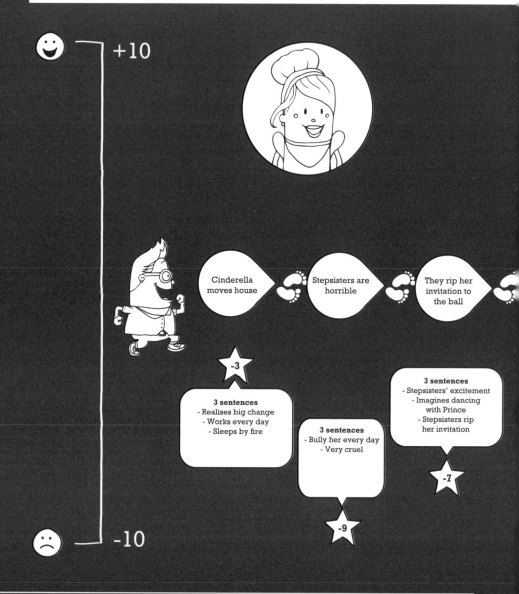

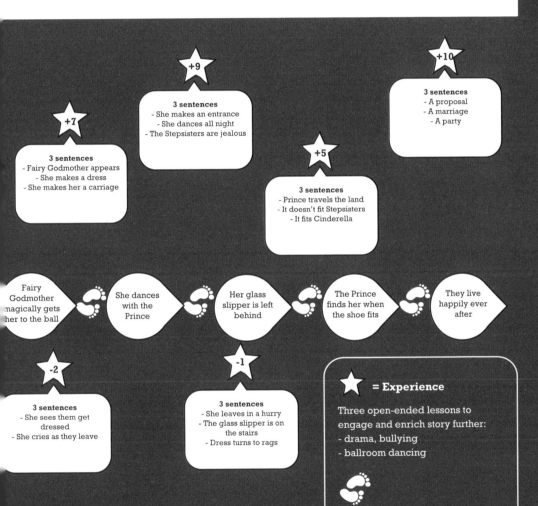

+9

3 sentences
- She makes an entrance
- She dances all night
- The Stepsisters are jealous

+10

3 sentences
- A proposal
- A marriage
- A party

+7

3 sentences
- Fairy Godmother appears
- She makes a dress
- She makes her a carriage

+5

3 sentences
- Prince travels the land
- It doesn't fit Stepsisters
- It fits Cinderella

Fairy Godmother magically gets her to the ball

She dances with the Prince

Her glass slipper is left behind

The Prince finds her when the shoe fits

They live happily ever after

-2

3 sentences
- She sees them get dressed
- She cries as they leave

-1

3 sentences
- She leaves in a hurry
- The glass slipper is on the stairs
- Dress turns to rags

★ **= Experience**

Three open-ended lessons to engage and enrich story further:
- drama, bullying
- ballroom dancing

Two lessons to focus on coherence, links and textual cohesion from plot point to plot point and within a plot point.

Examples of Nine Story Journey Pupil Work:

Happily Ever After:

Year 2 Pupil Work - Cinderella

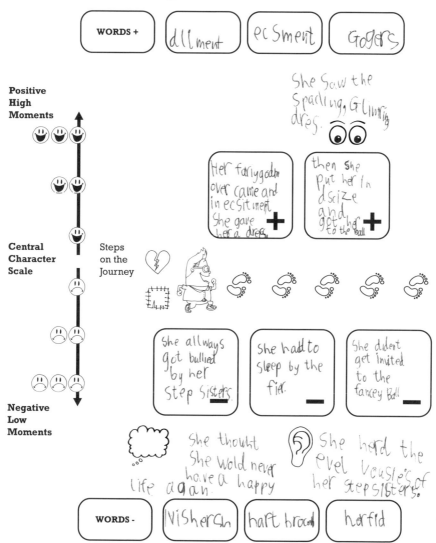

WORDS + | dllment | ecSment | Gogers

Positive High Moments

Central Character Scale

Steps on the Journey

Negative Low Moments

She Saw the Sparcling, GLinring dres.

Her fariygodm over came and in ecSitment She gave her a dres. +

then she put her In d scize and get her to the ball +

She allways got bullied by her step Sisters

She had to sleep by the fir. —

She dident get Invited to the fancey Ball —

She thoukt She Wold never have a happy life agan.

She herd the evel Vcusies of her step sisters.

WORDS - | visherSh | hart brocd | herfld

Pashent,

Jouies

sel brasen

WORDS +

When She was   She took the
danceling with carmina. hand of prinс
the prinс Shatfelt
like a Grlrmino startfelt

"I love you"
She wiped.

and She
dancet With
the prinс.

+

The prinс l na
Charming way
he trys the
sliper on eury
women in
the ville.

+

thay were
dlfted to Mary
and thay
lived happy
ever after.

+

then it was
midnight.
She runed
out the doк.
She lost her sh

in a Sad way
She clend up the
house.

d l ser ponted,

terfld

Wored

WORDS -

Year 6 Pupil Work - New Story In Search of a Goal

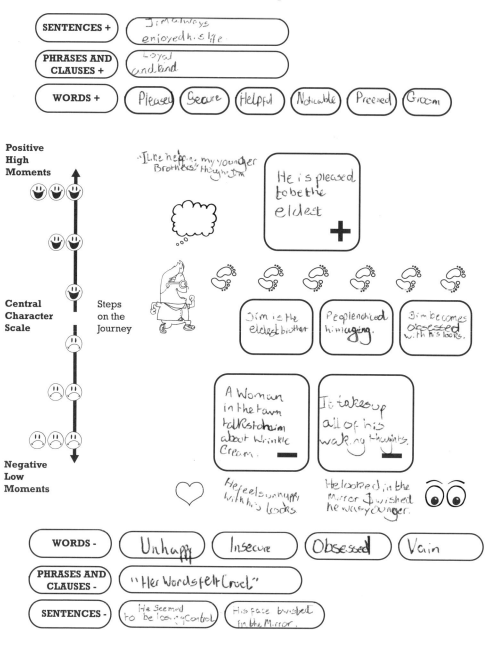

SENTENCES + Jim always enjoyed his life.

PHRASES AND CLAUSES + Loyal and kind

WORDS + Pleased | Secure | Helpful | Noticable | Preened | Groom

Positive High Moments

"I Like helping my younger Brothers" thought Jim

He is pleased to be the eldest **+**

Central Character Scale

Steps on the Journey

Jim is the eldest brother. | People noticed him aging. | Jim becomes obsessed with his looks.

A Woman in the town talks to him about Wrinkle Cream. **—**

It takes up all of his waking thoughts. **—**

Negative Low Moments

He feels unhappy with his looks.

He looked in the mirror I wished he was younger.

WORDS - Unhappy | Insecure | Obsessed | Vain

PHRASES AND CLAUSES - "Her Words felt Cruel"

SENTENCES - He seemed to be losing control | His face twisted in the Mirror.

Jim knew this was the right thing.

SENTENCES +

An optimistic walk.

a torrent of words

a magic realization

PHRASES AND CLAUSES +

Friends   Companion   Clever.   Outwitted   Realization   Hope

WORDS +

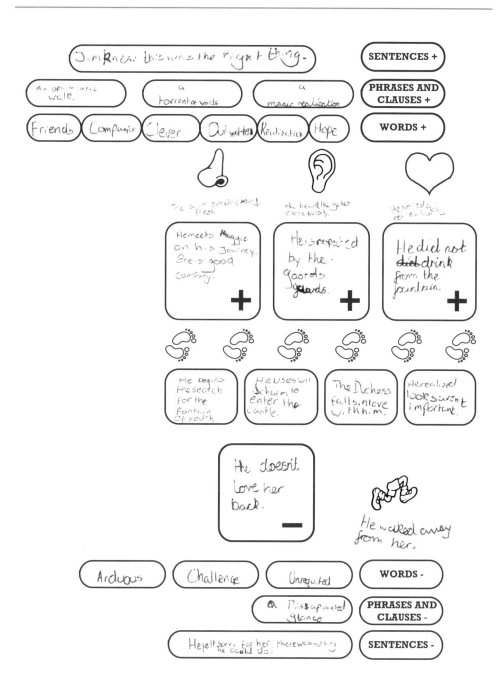

The air smelled clean & fresh.

He heard the gates close noisily.

He smiled as his reflection looked back.

He meets Maggie on his journey. She is good company.

He is respected by the qaords. guards.

He did not drink drink from the fountain.

+   +   +

He begins the search for the fountain of youth

He uses will & charm to enter the castle.

The Duchess falls in love with him.

He realized looks aren't important.

He doesn't love her back.

—

He walked away from her.

Arduous   Challenge   Unrequited

WORDS -

A Dissapointed glance

PHRASES AND CLAUSES -

He felt sorry for her, there was nothing he could do.

SENTENCES -

1

HAPPILY EVER AFTER

A character's journey to find lasting happiness

THE CHARACTER'S PATHWAY

The central character begins the journey as an unhappy and downtrodden individual.

Forms: All Genres
Typical Examples: Cinderella, Ugly Duckling, Annie

As he or she moves through the story, there are highs and lows
before reward and happiness.

Textual features of a 'Happily Ever After' story journey

A character's journey to find lasting happiness	Review	
Textual features	My Writing	My Friend's Writing
Central character is victimised or is a victim of circumstances.		
Central character is dignified during times of victimisation.		
Central character experiences lows which are contrasted with other characters' highs.		
Central character experiences highs (although sometimes these are followed by disappointment.)		
Central character experiences a short-term glimpse of life in a different place.		
Rivals are weakened by events. Central character finds 'inner strength' to escape their grip.		
Central character rises in social status and is recognised by community as deserving new status.		
A big event marks finale of story e.g. a wedding/a party etc.		

Happily Ever After				
1	2	3	4	5
Not even started	Early stage	Getting there	Well on your way	You've arrived. Jump for joy!

Find these features in the example story on the adjacent page. Include these features when writing your own unique 'Happily Ever After' story.

How many of the features have you or your friend included in the story?

Reading: Exemplar Story/Journey Text

1

HAPPILY EVER AFTER

A character's journey to find lasting happiness

Use the text to find evidence of key features.

Jack had lived with the Pettyworths for a long time: since he was four years old when his mother had died suddenly. The Pettyworths were neighbours and took Jack on as a trade for the farmland that his mother once owned. He tried hard to fit in and, even though Mrs. Pettyworth was kind-hearted, she was a weak figure in the family and it was Mr. Pettyworth and his two sons who dominated the household with strict regimes and cruel words. Jack was often the victim of spiteful practical jokes and brotherly tomfoolery.

A weary gloom hung over him.

"Jack, go outside and collect the chickens' eggs," ordered Jacob, the eldest of the brothers.

"Yeah, get on with it," Matthew reinforced. Jack didn't even mention it was his eighteenth birthday. He hadn't celebrated one since he was four. He always did as he was told. He had learnt the hard way that there was no point questioning anything. As always, he was suspicious of any duties he was asked to undertake.

As Jack moved forwards towards the barn, he noticed a shadowy figure slinking inside the building. His heart sank. This seemed to be another prank in the offing. Nonetheless, he continued forward, but - without warning - Matthew leapt out and smashed an egg violently in his face. Jack sighed heavily as raw egg slime dripped off the end of his nose. In contrast, the brothers ran back to the house chortling about their malicious deed. Jack didn't want to go back inside just yet and so he walked dejectedly over to a nearby wall and slumped down in a heap.

He was startled awake by a friendly "Hello". As he looked up, overshadowing him was a jolly-looking gentleman in a floppy hat. Jack was still half asleep but mustered up a vague smile. The gentleman said, "Here, take this ring. It belonged to your mother. When trouble strikes, rub it three times."

Jack was stunned. He rubbed his eyes to make sure he wasn't dreaming and tentatively took the ring from the kind stranger.

Instantaneously, the man disappeared.

Jack put the ring in his pocket and returned to the farmhouse.

"Where have you been, egg-head?" Matthew gruffed.

"Nowhere," Jack replied and put his head down and tried to busy himself by bottling up the milk.

"I saw you talking to someone, you weirdo, and there was no-one there!" announced Jacob, whilst poking at his arm.

Jack didn't feel so alone. He could feel his mother's ring in his pocket and knew he now had help. He felt relieved. Jacob could sense that Jack didn't feel so scared and he didn't like it. He pushed over a set of filled milk bottles and shouted, "Dad, look what Jack did on purpose!"

Mr. Pettyworth lunged into the kitchen, grabbed Jack by the collar and told him to sleep in the barn that night.

As the dark closed in, Jack made himself a makeshift bed in the barn amongst the hay and the chickens. It was warm, but a bit uncomfortable and smelly. Meanwhile, Jacob and Matthew snored comfortably in their soft, plumped-up beds.

While Jack was alone, he took out the ring, which glinted brightly in the moonlight. He rubbed it three times and a woman appeared before him. She wore a headscarf and her face was difficult to make out in the darkness, but Jack could see she had kind eyes.

"I am here to help." Her voice was soft and gentle and Jack felt comforted by her supportive words. "Follow me," she told him. The woman walked out of the barn, away from the farm and pointed towards the horizon.

"There is more farmland that is rightfully yours; you just have to find the documents." As Jack looked out expectantly across the land, he could see himself as a farm owner, happy and contented in his own space. He turned back around to find the woman had just vanished. The next day, after a restless night's sleep, Jack continued with his chores as normal. Jacob taunted him while he cleaned out the pigs, fed the chickens and milked the cows. Jack remained calm and unflustered by the onslaught of cruel words. His mind drifted back to the woman's words last night: "...you just have to find the documents." Jack was startled back to reality by a broom thrown at his body.

"Oi," yelled Matthew. "Clean up the yard!"

Jack moved outside and began sweeping. As he relaxed into a rhythmic movement, it dawned on him that he knew where the documents were all along. Mrs. Pettyworth had given him an envelope when he first moved in and she'd said it was a photograph of his Mum and some other information. Jack had been too upset to open it at the time and knew that looking at lots of photographs would have only made him feel worse.

Nonetheless, he had put the envelope in a safe place, under a floorboard in the pantry. Without warning, he dropped the broom where he was and raced indoors. He levered up the floorboard and scrambled for the envelope, tearing at it excitedly. Inside, was a picture of a beautiful woman, wearing a headscarf. This time he could make out her face; it was his mother. She seemed to be looking right at him and was smiling softly. Furthermore, the package contained official ownership documents for a nearby farm.

Jack was overjoyed. He hugged Mrs. Pettyworth. Jacob and Matthew looked stunned; they couldn't believe what was going on.

Two weeks later, Jack held a party at his farm for all the local villagers, including the Pettyworths. Jack was so pleased to start his new life and the villagers were delighted for him too. He glanced at the ring he was wearing and smiled.

2

IN SEARCH OF A GOAL

A character's journey to reach a goal

THE CHARACTER'S PATHWAY

Forms: All Genres
Typical Examples: The Hobbit, Finding Nemo, Myths and Legends

A central character embarks on a quest for a goal,
experiencing highs and lows on the journey before
finally achieving what he/she intended.

Textual features of an 'In Search of a Goal' story journey

A character's journey to reach a goal	Review	
Textual features	**My Writing**	**My Friend's Writing**
A central hero/heroine goes in search of a goal e.g. kingdom/prince/princess/holy grail.		
Hero/heroine stereotypical in their characterisation. Wildly enthusiastic, naïve but very determined.		
The journey they embark on is typified by both highs and lows.		
At low points, the central character doubts their capabilities to achieve what they set out to do.		
Story comes to a pivotal moment just before the discovery of the goal.		
Often an enormous battle where the central character is in a near-death situation.		
Central character reaches goal and is heralded as a true hero/heroine.		
A big event marks finale of story e.g. a wedding/a party etc.		

In Search of a Goal				
1	2	3	4	5
Not even started	Early stage	Getting there	Well on your way	You've arrived. Jump for joy!

Find these features in the example story on the adjacent page. Include these features when writing your own unique 'In Search of a Goal' story.

How many of the features have you or your friend included in the story?

Reading: Exemplar Story/Journey Text

2

IN SEARCH OF A GOAL

A character's journey to reach a goal

Use the text to find evidence of key features.

Marvin's Quest

Marvin hung on the periphery of some of the most important discussions of all time. Sir Paigant had called an urgent wizard and warlock meeting because Princess Eliza had gone missing, suspected of being snatched by Count Dastardly. Marvin had never quite worked out the magic ingredient that allowed you to enter into the noble and refined inner circles of wizardry. He was always left skirting around the edges, sorting out potions, tidying up after exciting events or packing other wizards' clothes and equipment before the next journey. Marvin was feeling fed up with this and longed to be at the centre of some clever magical problem solving.

Marvin heard Sir Paigant say,

"The only clue we have is that a boat was seen moving out of Rocky Edge Cove at an unusual hour."

Marvin concocted a plan. He would rescue Princess Eliza and then the others would notice him, and accept him properly into the group. Marvin knew he had to take up his one-man quest in secret, so he waited until later that evening, as dusk was drawing in, to escape the camp. Marvin was so excited and very determined. He began his quest by entering into 'Dark Firmley Woods'. It suddenly struck him that he was isolated and very alone. The darkness seemed to close in tightly around him. Ominous shadowy shapes moved across his eye-line, making him edgy and uncomfortable. Marvin knew these woods well but realised he had only passed through in daylight. The hoots of owls lingered for longer than usual and his feet felt 'off-balance' as he attempted to navigate the busy and tangled undergrowth. Marvin now wasn't sure if he was heading in the right direction to reach Rocky Edge Cove but nevertheless he continued like a determined deer trying to find her lost fawns. Marvin was unsure if he had made the right decision to go it alone and, just as the demons of doubt were closing in, he fell.

Marvin plummeted into a large cavernous hole, through the woodland floor, and imagined he was probably a long way from ground level. Nursing a scraped face from the hard, dusty descent, he slumped desperately at the bottom. He knew he had a sleeping potion in his pocket but that couldn't help him out of this problem. Suddenly, Marvin heard a rustling and scratching sound, but he couldn't make out what, or who, it was.

"Who's there?" Marvin mustered up a dusty plea. To his surprise, an angry voice replied, "What are you doing crash-landing into my home?"

Marvin was dumbfounded; he watched as a small light was put on to illuminate the darkness. Marvin couldn't believe what he saw. It was a miniature wizard and oversized rabbit, morphed into one. Two large ears poked through his hat, but his face was reassuringly familiar-looking, apart from the large white whiskers.

"I didn't...I didn't mean it," Marvin stumbled over his words.

The creature extended a hand-paw, which Marvin shook politely. He introduced himself very assertively:

"I'm Bobbin, and I am the leader of Burrow 740."

Marvin explained his dilemma and how he needed to reach Rocky Edge Cove quickly to continue his rescue mission for Princess Eliza. Bobbin was transfixed, and was particularly pleased as Burrow 740 linked up to the Cove. Bobbin began jumping up and down, thumping his paw-feet. Then, in a high pitched squeal, announced,

"Follow me!"

Marvin was unsure how easy this would be but Bobbin was on all fours, scrabbling through an enclosed and complex network of tunnels. He was fast and created a lot of back dust with his paw-feet. Marvin now regretted trying to follow him from behind and his eyes were starting to feel very gritty and sore. However, he knew this was his only hope as he was uncertain of his location and couldn't scramble back up the large drop. Step by step, he persevered and over time became more adept and rabbit-like in his manoeuvres.

"Here we are!" Bobbin cried, bubbling with excitement. Confidently, he poked through from the darkness into the light and Marvin could see that the sun was rising on the watery horizon. He thanked Bobbin and in a flash he was back down the burrow, pounding back to where he came from.

Marvin was a little stunned. The sun was stinging his eyes and he walked down to the water's edge to bathe them. As he looked down by the smooth wave-beaten shores, he noticed a piece of material. It was purple and had an embossed emblem on it; it seemed like a piece of clothing that had been ripped from Princess Eliza. Marvin was more determined than ever to save her. Without hesitation, he jumped into a nearby boat, unleashed the mooring rope and rowed out to the sea. After a few hours, Marvin was feeling exhausted. His arms were hurting from the incessant rowing and the sun was heating up the atmosphere, making it more difficult to keep going. Marvin let the boat drift for a while. The slow rhythmic rocking soon sent him into a deep and comforting sleep.

He was woken abruptly by a violent jerking of the boat. Marvin was under attack by a sea monster! He had heard stories about 'Rochveer: the Monster of the Deep,' but never believed them. Its green, slimy, lizard-like face was nudging the side of the boat and Marvin clung to the wooden seat with all his strength. Its yellow teeth were encased in black oversized gums, and a pungent smell exuded with every vicious roar it made. Marvin was pushed out of the boat whilst it was in mid-air and frantically gripped the edge, praying he would not be eaten by this strange creature. He could see an enormous drop below into the treacherous green depths. He knew if he stayed in this position it was likely he'd be lunch, so he cleverly clambered onto Rochveer's nose. With that, it tossed its head in an attempt to eat him but instead flung him sharply onto dry land.

Marvin was relieved. In front of him was a mysterious building; it was very picturesque and its dome-like roof glinted in the sunshine. Marvin was drawn towards it, and as he got closer, he could see the intricate carvings and jewels encrusted on the walls. He shuffled forward to some nearby foliage and crouched down in the bushes. At that movement, there was a kerfuffle in the doorway. Two men were jostling with a woman and Marvin could hear them saying,

"Tell us where the family jewels are?"

Marvin squinted and saw that the men had the woman in an arm-lock. As the woman was pushed forwards out of the shadows, her face was bathed in light, and Marvin realised it was Princess Eliza! What was he to do? Panic gripped him.

With no plan in mind, he raced towards the trio. As he ran, he felt the potion bottle in his pocket clink. He pulled it out and unleashed the stopper. As he grew closer, the two men set their eyes firmly on him. Marvin threw the sleeping potion into their eyes and their grips loosened as they crashed to the floor.

"Princess Eliza, I have come to rescue you," he announced proudly.

Eliza and Marvin jumped into a boat belonging to Sir Paigant and made their way back to Rocky Edge Cove. Rochveer was obviously busy hassling some other sea farers. On their arrival, Marvin called on the assistance of Bobbin and warned Eliza that it might not be an easy route but it was definitely a safe one. The challenge came when they arrived back at the deep hole, but between them, with some steady shoulder balancing, they were soon free to navigate Dark Firmley Woods. The sun was up and the walk was relatively easy. Marvin strode back into camp with Eliza not far behind him, and Sir Paigant called all the wizards and warlocks to silence.

"In our midst, we have a true talent. Marvin has been a diligent worker for many years and has not been given the respect he deserves. While we still argue about the details of our rescue mission, Marvin has already completed the task. Marvin, I declare you to be one of the Chief Wizards for our clan, as you have shown yourself to have exceptional and extraordinary abilities."

With that, Eliza turned around and gave Marvin a kiss on the cheek!

3

THERE AND BACK AGAIN

A character's return journey

THE CHARACTER'S PATHWAY

A central character goes on an unplanned journey.
Their destination is strange, curious, exciting or disappointing.

Forms: All Genres
Typical Examples: Alice in Wonderland, Where the Wild Things Are, Wizard of Oz

They live and experience but then they are pleased to go home.

Textual features of a 'There and Back Again' story journey

A character's return journey	Review	
Textual features	My Writing	My Friend's Writing
Central character embarks on a journey and finds themselves in a very different place.		
The new place is often very different from familiar surroundings and sometimes has magical or weird dimensions.		
Central character becomes involved in an adventure in their new place. They meet the locals and experience some of the local life.		
Central character is bemused and bewildered by some events.		
Central character remains 'in control' in the new place. Once this control is under threat, or the adventure is over, they find a way back home.		
Often an enormous battle where the central character is in a near-death situation.		
Central character reaches goal and is heralded as a true hero/heroine.		
A big event marks finale of story e.g. a wedding/a party etc.		

There and Back Again				
1	2	3	4	5
Not even started	Early stage	Getting there	Well on your way	You've arrived. Jump for joy!

Find these features in the example story on the adjacent page. Include these features when writing your own unique 'There and Back Again' story.

How many of the features have you or your friend included in the story?

Reading: Exemplar Story/Journey Text

3

THERE AND BACK AGAIN

A character's return journey

Use the text to find evidence of key features.

A Number of Times

Maggie put on her most whiney voice and said, "Are we there yet?"

The journey was hot and uncomfortable but they hadn't been on the road long. Maggie was looking forward to the picnic with her family.

After a couple of hours, they had arrived. Mum opened the car doors and a heavy and humid atmosphere hit them and made Maggie and her brother Malcolm drowsy. Dad was busying himself at the boot, unloading picnic bags, blankets and plastic bags of bits and bobs. Once they had unloaded, the four walked slowly down towards the river bank. The sun was hazy and groups of midges were gathered in busy clusters near the water's edge. Having found a shady tree, Dad waved the picnic blanket like a chequered flag, signalling everyone to stop and make their way to the official picnic location. Maggie slumped down, relieved there was not further walking on this muggy day. Whilst Mum

checked that the scotch eggs hadn't been forgotten, Malcolm ran down to the river and Maggie reclined on the sweet-smelling grass and closed her eyes. School holidays were great, Maggie thought. Had she been at school today, then she'd be sat in class doing maths...'Boring!' she thought.

Maggie was startled by a voice she recognised.

"Maggie Pickinson... Who would have thought it?" Mr. Charles bellowed.

Maggie's heart sank. She knew he would ask how her homework was coming along. However, she need not have worried; instead he wanted help with a situation further up the river. Maggie joined Mr. Charles and raced to the incident, intrigued about what it could be.

In the distance, she could see a boat that was half-stuck under a bridge and some frantic people on board, whilst others on the riverbank were shouting instructions and advice to no avail. Mr. Charles explained to Maggie that he felt that the situation could be resolved mathematically. Maggie was not convinced, but Mr. Charles was adamant and asked her to work out the area of space under the bridge whilst he undertook some of the calculations.

After a few moments, Mr. Charles shouted "Eureka!" and explained to the distressed crew that he had a solution. He told Maggie to clamber onto the boat as he needed someone to relay instructions to. Maggie did as she was told and, as she got closer to the people on board, she noticed something really strange. The two men near the engine had unusual tattoos - they had numbers and mathematical equations etched onto their arms. A woman who was ruffling the sail and tying up ropes had mathematical operations on her clothes, a division print shirt and multiplication print trousers.

Mr. Charles shouted to Maggie, "What is 30 x 9?"

"270," Maggie called back and with an almighty lurch the boat plummeted forwards out from underneath the bridge and moved quickly towards the sea. Almost immediately, the horizon opened to an expanse of blue and Maggie realised she was trapped on board. The unusual woman she'd noticed earlier was calling her over with a wave. Maggie moved tentatively towards her and heard her trill,

"Have some lunch with us, girlie. What's your name?"

Maggie replied daintily.

"I'm Dee Vision," said the woman. "You can call me Dee."

Maggie sat down. She was hungry as she'd missed out on her picnic. The food was really tasty although a bit unusual: number-shaped fish fingers, chips displayed as maths signs and strangely-shaped sauce bottles! Dee announced that they should have a quiz. Maggie asked the first question, about who was number one in the music charts. Dee didn't know the answer, but she asked a really complicated division sum, "What is 136 ÷ 8?" Maggie huffed as she felt it wasn't fair. They finished eating together and Maggie was curious to find out where the other two men who were on board had gone. Maggie saw some steps going downstairs and decided to investigate what was down below the deck. There was a small doorway and Maggie cautiously opened it.

"Come in!" said one of the men. He was rough-looking with a beard but he had a kind face. "I'm Adam Mupp and this is Matty Matticks."

Maggie entered the room. On the floor were large 3D shapes and on the walls were endless bar charts and pie charts.

"Thank you for coming on board, Maggie. We are the Maths Crew. It is our job to keep the excitement of maths alive. We make it our business to make maths fun and dispel any myths that maths is boring…You don't think maths is boring do you Maggie?"

"Umm…no," she mumbled. "Do you do maths all the time?" She was intrigued.

"Yes. In fact we are going to play a game called '3D bar charts'. Would you like to play?"

Maggie was interested to find out what it was about. Adam and Matty were building a bar chart from 3D blocks, to represent the number of children they'd met who'd thought maths was boring. One block represented one child, and when Matty and Adam had finished, there was one block spare.

"Who does that represent?" Maggie asked. Adam and Matty both shrugged their shoulders. Maggie laughed. They spent the afternoon doing puzzles, word problems and practical games. Maggie really enjoyed herself and used a human-sized multiplication table to work out $136 \div 8$. Maggie shouted over to Dee, "It's 17, it's 17!"

Instantaneously, the boat came to a halt.

"It's time for you to go now," Dee whispered. "Oh," grumped Maggie. "I was enjoying that."

"You can stay for the maths test if you want," said Dee.

"No thanks, I want to go back to my picnic," Maggie replied without hesitation.

Maggie waved goodbye to her three new friends and left the boat, stepping onto dry land. She could see her picnic blanket in the distance and raced up to it.

"Hurry up!" her Mum said. "I had twelve scotch eggs this morning, and five have been eaten already."

"That means that there's only seven left," Maggie said.

"Look at you and your maths skills. I'll have to tell Mr. Charles about this."

"I think he already knows!" said Maggie with a wry smile.

Her Mum looked at her strangely and passed her a scotch egg. Maggie was glad.

4

DEFEATING THE ENEMY

A character's journey to overcome evil

THE CHARACTER'S PATHWAY

The central character embarks on a journey as an optimistic individual.

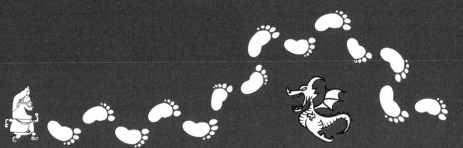

Forms: All Genres
Typical Examples: Jack and the Beanstalk, Wolves in the Walls,
Little Shop of Horrors

As he or she moves through the story, they come face to face
with the enemy and defeat them.

Textual features of a 'Defeating the Enemy' story journey

A character's journey to overcome evil	Review	
Textual features	My Writing	My Friend's Writing
The enemy of the piece is described in immense detail.		
The enemy is often referred to in an ambiguous way.		
Tension and suspense are created through central character's viewpoint.		
Focus on hero's/heroine's mission to defeat the monster. Obstacles on the journey.		
Hero's/heroine's feelings are explored at every stage of the journey.		
Face to face with the 'monster', with a focus on the senses to heighten the experience.		
Hero/heroine defeats the enemy and the community shows its appreciation.		
The community changes.		

Defeating The Enemy				
1	2	3	4	5
Not even started	Early stage	Getting there	Well on your way	You've arrived. Jump for joy!

Find these features in the example story on the adjacent page. Include these features when writing your own unique 'Defeating the Enemy' story.

How many of the features have you or your friend included in the story?

Reading: Exemplar Story/Journey Text

4

DEFEATING THE ENEMY

A character's journey to overcome evil

Use the text to find evidence of key features.

A Dark Day

A grey world. Mariville had been like this ever since the dreaded beast had rampaged through the village. No one who'd survived could ever forget that day.

It had felt like just another ordinary market day. Fruit stalls displayed an array of colours and smells. Zesty oranges burst with brightness in bowls; sweet reds of all hues featured in cherries, strawberries and rich ripe peaches; waxy aubergines glinted in the sunshine, and deep green Savoy cabbages were piled in pride of place on vegetable stalls. Mariville was alive with colour and community excitement.

A slowly-moving shadow edged deliberately across the market place pavement. Villagers felt instantly cold and alarmed by what was happening. Lisa looked up. She could hardly take in what she'd seen. This was a beast of enormous proportions; his furry body was matted like that of an unloved dog. His eyes were dark, treacherous sandstorms spinning in

anger and his mouth a dark cave expelling echoey lonely roars. The village let out a communal scream and raced desperately away from the ominous beast.

Lisa just stared. It was from this position she was able to see, close up, the malicious act as it happened. The unknown creature belched out a damp and overbearing stench. Lisa wretched but tried to stay in control. She looked on in horror. It then drew in a cavernous deep breath that nearly pulled Lisa off her feet, and she felt her hair stretching towards the inhaled air. Lisa squinted and through the smell and the blur she could see a rainbow-mix of colours being drawn towards its dark mouth. The thing was actually swallowing colours: rich purples, robust reds, bright oranges and deep greens. The monster was stripping Mariville of its colour. It feasted on everything around itself. The blue canvas on the stalls, the fresh green of the grass, and the yellow from the daisies that were intermittently scattered on the village green.

Lisa watched as it bleached every last drop

of colour from the place. The unknown creature then moved away as quickly as it had arrived. Lisa looked down, her once bright yellow t-shirt was now a drab neutral tone, and her jeans were no longer blue. The people who had been huddled on the floor slowly rose to their feet and there was a shocked silence from all that had witnessed this event.

What had happened?

What were they to do?

A few days passed. The people of Mariville began to get back on with their lives. They felt fragile and shocked but everything they had known was still intact, albeit colourless. The shops began to open, the children went back to school, and cars reappeared on the roads. Life continued but it was very bleak. Lisa missed the soft pink of her favourite party shirt; the warm brown of her favourite teddy bear and the cheerful yellow banana skins in her packed lunches. She noticed that people's faces were sadder and the once-bright sparkles in their eyes were now muted. Was Mariville destined to be sad and grey forever?

That night, when Lisa lay awake in bed, she felt frustrated that there was nothing that could be done to redress this tragic situation. As her mind flooded with crazy plans of how to turn back time, she drifted uneasily into a deep but fretful sleep. During her dream, she imagined all of the colours of Mariville, its individual hues and tones, slowly drifting back to the town. The powdery reds of the house bricks, the brightly-painted front doors, the sparkling

oranges, blues and greens. The intense floral patterns on the curtains all became alive with colour. In her dream, people were laughing again, and the children danced on the green, playing with the colourful maypole ribbons.

Suddenly, she opened her eyes, scrambled out of bed quickly and pulled the curtains back. A fog had descended over Mariville and, as her eyes adjusted to the darkness, she saw that it was still a place shrouded in grey. Lisa spent the rest of the night restless and unable to settle back to sleep. As dawn broke, she missed the warming sunlight filtering through her window. Lisa knew she had to do something about it but she didn't know what. She dressed for the day and decided to go down to the market place. It was deserted and cold. She wanted to come face to face with the monster. She called out desperately for it to return. An hour later, she reluctantly left - still not having glimpsed the strange entity.

Every night, she had the recurring dream. It was as if paint pots of colour were spilt and defying gravity, moving upwards to cling onto the appropriate things. Once again, Lisa tried to entice the monster to meet her at the market place. This time she remembered that it was the fruit and vegetable market that had attracted it before, so she had brought a collection of these from the nearby village. There was a range of different palettes: aubergines, carrots, courgettes, and sweetcorn, oranges, apples, strawberries and bananas. She placed the bowl down gently and watched. Instantaneously, Lisa heard a strange gurgling and breathing sound.

It was the evil creature. The shadowy mass edged slowly towards the fruit and vegetables, and it inhaled the colour from each item. Lisa closed her eyes as she replayed the dream she'd had last night, and the previous nights before that, in her mind. A vast array of spilt paint pots oozing with illuminous colour. When she opened her eyes, the monster was gone and the grey landscape looked back at her, disappointed and saddened. Lisa had another plan. She raced back towards the shops and encouraged Mrs. Pickering from the bakery, and Mr. Clegg from the sweetshop to come out onto the street and join her.

"I've got a plan. Get your friends. Get your family. Get anybody!" she yelled.

There was a hubbub in Mariville. People were pouring into the streets, whispering, "Lisa's got a plan...That girl there, she's got a plan." Teachers left the school with the children in tow, the workers left the factory, and the elderly left the bridge club. A crowd was growing rapidly and Lisa stood up on the steps to oversee the numbers. As she looked out on the drab and gloomy crowd, she could see an expectant look in every pair of eyes.

"I don't know if this will work. But I am sure, like me, you still dream in colour. The monster couldn't strip us of our rich and vivid memories. We need to use these memories to fight back together, as a team."

Lisa led her army towards the market place. They stopped in unison at the edge of the original incident. People fidgeted nervously as Lisa reached out to hold the hands of Mrs. Pickering and Mr. Clegg. In turn, everyone extended their hands and gripped the hand of the person next to them. The group stood there in quiet solidarity for a long while. In the distance, the crowd could see a dark, menacing shadow approaching.

"Hold hands!" Lisa shouted. "As it gets nearer, close your eyes and relive your dreams, and do not open them again until I say so."

Lisa could feel Mrs. Pickering's fragile hands shaking in her grip. The frightening, threatening beast moved closer. A stagnant smell strayed towards the congregation, and hands tightened amongst pairs. Some had already closed their eyes instinctively, and the rest of the community followed. Each and every person visualised colour in their world. Mrs. Pickering thought of the yellow-brown crust of a newly-baked loaf, and of the glistening pink icing on top of the iced buns. Mr. Clegg thought of the dark, rich browns of his chocolate toffees and the rainbow hues of his multicoloured sherbet. Lisa thought of the warm sunlight bursting through her curtains and brightening up her mornings. Everyone's eyes were clenched shut as they concentrated on their colourful dreams and memories. Lisa noticed the smell of freshly cut grass. The overpowering smell of the creature had gone. She opened her eyes and yelled, "We did it!"

Everyone cheered and hugged Lisa. Mariville was beautiful again. It exploded with a kaleidoscope of colours. The people of Mariville were overjoyed and the sparkle returned to their eyes.

Lisa looked to the ground, and saw a grey liquefied sludge splattered across the market place. It looked like a spilt bit of discoloured grey paint. Lisa knew Mariville would always be colourful!

5

ACHIEVING THE IMPOSSIBLE

A character's journey to achieve the unthinkable

THE CHARACTER'S PATHWAY

A central character has a dream or is put in a difficult situation. They are determined to achieve success or overcome the situation.

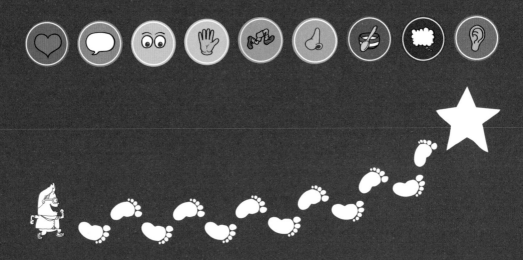

Forms: All Genres
Typical Examples: Mrs Frisby and the Rats of Nimh, The Firework-Maker's Daughter, Mulan, Billy Elliot

Those around the protagonist are unsupportive, but a mentor appears and helps him/her to eventually exceed expectations.

Textual features of an 'Achieving the Impossible' story journey

A character's journey to achieve the unthinkable	Review	
Textual features	My Writing	My Friend's Writing
Situations, problems and challenges build up to such a degree they almost suffocate the central character.		
Stereotypes and expectations of the central character are negatively reinforced.		
Central character discovers a talent they have or a particular dream they want to chase.		
Most people do not support central character in their pursuit of talent/dream.		
A significant other, who is close to central character, supports their cause.		
Central character's determination is evident.		
Central character is put under pressure, emotionally/physically or both.		
Central character reaches their goal and is accepted by those who didn't believe they could make it.		

Achieving The Impossible				
1	2	3	4	5
Not even started	Early stage	Getting there	Well on your way	You've arrived. Jump for joy!

Find these features in the example story on the adjacent page. Include these features when writing your own unique 'Achieving the Impossible' story.

How many of the features have you or your friend included in the story?

Reading: Exemplar Story/Journey Text

5

ACHIEVING THE IMPOSSIBLE

Use the text to find evidence of key features.

One Girl and her Dog

Martha had a dog...a dog called Tiger. Tiger had Martha. They had each other. Most days were filled with playful games in the park, a good walk around the streets, and dog-smell cuddles in the evening.

School wasn't going well for Martha. She'd had a few weeks off because her Mum had been in hospital for an operation, and her Dad hadn't got her up in time. Anyway, he needed the company. Martha went back one week and the class was in the middle of a space project. She didn't know what was going on and, to make matters worse, she was put in Abigail's group. Her heart sank. Abigail and Martha had clashed since Reception. Abigail was dominating, very self-confident and annoyingly popular. Martha was none of the above but was self-assured enough to disagree with Abigail, and years of bickering had cemented their dislike for each other. However, Martha was powerless in this situation, as she didn't understand what they needed to do for this project: Who was – or wasn't – NASA Management? What were the requirements for the Lunar Spacecraft? What were the success criteria for the whole project?

Unfortunately for Martha, Abigail was team leader and she took great delight in putting Martha 'to task'. Martha was left with a tub of straws and told to join them together in the most effective way possible. Martha sat there amidst thousands of straws and mounds of sticky tape.

School was getting her down. She fixed about twenty pairs of straws together in an assortment of ways: bound string, tangled tape, precision arts, and a stapler. Martha's eyes glazed over. She thought about Tiger. She remembered the picnic they'd had together on Sunday, under the large oak in the park. After eating, they'd run in unison to the bottom of the hill. He'd scampered across the damp-smelling grass, nipping playfully at Martha's jean flares. Tiger had got in her way and she'd tumbled towards the grass, landing in a giggling heap, with Tiger bouncing around her and licking her face. They were really good friends.

"Get on with it!"

Martha was startled from her daydream by Abigail's shrill, annoyed voice. Martha didn't want to be cooped up in school with Abigail and an abundance of straws.

"You're so slow Martha...and rubbish."

Martha couldn't bear it for much longer. She felt suffocated and misunderstood at school. She couldn't see how she could ever make it work. Martha longed to be outdoors, out in the world with Tiger.

For two torturous weeks, the space project continued: loo roll joins, painted plastic cartons and paper mâché glue. The whole thing was a sticky mess and that wasn't just their collapsing 3D model. Martha just wanted to leave school... forever. She couldn't tell her Mum and Dad, and even though Tiger listened, his advice was limited.

One day, when Martha got up, she decided to tell her Dad about her plan to leave school.

"Don't stress me out with your attention-seeking tricks. You'll have no future if you do that," he snapped.

Martha continued to attend school, but she couldn't think of anything else during every minute she was there. She was overcome with a desire to leave...but she also knew that she needed a survival plan. During an afternoon geography lesson, Martha looked out of the window. It was a clear day and she could see the park that joined onto the school grounds. In the distance, she spotted a woman standing in a circle with lots of other people. All of them had dogs, and from where she was sitting, Martha could tell they were young dogs because they were quite snappy and kept jumping up. Martha looked on admiringly, as she realised what she wanted to do when she grew up.

At the end of the school day, Martha took a deliberate detour to read the park's noticeboard. Plastered in the middle of the board was a poster that read:

Puppy Training Classes
Do you need help with training
your puppy?
Help and advice given on:
• Walking in public places
• Appropriate behaviour with others
• Dealing with common problems
COME ALONG! ALL WELCOME!
Wednesday 11:00 - 12:30
Thursday 4:00 - 5:30
Saturday 12:00 - 1:30
Meet at the park by the main entrance
with your dog on a lead.
SUE WILLING – Dog Trainer
£2.50 fee per session

"Great!" thought Martha. "There's a slot after school tomorrow, I'll bring Tiger along."

Martha could hardly concentrate at school the next day. She was too busy thinking about the training classes. When she told her Dad about her plans, he just grunted and said, "That stupid dog will be your downfall."

During the late afternoon, Martha stood patiently by the park gates, with six other dog owners and their rather lively puppies. Tiger just sat quietly looking up into Martha's eyes. Martha recognised Sue, the trainer, as she approached the main entrance. She welcomed everyone and turned to Martha and said quietly,

"This class is only for adults."

"Oh but..." Martha groaned.

"And," she continued, "that dog is not a puppy, he is a very well-trained dog, and does not need training."

Martha looked devastated and despondent. "Can I at least stay and watch?" she begged.

"Okay," Sue smiled.

Martha looked on in complete admiration. Sue was so calm and in control of all the puppies. She gave the owners clear and friendly advice. At the end of the session, Martha said goodbye to Sue, who bent down to stroke Tiger. Sue wasn't expecting to see Martha again, but every Thursday afternoon, and every Saturday lunchtime, Martha was there. She was always the first to arrive and the last to leave. One time after class, Martha told Sue that she wanted to do her job when she grew up. Sue explained that this wasn't her day job but that she'd spent a lot of time breeding dogs and taking them to shows.

"Tiger's a good standard for his breed. You could show him!" Sue said.

This got Martha thinking. In fact, she could think of nothing else. During a PE lesson, when she had to complete an obstacle course, she imagined it was a course at a dog show, and she and Tiger were navigating it together. Mr. Morley was really impressed with her sequence and didn't know she was such a talent! When Martha told him what she planned to do when she was older, he said, "What a foolish job! You're a bright girl Martha, and you could do so many things."

Martha stopped telling anyone but Sue. One Saturday after class, Sue spent some time with her, showing her how to practise with Tiger to get him to do a show stand. It was difficult at first, as he kept wanting to sit down. Martha persevered and, long after the initial input, continued to practise with Tiger every single day. A few weeks later, Sue showed Martha how to walk her dog in a ring, as well as the importance of the dog's eye contact with its owner. Again, Martha listened avidly to all Sue said and relentlessly went over the routine with Tiger. Sue could see that Martha was determined to devote her life to dogs and she was an excellent student to prepare for dog shows.

Impressed with her young trainee's commitment, Sue made contact with Martha's Dad to inform him of the work they were going to do together. She was keen to prepare Martha for local, regional and national dog shows. In Martha, Sue had found the model owner, and in Tiger, the most obedient dog. In the run-up to Blakesley's Dog Show, the training became more onerous and tiring. Sue expected perfection and Martha was becoming exhausted. Sue knew that Martha and her dog would be stars in the ring; Martha just hoped she didn't run out of energy.

A brisk Saturday morning at 7:00am, Sue knocked on Martha's door. The day began with a chaotic bath for Tiger – this was one department that Tiger didn't score highly in for his obedience. A small flood later, and with some spilt dog shampoo, Tiger was smelling fresh and was ready to go.

At the show, Martha was feeling really nervous but Sue reminded her of all the practice she had undertaken and how prepared she was. Before long, the dogs were called into the ring. Martha walked Tiger in a circle whilst he looked up dotingly into her eyes. She then stood him still for the judge's inspection. He stood perfectly, stretched out and proud, with his neck slightly lifted. Within a few minutes (which felt like hours), the judge announced first, second and third place...

Tiger had won!

Martha laughed!

Sue cried!

Martha's Dad winked from the ringside and said, "I knew you could do it!"

After that, school wasn't so bad for Martha. She still stayed out of Abigail's way, but when she brought in certificates and rosettes to assemblies, Abigail was really interested in her achievements. She even heard a rumour that Abigail had bought a puppy!

6

EVERYDAY LIFE DISRUPTED

A character's journey where a new person leads to a changed outlook

THE CHARACTER'S PATHWAY

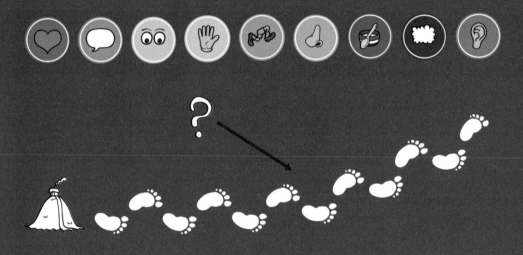

Forms: All Genres
Typical Examples: Mary Poppins, ET, Nanny McPhee

A central character begins the journey experiencing their everyday life.
Suddenly, an invited or uninvited guest brings enormous change to their world
and they learn from them.

Textual features of an 'Everyday Life Disrupted' story journey

A character's journey where a new person leads to a changed outlook	Review	
Textual features	My Writing	My Friend's Writing
Author creates calm and tranquil setting, e.g. ordinary, quiet village.		
False sense of security built up by author through emphasis on the quiet/ordinary dimensions of the locality.		
Sense of the ordinary depicted through mundane activities.		
Sudden and shocking arrival of invited or uninvited guest.		
Invited/uninvited guest provides a chaotic element through: • challenging the current 'status quo' • modelling a different approach to life.		
A bond occurs between central character and the visitor.		
The invited/uninvited guest has an impact on their new surroundings.		
Invited/uninvited guest has to return to where they came from. Main character misses them but there is evidence they have left their mark.		

Everyday Life Disrupted				
1	2	3	4	5
Not even started	Early stage	Getting there	Well on your way	You've arrived. Jump for joy!

Find these features in the example story on the adjacent page. Include these features when writing your own unique 'Everyday Life Disrupted' story.

How many of the features have you or your friend included in the story?

Reading: Exemplar Story/Journey Text

6

EVERYDAY LIFE DISRUPTED

A character's journey where a new person leads to a changed outlook

Use the text to find evidence of key features.

Life is Full of Surprises

Mr. Colin looked out of the classroom window. A thought flashed across his mind right in the middle of a maths lesson. It was one of those overwhelming and worrying thoughts that shocks you so badly you feel a little stunned afterwards. Mr. Colin was certainly in a state of confusion. Ryan and Connor picked up on this and started making paper aeroplanes out of their cube net-shaped paper outlines. It didn't take him too long to register what was going on. However, it did take a paper aeroplane making contact with his shoe before he shouted, "Ryan, Connor! Stay behind at the bell."

What was this thought of Mr. Colin's? It was short but very unexpected...

'Why did I become a teacher? I'm not sure I want to do this.'

How strange! Mr. Colin had spent four years of his life training to be a teacher,

then a year of late nights and hard slog to pass his first year in a school. He had even lived through a visit from the school inspectors. Mr. Colin, real name Nigel, was not sure he'd done the right thing, or followed the right profession, but he was here.

"Now boys...what should you have been doing with those nets?" asked Nigel in an expertly teacher-like way.

"Making cubes," Ryan mumbled.

"Exactly. Now go out to play," he ended the interrogation quickly. Ryan and Connor scarpered out of the class, a little bemused that it was over so abruptly.

Nigel was alone. He reflected on his previous thought. He couldn't understand it. Primrose Park School was a good school: the other staff were friendly, the Headteacher was supportive, and the children – well they were kids! Nigel decided to talk it over at home with his wife, Jessica. He picked himself up from his desk, huffed, and walked over to the staffroom for a coffee.

The rest of the school day was an average Tuesday, an overly-long assembly, a rushed history lesson, two leaking flask incidents at lunchtime, a 'not-quite-get-the-apparatus-out' PE lesson and messily disappointing results from the painting session in art.

On the drive home, Nigel suddenly remembered that Jessica's Auntie Barbara was coming to stay. This was disastrous! He really needed to talk. He'd never met Auntie Barbara before and it wasn't appropriate to start a crisis debate about careers during their first meeting. Nigel was deflated but nonetheless called in at the local supermarket and picked up some extra milk, as Jessica had instructed him to do. No sooner had he arrived home than the doorbell rang. Jessica whooped, "That's her!" and raced to open the door. Nigel just stood bemused in the kitchen. Auntie Barbara was welcomed in, hugged excitedly and ushered into the kitchen to meet Nigel. Auntie Barbara was unusual to say the least: she had green and purple dyed hair, spiked at the front and tousled at the back. Her orange dress screamed at Nigel and, as he hugged her, he noticed the parrot earrings and rainbow print boots.

"It's great to be here!" she announced. "I'm dying for scrambled eggs! Will you help?" She looked at Nigel, and he nodded in response. Two minutes later, they were both whisking in unison in the kitchen, while Jessica pottered about and put Auntie Barbara's suitcase in the spare bedroom.

"Eggs help you see life differently. You see, they can be one thing or another, or another, or another. It depends on what you make of them. Careful cracking and gentle heat, a fried egg. Keep contained but warmed in water, a boiled egg. Or a vigorous beating and you get scrambled! Isn't life full of surprises?"

Nigel looked dumbfounded but kept whisking. Nigel sensed that Auntie Barbara was going to become a lively member of the family for the next few weeks. He wasn't sure he had prepared himself. He joined her with her feast of scrambled eggs and listened to her story of the journey, all the people she'd met and grew to know.

"I love getting to know people," she remarked. Nigel wasn't sure if he felt the same.

Later that night, when Nigel decided to go to bed, Auntie Barbara decided to stay up. The second his head hit the pillow, he was disturbed by loud thuds from downstairs. Someone was dancing - tap dancing in fact. He couldn't sleep. Shuffle ball change rhythms filled the air. Nigel knew it was going to be a long night.

The next day, Nigel dragged himself out of bed, got ready for work, and went downstairs for breakfast. Auntie Barbara was sitting at the table, knitting. She had two oversized knitting needles and an abundance of cerise-coloured, mohair-type wool cascading towards her toes. Nigel felt her larger-than-life presence more keenly than ever.

"Wool helps you see life differently. You see it can be one thing or another, or another, or another. It depends what you make with it. Repeated stitches and regular amounts, a scarf. A mixture of movements and some sewing, a jumper. Or a complicated pattern and some patience, a teddy bear! Isn't life full of surprises?"

Auntie Barbara's energy was exhausting Nigel. He grumped as a reply, ate his porridge and went to work.

At school, Nigel was probably having the worst Wednesday since starting the job. He'd wanted the children to complete a story by the end of the English lesson, and not one of them had. They'd all found science too difficult and PE had been another lesson without apparatus. Nigel went home feeling more than ever that teaching wasn't for him. Worse than that, he had to face Auntie Barbara when he got in!

At home, Nigel opened the door cautiously. What was going to face him? A tap dancing eccentric woman knitting scrambled eggs and eating wool. Well, life is full of surprises!

When he got in, he couldn't believe what he saw: Auntie Barbara's hair was now a shade of pink, and in the dining room was the most fabulous spread. A golden chicken cooked to perfection, a whole range of colourful dishes, and the largest fruit pavlova he had ever seen. This was a surprise. Everyone had a great evening, with wonderful food and relaxing chat. Nigel told Auntie Barbara how he was feeling about teaching, how he didn't know if it was the job for him or if he was enjoying it anymore. Jessica looked stunned by Nigel's admissions. They talked for a long time and eventually went to sleep in the early hours of the morning.

Exhausted, Nigel got up for work. Downstairs, he was expecting to see Auntie Barbara, but she wasn't there. She must still be in bed. He missed her little anecdotes and her wise words. He ate his breakfast in silence. As he was just about to leave the house, he heard a shriek.

"Wait for me!"

He turned around. Auntie Barbara was stood at the top of the stairs wearing a flamingo-pink coat and an enormous green feathered hat. Her smile filled her face.

"Why?" said Nigel, bemused.

"I'm coming with you. I'm coming to school."

"Hurry up then," he replied affectionately.

Nigel sneezed during the whole duration of the car journey to work. He was allergic to feathers. When he got there, he explained to the head teacher that he had a surprise visitor to meet his class.

After the register, Nigel announced his guest to the class, and Auntie Barbara made a flamboyant entrance. Ryan's eyes widened and Connor sat upright on the edge of his seat. She sat down and removed her hat.

'Thank goodness,' Nigel thought, and put it in the stock cupboard. Auntie Barbara told the class a story. It was a story about her own schooldays and what had excited her in the classroom, and helped her to learn. It was all about how she'd enjoyed lessons full of surprises. Every child in Mr. Colin's class was captivated by the story, including Nigel. At the end of the story, she took out a bag and pulled out knitted cerise pink fluffy chicks with eyes and gave one to each pupil. She then left as suddenly as she'd arrived, and told Nigel she would catch the bus back home.

That evening, and every subsequent evening, Nigel and Auntie Barbara would stay up for hours talking about how to make lessons surprising for the next day. Sometimes, Nigel laughed so much his stomach hurt, and often at school the following day, the children laughed so hard that they found their stomachs hurting.

Eventually, it was time for Auntie Barbara to go home. Nigel knew he was going to miss her and told her so. All she said was, "Kids help you see life differently. You see they can be one thing or another, or another, or another. It depends what you make of them. Isn't life full of surprises?"

"Thank you so much," he whispered. He was so very grateful.

The next day at school, after a lively science lesson, Mr. Colin opened the stock cupboard, and lying there on the floor was a large green feather.

Atchoo!

Wasn't life full of surprises? And Auntie Barbara was one of them!

7

CHAOS TO CALM

A character's journey to harmonious union

THE CHARACTER'S PATHWAY

A central character misunderstands another character and further chaos is caused as communication continues to break down.

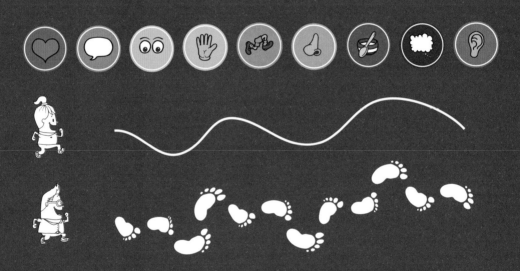

Forms: All Genres
Typical Examples: The Gardener, BFG, Midsummer Night's Dream

Calm is restored when characters resume direct communication.

Textual features of a 'Chaos To Calm' story journey

A character's journey to find harmonious union	Review	
Textual features	**My Writing**	**My Friend's Writing**
Misunderstandings from the outset between main characters e.g. crossed wires, lack of communication and near misses to clarify situations.		
Main characters are confused about their positions in relation to others. Erratic behaviour typical.		
Opportunities for understanding between the two parties are thwarted by outside influences or others.		
A defining moment occurs and the two parties become synchronised, e.g. kiss, shared laughter, a look.		
Harmonious ending. Celebratory event of some kind, e.g. picnic, party, wedding.		
A bond occurs between central character and the visitor.		
The invited/uninvited guest has an impact on their new surroundings.		
Invited/uninvited guest has to return to where they came from. Main character misses them but there is evidence they have left their mark.		

Chaos to Calm				
1	2	3	4	5
Not even started	Early stage	Getting there	Well on your way	You've arrived. Jump for joy!

Find these features in the example story on the adjacent page. Include these features when writing your own unique 'Chaos To Calm' story.

How many of the features have you or your friend included in the story?

Reading: Exemplar Story/Journey Text

7

CHAOS TO CALM

Use the text to find evidence of key features.

Walks Home

Sometimes, you stumble across things you don't intend to. This happened to Maggie. Maggie even wished she hadn't stumbled into it. Now there was no turning back. This defining moment happened one day at school in the cloakroom. Maggie was a bit clumsy and had lost her reading book, so she was sent by the teacher to her bag to try and find it. Whilst she was tipping her bag out to hunt for the book, her favourite gold gel pen rolled under the cloakroom benches. As she was small-framed, she crawled under them to retrieve it. At this very moment, Katrina and Abigail walked into the cloakroom, talking:

"Well, all I can say is that I think she is making a fool of herself. All she does is giggle around Gary Bodkin, and is making it so obvious she likes him. It's just embarrassing."

"Yeah, I know. She is like 'yeah Gary, whatever you say Gary.' I wish she'd stop it!"

Maggie was in a frozen huddle, holding her breath and listening to the entire conversation. She was also bright red because she knew it was her they were talking about. She waited until the girls had gone back to class and then crawled out, thinking hard about what they'd said.

'They were right,' she thought. She and Gary had walked home together since Year 4. They both lived near the school and didn't have to cross any roads. Every afternoon after school, they would chat, argue, or even walk in silence until they were both at home. They got on really well together; Maggie knew who Gary's favourite teachers were, who blocked the boy's toilets last year, and how he liked his bacon sandwiches cooked. Likewise, Gary knew Maggie's most annoying habit, what her dog liked to eat, and all about her gel pen collection. However, in the last few weeks, something had changed. On one of their walks home, Maggie had stopped listening to Gary explaining how to beat the baddies on level four of his computer game, and was instead looking at how his lips moved. She'd found the way he flicked his hair up – until recently – really annoying, but now she thought it was quite cute. She'd also noticed he had soft, chocolate-brown eyes...

"Maggie, get back to class!" Mr Brown shouted from the classroom door. She was startled back to her senses.

"Have you found your book yet?"

"No, Sir."

"Find it by tomorrow."

Maggie returned to her seat. She felt the glare of Katrina and Abigail on her back. She couldn't believe that her secret was out. For the rest of the day, Maggie couldn't concentrate. She was distracted during PE and kept dropping the ball during bat & ball skills. Later, in geography, she didn't finish her map work and finally, in English, she felt like she had writer's block. At half past three, the bell rang and school was over. It was time to meet Gary at the school gates. Maggie felt mortified; what if Katrina and Abigail had said something to him? It suddenly struck her what she could do to avoid the situation. She made sure she was the first out of class, grabbed her coat and bag and ran wildly, like a terrified animal, until she got to her front door. Her Grandma let her in.

"You're early!" she said.

"Yeah, I know!" Maggie panted.

"Sit down darling, you're out of breath. Are you okay?"

Ten minutes, and a cup of tea later, and Maggie had told Grandma the whole story. "Oh well," said Gran. "Maybe it's for the best that you walk home on your own." Maggie started crying. Then the doorbell rang.

"That's probably one of your friends."

"Just ignore it, Gran, I'm not in the mood." The doorbell went again. A minute passed, and then faint footsteps could be heard leaving the front garden pathway.

The next day, Maggie reluctantly dragged herself into school. She could see Abigail and Katrina huddled together on the playground, giggling, and Gary was playing football. She just sat quietly on the bench with her head down. The sky darkened and Maggie looked up to see a figure overshadowing her – it was Gary.

"What's wrong with you?" he asked.

"Nothing, I hate you," she said abruptly.

Sometimes, you stumble into things you don't intend to. This had just happened to Maggie. Maggie wished she hadn't said that. Now there was no turning back. Gary was stunned, and there was a long, awkward pause.

"I hate you too," he said.

He turned on his heels and kicked a stone across the playground. A tear rolled down Maggie's face, but she quickly wiped it away.

School for Maggie for the next few weeks was really difficult, especially home times. Then one Tuesday, out of the blue, Lorraine said,

"Shall we walk together Maggie?"

"Erm, yeah, sure." Maggie was slightly taken aback. "I didn't know you lived near me?"

"I do now, I've moved," Lorraine replied.

Lorraine and Maggie became really good friends. Every afternoon after school, they would chat, argue, or even walk in silence until they were both at home. They got on really well together; Lorraine knew who Maggie's favourite bands were, how she liked her bacon sandwiches cooked, and all about her gel pen collection. Likewise, Maggie knew the names of all of Lorraine's siblings, where she kept her secret diary, and that she fancied Gary Bodkin and couldn't stop giggling at everything he said!

The next day at school, Maggie found Gary on the playground.

"Are you alright?" she asked.

"Yeah...are you?"

"Yes thanks, but I'm really sorry about what I said."

"Me too!" At last, they were friends again. They both smiled. Later, after school, Gary said to Maggie, "Do you and Lorraine want to walk with me and Thomas?"

So they did. And Maggie giggled all the way home at Thomas' jokes.

8

ENLIGHTENMENT

A character's journey of positive inner change

THE CHARACTER'S PATHWAY

Forms: All Genres
Typical Examples: A Christmas Carol, The Red Tree, About a Boy

A central character has a negative outlook on life.
A significant event or person jolts them to a new, more positive way

Textual features of an 'Enlightenment' story journey

A character's journey to find inner change	Review	
Textual features	**My Writing**	**My Friend's Writing**
Central character is trapped in a shadowy mindset; a negative outlook on life.		
Central character's actions are described in detail and reinforce their cold-hearted approach to life.		
Central character practises their behaviour in a range of differing situations.		
Weather often dismal/bad to parallel the characteristics of main character.		
Central character gets a jolt about their actions and behaviour.		
Reformed personality shows examples of 'giving back' to others and the world at large.		
Backdrop to story improves. Weather becomes good to parallel central character's more charitable approach to life.		
Invited/uninvited guest has to return to where they came from. Main character misses them but there is evidence they have left their mark.		

Enlightenment				
1	**2**	**3**	**4**	**5**
Not even started	Early stage	Getting there	Well on your way	You've arrived. Jump for joy!

Find these features in the example story on the adjacent page. Include these features when writing your own unique 'Enlightenment' story.

How many of the features have you or your friend included in the story?

Reading: Exemplar Story/Journey Text

8

ENLIGHTENMENT

A character's journey of positive inner change

Use the text to find evidence of key features.

Umbrella

Charlie was naughty. In fact, he couldn't remember a time he hadn't been renowned for his naughtiness. Unlike some children, who were perhaps naughty in some situations, Charlie prided himself on his consistent bad behaviour, wherever he was.

Charlie was 'down' on life and this translated into all that he did. At home, he had managed to cultivate a situation that meant he was never asked to do anything to help. The reason for this was that the rest of the family had given up asking because they knew he just wouldn't do it. Charlie's bedroom was a state and his Mum had learnt to cope with the mess by just shutting the door on it. Unfortunately, it never got tidied, and the condition of it was out of control. It was a dark and dingy room with breakfast bowls containing remnants of cereal shoved under his bed. Clothes were strewn all over the floor like it had just been hit by a whirlwind. Bits of broken toys and games were randomly scattered in a strange array of places: by the broken

bookshelf, or amongst his clothes drawers. Charlie didn't care and didn't respect anything.

At school, Charlie was equally despicable. He would deliberately pull two coats off their hooks in the cloakroom before hanging up his own. In class, he would scribble graffiti on school books and draw fake moustaches and glasses on beautifully-illustrated stories. At lunch time, he'd make other children hand over their treats and would take great delight in making others very nervous, or even reducing them to tears. Mr. Jackson, his class teacher, tried to talk to Charlie about his behaviour, but Charlie always had the same reply:

"Stop picking on me."

Mr. Jackson didn't know what to do.

Charlie's Mum didn't know what to do.

The children in Charlie's class didn't know what to do.

And Charlie just didn't care. There was a coldness in his eyes.

One particular day, when Charlie got up for school, the sky was dark grey and rumbles of thunder were threatening in the distance. It was a heavy and humid atmosphere, and Charlie felt particularly angry. When he got downstairs, he demanded that he wanted *'Sugarwheats'*. "Sorry Charlie, I haven't got any of those," his Mum whispered timidly.

Charlie pushed her books off the table and stormed out to school, without any breakfast. On his way to school, he could see Rosie walking in front of him. The thunderstorm was closing in and the rain was becoming stronger. Charlie began to run and, without warning, he snatched Rosie's umbrella with such stealth that she didn't even have time to cling on to it. Rosie was so shocked, but even as she watched her umbrella disappearing in the distance, she knew that it was Charlie who had taken it. Her tears were unnoticed in the storm and, rather reluctantly, a very drenched Rosie arrived at school ten minutes after Charlie.

Rosie didn't know what to do.

Later that day, Mr. Jackson wanted the class to write stories. Rosie was an excellent writer, and she enjoyed creating magical worlds woven from a mixture of real and imaginary people and events. Near the end of the lesson, Rosie was asked to read her story so far. She stood up in front of the class and began to read. Her voice was very soothing, comforting to listen to.

"One thunderous morning on the way to school, I was walking quite hurriedly to make sure I got out of the rain quickly. Inside, I was regretting that my coat didn't have a hood, because then maybe I could have prevented the large, cold droplets running down my back and making me feel chilly and uncomfortable. Just as I was jostling with the idea of running the rest of the way, I heard footsteps behind me, splashing through the puddles. I turned round to take a look. It was Chris, from my class.

"Hi, Rosie," his friendly smile cheered me up. He then looked in his bag and pulled out an umbrella. It opened instantaneously and he held it over both our heads, like a much-needed shelter.

"Thanks," I said, and I really meant it.

Rosie broke off and then said, "That's as far as I got, Sir." Rosie looked up to her captivated audience and caught sight of Charlie. His face looked different; his frown had fallen away and his eyes were wide and contemplative. Unusually, Charlie put his hand up.

"Can I go to the toilet please, Sir?"

The class couldn't believe what they were hearing. It had probably been two years or more since anyone had heard Charlie say 'please'. Mr. Jackson nodded, himself a little stunned.

That night at home, Charlie thought again and again about Rosie's story. He knew it was a message for him, and he also knew that Rosie hadn't told anyone about the umbrella-snatching incident. Her kindness to him made him care.

Charlie really cared.

Charlie didn't know what to do.

The next morning, Charlie's Mum had bought him *Sugarwheats*.

"You shouldn't have done that, Mum. I'm sorry."

Charlie's Mum started crying. She couldn't believe what she was hearing. It had probably been two years or more since she had heard Charlie say 'sorry'. Charlie ate his breakfast and left a little earlier than usual to go to school. The storm yesterday had broken the heavy atmosphere, and today the sun was warm and fresh. Charlie called in at the corner shop and bought an umbrella. The shopkeeper gave Charlie a puzzled look and remarked,

"The weather report says 'sunny'."

Charlie merely smiled, and went to wait on the wall outside. In the distance, he could see Rosie walking towards him. He was feeling very nervous and a bit afraid about what he had to do next. Rosie approached him. He tentatively handed her the new umbrella. She took it and grinned. Rosie proceeded to push it up until it clicked, then looped her arm under his and held it equally over both of their heads.

Charlie laughed.

The sun warmed their smiles.

9

MISGUIDED

A character's journey of negative inner change

THE CHARACTER'S PATHWAY

A central character begins the journey driven
and goal-orientated.

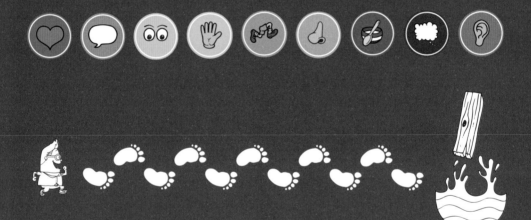

Forms: All Genres
Typical Examples: Matilda Told Such Dreadful Lies (poem), Romeo and Juliet,
The Bicycle Thieves

As he or she moves through the story, they hurt others with
their immoral decisions and actions - fuelled by a relentless
determination to get what they want.

Textual features of a 'Misguided' story journey

A character's journey to find lasting happiness	Review	
Textual features	**My Writing**	**My Friend's Writing**
Author builds central character empathy from the outset.		
In the early part of the story, the central character has noble missions and virtuous moral goals.		
The central character cannot get what they want easily.		
Insight into character's perceptions and motives are drawn out in extensive detail.		
Heightened emotions are exposed by author at various trigger points.		
Central character is tempted to do 'dark' acts to get what they want.		
The central character begins to commit 'dark' acts so as to achieve personal goals.		
The central character's lies are unscrupulous.		
Events escalate and crisis occurs.		
Reader's empathy is with the central character. We can recognise how they have taken the wrong path, even though we disagree with it.		
The story comes to an abrupt end. People are hurt and death is often a feature (tears or blood are spilt.)		
Moral lessons are learnt by observers/significant others.		
The tragedy of the situation is overwhelming.		

Misguided				
1	2	3	4	5
Not even started	Early stage	Getting there	Well on your way	You've arrived. Jump for joy!

Find these features in the example story on the adjacent page. Include these features when writing your own unique 'Misguided' story.

How many of the features have you or your friend included in the story?

Reading: Exemplar Story/Journey Text

9

MISGUIDED

A character's journey of negative inner change

Use the text to find evidence of key features.

Who Done It?

Jessica was well-liked at school. She had many friends and prided herself on her popularity. She had some friends she played rounders with, other friends she made up dances and skipping games with, and a whole group she enjoyed chatting to. Jessica kept a diary and each day after school she would scramble up to her bedroom and pull out the glittery pink book that was hidden under her pillow. Today, when she raced upstairs, she retrieved her diary and re-read yesterday's entry:

Dear Miss Diary,
Today was really cool! Amanda and I invented a new song about kittens. Loads of people came and listened to it. We even got a round of applause from our audience. Tomorrow, we're inventing the dance moves to go with it. Molly and Phoebe so want to be in our gang. We'll let them join in tomorrow.
See you soon, J x

Jessica enjoyed being the inventor of new and exciting playground games, and relished the fact that others often begged to join in.

Dear Miss Diary,
I am going to make it a personal challenge of mine to capture the interest of as many people as possible through my amazing games. I will be the most exciting person to play with in the whole of Barkington School. That's a deal, J x

Jessica sat and pondered for a while. Amy's words popped into her head. Amy had said this to Jessica in Year 1 and Jessica had hoped she would be able to get over it by now. Intermittently, the words would drift back into her mind:

"You're boring Jessica. Your games are boring. I don't want to play with you."

Amy had meant it. Amy and Jessica just didn't get on any more.

Back at school the next day, Jessica put on a show at lunchtime and showcased the kitten song and dance – by now, six other girls had joined in, and it was performed to a large audience. Jessica felt overjoyed and began planning the next playground game that could generate the same excitement, and perhaps even interest the boys.

This was causing Jessica more difficulty than she anticipated, but eventually she decided on a game based around a detective agency. Jessica was the inspector in charge at the agency, and she would only consider the crime solved if the detectives could explain what had happened, in detail, in the time leading up to the crime - and declare who did it. Jessica knew that this game was a master stroke of genius. Maybe this was the game that would convince Amy that she was interesting, and possibly even be enough for Amy to ask to join in.

Dear Miss Diary,
There are now 12 people enlisted in the detective agency game, and four of them are boys! We spent time today sorting out the rules properly and giving everyone roles within the agency. We even have a caretaker, who offers helpful advice and clues – Jack's doing a great job at that. Amy was playing 'tig and tag' today. She'll soon get bored of that.

Write soon, from Inspector Gardener (Me!)

At playtime, two more children joined the group and it was decided that the agency was ready to deal with its first crime. Jessica spent a lot of time orchestrating the complexities of the crime scene, and then she took the group over to a wooded area at the back of the playground. Jessica composed herself, coughed, and announced to the huddled crowd of detectives:

"Yesterday, at some point, a crime was committed here. Someone had their bag stolen with all its contents. Strangely, that person never reported the crime, but an anonymous call to the station revealed the theft, and the details of that call will provide us with clues."

Jessica stayed in the role for the duration of the explanation. As she set the scene, all the children who were playing detectives were completely engrossed by her very serious and expressive tone of voice.

"It is our job to find the bag and its contents and return it to the owner, even though they have not declared the crime. Search around this area and return to the station if you discover any clues or anything worth reporting."

There wasn't much of playtime left, but all the detectives were completely absorbed in the 'task at hand'. Many were looking around the base of trees, or scrabbling around in the undergrowth. Others were huddled together discussing the best course of action, whilst a few were questioning other pupils on the playground.

'What power I yield,' thought Jessica as she walked back to the bench in the quiet area, which marked the office base of their work. She caught a glimpse of Amy laughing with Tamsin over a skipping game. Jessica had invented the best game of her life, but in terms of luring Amy over to play, it just wasn't going to plan.

Dear Miss Diary,

The detective agency is going strong. Everyone is so involved. Loads of evidence came back today, a thread from someone's jumper, a screwed up note with indecipherable handwriting on it, and a broken pen. Tomorrow, I'm going to announce that the game is starting and it is the last chance for anyone (including Amy) to join. J x

Jessica stood on the corner of the playground (in the same position that teachers stood when they wanted to make an announcement). In her loudest voice, Jessica belted out an outline of the game, and the fact that it was the last opportunity to join up. Two minutes later and two more recruits had joined: Thomas Bickle, a small and friendly dinosaur enthusiast, and his friend Kyle, a very shy and quiet individual. Anger welled up inside Jessica. What more could she do to entice Amy? All she wanted was to be friends with her, and for her to reconsider her as not boring.

Jessica thought about how she could grab Amy's attention. Suddenly, it came to her! She could make Amy the victim of the crime and that way she'd be forced to join in.

At the next detective agency meeting, Jessica revealed a vital piece of evidence.

"This pen was found on the ground near the back of the woodlands," she explained. "It is very distinctive and popular with girls, and narrows down our search for the victim of this crime."

As Jessica rolled the pen in her hands, she knew it would cause a stir as this really was Amy's pen. Over lunch yesterday, she had crept back into the cloakroom and surreptitiously stolen a pen from Amy's pencil case. The others started whispering amongst themselves – it was clear that five girls in the class had one of those pens, and three of them were involved in the game. That left just two.

Dear Miss Diary,

The game is hotting up. How much more interesting to use real artifacts from a real person! She doesn't even realise what I've done, yet this way she's playing my game and doesn't even know it! It's all good fun and nobody's getting hurt... J x

Jessica couldn't believe how easy it had been to pilfer items from Amy's bag, and so, just in time for afternoon play, she took another item. This time it was a reading book. As Jessica explained the next piece of evidence, she talked in detail about this child's reading level, and how it could be the link to solving the case. Many of the detectives were getting really excited by the realness of the game and Jessica was thrilled by the way she was manipulating Amy's involvement. 'Boring?' she thought to herself, 'I'm not boring!' Jessica knew that the next course of action she took was a little dangerous but she was frustrated that Amy had not once come to ask her what was going on. She had been interviewed six times by Jessica's officers but had just told them she didn't know what they were on about. Jessica called an emergency meeting. While everyone was gathering near the woodland, Jessica boldly marched up to Amy's back-pack and pulled out her diary. She then proceeded to walk back to the congregation, calling everyone to attention.

"I have found one significant piece of evidence - the victim's diary. This will enable us to solve the crime. I am going to read a page at random from this."

Jessica opened the diary. Not only were all the detectives looking on aghast, but other pupils from the playground had also stopped what they were doing. Jessica felt that this was the only way to get Amy to take notice of her. With regret, she opened up the diary and read,

Dear Polly-Anne,
School is just awful. I try to go in and keep myself to myself, and play with others who like me. I'm so unpopular and Jessica seems to be gaining in popularity every day.

Tamsin has stopped playing with me and has joined the police game. I don't know why Jessica doesn't like me: she seems to be deliberately hurting me and pushing me out at the moment. Worse than that, she is sending her cronies to tease me about some pretend crime.

I wish I could move schools...

At that moment, Jessica looked up into the crowd. Amy was stood aghast, watching the performance. Their eyes made contact and then Amy ran off with tears pouring down her face.

"You shouldn't have done that!" Tamsin shouted angrily from the crowd. Jessica hung her head.

The detective broke out of role and walked away, leaving Jessica standing alone.

Children mark milestones on narrative journeys so they have clear ideas about sentences that can be used in their stories.

Consider

Watch *Blue Umbrella*, the Pixar short film, and bare-bone the key plot points in the frame below. Subsequently, mark in the positive and negative aspects for Blue Umbrella on his journey.

The Blue Umbrella

School Impact Points

Discuss the Nine Story Journeys as a staff team - talking about the journeys your classes will most likely meet in the stories you read, share and model.

Build a long-term view, by year group, of the types of stories your pupils experience. Next, map in the journey-types of those stories (and build the processes into your teaching sequences for writing).

Oscar, Year 2

What are the Three Zones of Writing?

A good place to start is at the beginning. The problem is knowing what is the beginning and what is the end.

Chapter 6

Summary

☑ Teaching and learning can be significantly improved in writing lessons if teachers 'sharpen up' how they model writing, and showcase how it is constructed using sentences.

☑ The FANTASTICs system uses a child-friendly acronym to represent the nine idea lenses through which pupils can craft their writing. (This is discussed in detail in *Chapter 7: What is the FANTASTICs System?*).

☑ The tools of writing are the grammar rules of our language system. The GRAMMARISTICs are an accessible way to target key weaknesses in pupils' grammatical and linguistic structures (This is discussed in detail in *Chapter 8: What is the Grammar of Sentence Building?*).

☑ The techniques of writing are brought to life by the BOOMTASTICs - the magic ingredients children need to begin developing their own unique writing voices. (This will be discussed in detail in *Chapter 9: How Can We Teach Personal Style?*).

What are the Three Zones of Writing?

To be great writers, children need to know about these three essential components:

1 Ideas

2 Tools

3 Techniques

From the youngest of ages, pupils love to see their shared compositions on display. This work is based on the Nick Sharratt — Elizabeth Lindsay book, *Socks*.

"Words create sentences; sentences create paragraphs; sometimes paragraphs quicken and begin to breathe." **Stephen King, 2000 On Writing: A Memoir of the Craft**

Pupils are particularly poor at textual cohesion. Seeing modelled examples of writing, built up over time, that exemplify writing with clear guidance on paragraphing helps them understand links and joins.

When supporting pupils as writers, we need to provide a framework for them to build their fledgling ideas into sentences. As teachers, we need to be clear about the ways in which we can support pupils through this messy business, enabling them to move towards more skilled constructions and to create particular effects.

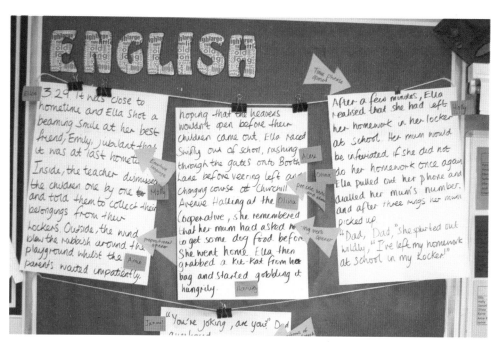

Children's work is displayed large - on washing lines - in these classrooms, so there is high celebration of individual contributions to the final piece.

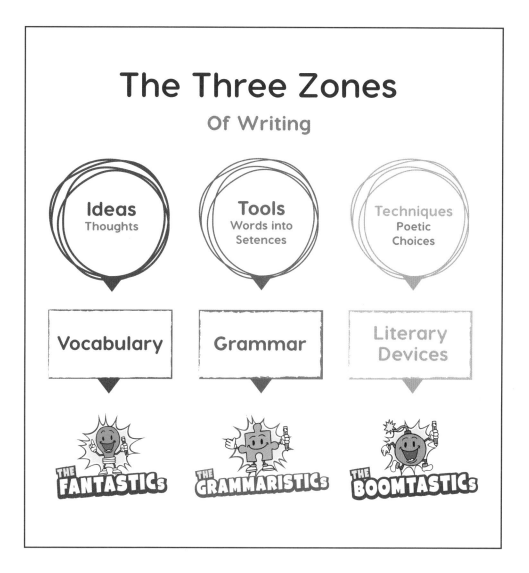

Once we recognise these areas as the most vital to support children through the writing process, we can begin to take a systematic approach to helping them very explicitly at every stage.

① Ideas

Where do you get your ideas?

Pupils find it hard to get going with their writing and often get stuck before they begin. Children who enjoy reading for pleasure tend to be the ones with the most ideas. A report for the Scottish Executive Education Department entitled, *Literature Circles, Gender and Reading for Enjoyment (Allan et al., 2005:5)*, sums up the benefits of reading for pleasure:

"Children who say that they enjoy reading, and who read for pleasure in their own times, do better at school. Reading for enjoyment is positively associated with writing ability **(OECD 2002)**. *Pupils who read for pleasure also demonstrate a wider general knowledge* **(Wells 1986)**, *a better understanding of other cultures* **(Meek 1991)**, *and more complex insights regarding human nature, motivations and decision-making* **(Cunningham and Stanovich 1998, Bruner 1996)**.*"

The link between reading and writing is strong. Reading not only exposes us to formal and informal sentence constructions but it also enhances vocabulary and helps us to understand the rhythm of writing. Schools that are desperately working on raising attainment in writing need to be sure they have a rich reading curriculum that actively promotes a love of books. If a school is focusing on a writing agenda, it won't get very far without bringing reading standards with it. Reading is a rich source of ideas and will directly support pupils with vocabulary choices and descriptive techniques. After all, description is a vehicle to make the reader a sensory participant in the story.

"Description begins in the writer's imagination, but should finish in the reader's."
Stephen King, 2002

Reading for pleasure helps pupils discover how authors construct and craft their writing. Deep discussion about language and structure awakens them to the immense power of words.

Children need time to think,
reflect and consider their ideas.

Generating ideas is very difficult for children who are not regular readers, as they are unsure of the focus points within stories and in non-fiction. Without reading, children do not understand the shapes of texts and the writers' abilities to zoom in and out, quicken and slow, and look up and down within their work. Reading for enjoyment is sharply divided between boys and girls and the National Literacy Trust's annual survey in 2015 revealed that 64.2% of boys did not enjoy reading (32,026 8-18 year olds).

The top three types of reading all children found the most fun, and read for pleasure, were: websites, social media and song lyrics. However, these texts do not require reading stamina or a sense that they require completion to obtain a whole meaning. All have a 'dipping in and out' quality and do not necessarily provide pupils with the delicious language of the well-told tale or engaging and thought-provoking non-fiction piece.

"You get ideas from daydreaming. You get ideas from being bored. You get ideas all the time. The only difference between writers and other people is we notice when we're doing it." **Author Neil Gaiman, Where do you get your ideas? blog.**

Writing can be a slog, even with ideas. Children often need more help than we allow for within our teaching units. It is our job, through a combination of: quality texts, real and imagined experiences, and clear modelling of expectations, to help mould their writing brains.

The Ideas of Writing

Vocabulary helps pupils to build vivid images in the reader's mind. Children struggle with this and need their thinking to be deepened, stretched and organised. In our world of information overload, even a thesaurus can be an overwhelming place to gather words to use in sentences. Prior to this, children need a structure to develop their ideas and, in Chapter 7, I will explore in detail the FANTASTICs system, nine big ideas to spark off winning words, fabulous phrases and creative clauses.

> ❝
> ## Words do not always need to wear a bowler hat and a monocle
> ❞

Words are the building blocks of sentences and sometimes children, and teachers, believe that the best word is a fancy, embellished word. It often isn't. Writing needs to be clear and, as writers, we need to find the best words for the job.

Pupils need to organise the language they collect under the nine lenses so they have a system for categorising their ideas.

In June 2015, The Guardian reported that a group of acclaimed children's writers, including the Carnegie winning author Tanya Landman, had contacted education secretary Nicky Morgan about the 'very damaging' tendency for primary school teachers to steer children's creative writing towards 'too elaborate, flowery and overly-complex' words. In classrooms up and down the country, the most complicated words are often presented as 'better' alternatives. The authors' open letter explained that this emphasis on ambitious words meant that children:

"fail to understand the nuances of their use, and they also fail to realise that they are used relatively sparingly".

Words do not always need to wear a bowler hat and a monocle. This is not to say that vocabulary is not important. It is. Words are the 'bread and butter' of writing. Without words, meaning cannot be communicated. More often than not, as an adult, the first word that pops into your head to explain something is likely to be the nearest to express meaning. But sometimes, as adults, we say we don't

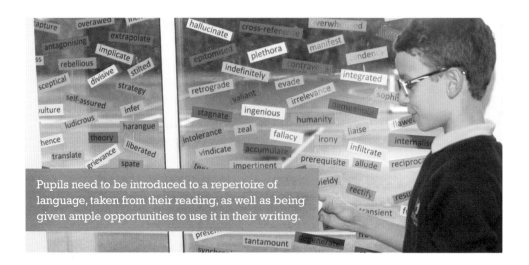

Pupils need to be introduced to a repertoire of language, taken from their reading, as well as being given ample opportunities to use it in their writing.

know how to describe something. Children experience this even more so, and feel even more frustrated when they cannot express what they mean. The nub of the problem is that children do not have a vast repertoire of language, clear or otherwise, to draw on. Ultimately, it is our professional duty to help pupils discover new words and discuss their nuances so they can be used correctly. We need to help children strive for both clarity and beauty in their writing.

 Tools

What are the tools of writing?

Kolln (2006) argues that knowledge of grammar is a:

"rhetorical tool that all writers should understand and control".

As writers, we need to be technically in control of the grammar principles of our language. Grammar enables the writer to make effective choices. It can, however, be a challenging aspect of our work with children, and the new national curriculum has added to this burden by cranking up expectations. There are SPaG (Spelling, Punctuation and Grammar) tests in Years 2 and Year 6 in primary school. Year 2 pupils will be tested on the use of the apostrophe in contracted forms, fronted adverbials followed by a comma and knowing the difference between coordinating and subordinating conjunctions. We have to keep reminding ourselves that children in Year 2 are only six and seven years old. By the time pupils are in Year 6, they are being quizzed on complex sentences, the active and passive voice, the full range of word classes and how to label a sentence's component parts.

Outlined below are the expectations from Years 1 to 6 for grammar in the UK's national curriculum.

Year 1: Detail of content to be introduced (statutory requirement)	
Word	Regular **plural noun suffixes** –s or –es [for example, *dog, dogs; wish, wishes*], including the effects of these suffixes on the meaning of the noun **Suffixes** that can be added to verbs where no change is needed in the spelling of root words (e.g. *helping, helped, helper*) How the **prefix** *un–* changes the meaning of **verbs** and **adjectives** [negation, for example, *unkind, or undoing: untie the boat*]
Sentence	How **words** can combine to make **sentences** Joining **words** and joining **clauses** using *and*
Text	Sequencing **sentences** to form short narratives
Punctuation	Separation of **words** with spaces Introduction to capital letters, full stops, question marks and exclamation marks to demarcate **sentences** Capital letters for names and for the personal **pronoun I**
Terminology for pupils	letter, capital letter word, singular, plural sentence punctuation, full stop, question mark, exclamation mark

Year 2: Detail of content to be introduced (statutory requirement)	
Word	Formation of **nouns** using **suffixes** such as –*ness*, –*er* and by compounding [for example, *whiteboard, Superman*] Formation of **adjectives** using **suffixes** such as –*ful*, –*less* (A fuller list of **suffixes** can be found on page 56 in the Year 2 spelling section in English Appendix 1) Use of the **suffixes** –*er*, –*est* in **adjectives** and the use of –*ly* in Standard English to turn adjectives into **adverbs**
Sentence	**Subordination** (using *when, if, that, because*) and **co-ordination** (using *or, and, but*) Expanded **noun phrases** for description and specification [for example, *the blue butterfly, plain flour, the man in the moon*] **How the grammatical patterns in a sentence indicate its function as a** statement, question, exclamation or command
Text	Correct choice and consistent use of **present tense** and **past tense** throughout writing Use of the **progressive** form of **verbs** in the **present** and **past tense** to mark actions in progress [for example, *she is drumming, he was shouting*]
Punctuation	Use of capital letters, full stops, question marks and exclamation marks to demarcate **sentences** Commas to separate items in a list **Apostrophes** to mark where letters are missing in spelling and to mark singular possession in nouns [for example, the *girl's name*]
Terminology for pupils	noun, noun phrase statement, question, exclamation, command, compound, suffix adjective, adverb, verb tense (past, present) apostrophe, comma

Year 3: Detail of content to be introduced (statutory requirement)	
Word	Formation of **nouns** using a range of **prefixes** [for example *super–, anti–, auto–*] Use of the **forms** a or an according to whether the next **word** begins with a **consonant** or a **vowel** [for example, *a rock, an open box*] **Word families** based on common **words**, showing how words are related in form and meaning [for example, *solve, solution, solver, dissolve, insoluble*]
Sentence	Expressing time, place and cause using **conjunctions** [for example, *when, before, after, while, so, because*], **adverbs** [for example, *then, next, soon, therefore*], or **prepositions** [for example, *before, after, during, in, because of*]
Text	Introduction to paragraphs as a way to group related material Headings and sub-headings to aid presentation Use of the **present perfect** form of **verbs** instead of the simple past [for example, *He has gone out to play* contrasted with *He went out to play*]
Punctuation	Introduction to inverted commas to punctuate direct speech
Terminology for pupils	preposition, conjunction word family, prefix clause, subordinate clause direct speech consonant, consonant letter vowel, vowel letter, inverted commas (or 'speech marks')

Year 4: Detail of content to be introduced (statutory requirement)	
Word	The grammatical difference between **plural** and **possessive** –*s* Standard English forms for **verb inflections** instead of local spoken forms [for example, *we were* instead of *we was*, or *I did* instead of *I done*]
Sentence	Noun phrases expanded by the addition of modifying adjectives, nouns and preposition phrases (e.g. *the teacher* expanded to: *the strict maths teacher with curly hair*) Fronted adverbials [for example, *Later that day, I heard the bad news.*]
Text	Use of paragraphs to organise ideas around a theme Appropriate choice of **pronoun** or **noun** within and across **sentences** to aid **cohesion** and avoid repetition
Punctuation	Use of inverted commas and other **punctuation** to indicate direct speech [for example, a comma after the reporting clause; end punctuation within inverted commas: *The conductor shouted, "Sit down!"*] **Apostrophes** to mark **plural** possession [for example, *the girl's name, the girls' names*] Use of commas after **fronted adverbials**
Terminology for pupils	determiner pronoun, possessive pronoun, adverbial

Year 5: Detail of content to be introduced (statutory requirement)	
Word	Converting **nouns** or **adjectives** into **verbs** using **suffixes** [for example, *–ate; –ise; –ify*] **Verb prefixes** [for example, *dis–, de–, mis–, over– and re–*]
Sentence	**Relative clauses** beginning with *who, which, where, when, whose, that,* or an omitted relative pronoun Indicating degrees of possibility using **adverbs** [for example, *perhaps, surely*] or **modal verbs** [for example, *might, should, will, must*]
Text	Devices to build **cohesion** within a paragraph [for example, *then, after that, this, firstly*] Linking ideas across paragraphs using adverbials of time [for example, *later*], place [for example, *nearby*] and number [for example, *secondly*] or tense choices [for example, *he had seen her before*]
Punctuation	Brackets, dashes or commas to indicate parenthesis Use of commas to clarify meaning or avoid ambiguity
Terminology for pupils	modal verb, relative pronoun, relative clause, parenthesis, bracket, dash cohesion, ambiguity

Year 6: Detail of content to be introduced (statutory requirement)	
Word	The difference between vocabulary typical of informal speech and vocabulary appropriate for formal speech and writing [for example, *find out – discover; ask for – request; go in – enter*] How words are related by meaning as synonyms and antonyms [for example, big, large, little].
Sentence	Use of the **passive** to affect the presentation of information in a **sentence** [for example, *I broke the window in the greenhouse versus The window in the greenhouse was broken (by me)*]. The difference between structures typical of informal speech and structures appropriate for formal speech and writing [for example, the use of question tags: *He's your friend, isn't he?*, or the use of **subjunctive** forms such as *If I were* or *Were they* to come in some very formal writing and speech]
Text	Linking ideas across paragraphs using a wider range of **cohesive devices**: repetition of a **word** or phrase, grammatical connections [for example, the use of adverbials such as *on the other hand*, in contrast, or *as a consequence*], and ellipsis Layout devices [for example, headings, sub-headings, columns, bullets, or tables, to structure text]
Punctuation	Use of the semi-colon, colon and dash to mark the boundary between independent **clauses** [for example, *It's raining; I'm fed up*] Use of the colon to introduce a list and use of semi-colons within lists **Punctuation** of bullet points to list information How hyphens can be used to avoid ambiguity [for example, *man eating shark versus man-eating shark,* or *recover versus re-cover*]
Terminology for pupils	subject, object active, passive synonym, antonym ellipsis, hyphen, colon, semi-colon, bullet points

When the overall detail of the national grammar expectations is viewed like this, it is a sharp reminder of the depth of subject knowledge required. Professor David Crystal explains the importance of grammar:

"Grammar is what gives sense to language... Sentences make words yield up their meanings. Sentences actively create sense in language and the business of the study of sentences is the study of grammar."

Other than for banal testing reasons, there are few benefits to teaching grammar in its own right. Most importantly, it is about making children aware of key grammatical principles, and their effects, to increase the amount of choices open to them when they write. What children learn about grammar should help them to make appropriate choices, not just enable them to write complicated sentences.

Grammar allows writers to see language as an organisational system, and once children understand the basics (such as nouns, verbs, adjectives etc.), they are able to play with language and substitute words. The most interesting study of grammar in education is from *Myhill, Lines and Watson (2011)*. In their research, *Making meaning with Grammar: A Repertoire of Possibilities*, they explored the effectiveness of embedded grammar teaching in developing young writers' skills. They studied two groups and discovered that both the pupils taught decontextualised grammar, and the pupils who used grammar in context, made progress. However, it was the group who analysed grammar as part and parcel of real texts that made a 20% improvement in their writing skills, compared to 11% in the other group. Myhill (2010) states:

"The contextualised teaching of grammar has a significantly positive effect on pupils' writing development."

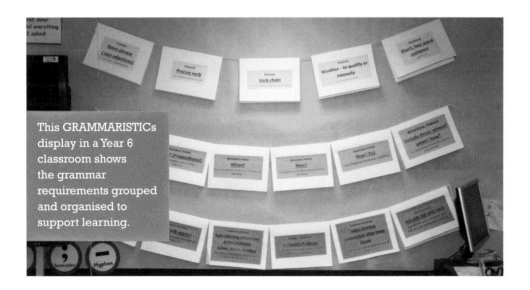

This GRAMMARISTICs display in a Year 6 classroom shows the grammar requirements grouped and organised to support learning.

The Tools of Writing

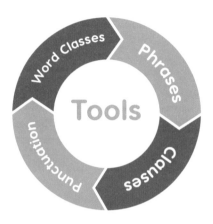

Grammar is powerful. It enables young writers to explore the infinite choices available to them in shaping creative stories and building critical, effective, non-fiction texts.

In Chapter 8, I will explore how we, as teachers, can use grammar as a sentence-building device and how the GRAMMARISTICs for different Key Stages can focus our teaching on the aspects that will both support our testing system as well as strengthening the quality of pupils' writing.

 # ③ Techniques

What different devices in writing can I employ?

Creative writing is all about conjuring up images in the reader's mind, and it is the writer's job to paint clear and vivid word pictures. Poetic and figurative language is a wonderful way to serve up a scenario, or character, to help readers to visualise what you are trying to create as a writer. These artistic structures can help writers make new, intriguing parallels or succinctly serve up an unexpected adjective or precise verb to make interesting connections. Children need to be taught a vast range of poetic devices and, as teachers, we also need to guard children against falling into the pitfalls of haggard similes and overused metaphors. The majority of our work in this area can be based on showing children what the best authors do in their writing. Noticing, collecting and grouping

language, into different types of poetic description and devices, will help pupils see the wealth of styles and strategies at the writer's disposal. One of my favourite lines of all time in a children's book is from *Wolves in the Walls* by Neil Gaiman. Heroine Lucy realises that if the wolves can come one way through the walls to scare her at night, then she can also move through the walls to their world and sort them out. The line showcases two poetic devices: internal rhyme within the line itself and a simile that further emphasises the darkness and horror of this tale.

"Quick as the flick of the wing of a bat, Lucy slipped into the wall."

Children need to be made overtly aware of all the aspects of writing that can provide control of the effects they are trying to create. Producing writing that is more precise, varied, engaging and fit for purpose is not an easy task, but exposure to the best of texts (with a teacher who knows how to draw children's attention to successes and weaknesses in writing) will grow and nurture the best writers. Gillespie and Graham's 2010 study found that what contributes to the effective teaching of writing is a classroom that creates an engaged community of writers. The most successful ways to develop that community are:

► Teachers modelling very closely how writing is constructed. Discussing and explaining why one decision might be preferable to another. Making deliberate errors and letting pupils see the internal monologue of a writer during the composition process.

Discussion about the ten techniques, and what they mean, supports children's understanding. Using examples from their reading books enables them to see commonalities between the techniques.

▶ Encouraging collaborative writing. Ensuring that pupils know the audience and purpose of the writing. Cumulatively rereading work to establish the flow and direction of writing.

▶ Ensuring that pupils and teachers give and receive constructive feedback through the writing process. Drilling down to the smallest parts of composition, so there is sharp attention to the smallest of details.

Grammar for Writing, a Department for Education booklet (2000), provides a useful guide to the three types of shared writing at a teacher's disposal during the demonstration of the writing process.

Key features of shared writing

During shared writing, it is important to:

▶ Agree how the audience and purpose

of the writing task will determine the structure, grammatical features and content.

▶ Use the specific objectives from the text, sentence or word-level work.

▶ Rehearse sentences before writing them down. In this way, pupils are more likely to learn how to compose in sentences. This habit can also help pupils to 'get it right' first time as sentences are orally revised before being committed to the page.

▶ Encourage the automatic use of basic punctuation.

▶ Constantly and cumulatively reread to gain a flow from one sentence into another – as well as checking for possible improvements or errors.

▶ Discuss and explain why one decision might be preferable to another.

▶ Pause during the writing to focus discussion upon the specific objective, but otherwise move the rest of the composition on quickly so that pupils' attention is not lost.

▶ Take suggestions from pupils who make effective contributions but also ask pupils who may struggle, in order to check misconceptions and provide further opportunities for explanation. These pupils should be specifically checked up on when they are using wipe boards, to ensure the quality of their writing. Where a small group remains uncertain, they may be targeted as a guided group.

▶ Make the occasional deliberate error to hold pupils' attention and focus on common errors (or an error related to the specific objective being taught).

A shared writing session should be clearly focused upon one or two specific teaching objectives at sentence and text level. There are three broad teaching techniques which can be used during a shared writing session to help children move towards greater independence.

Teacher demonstration

Most shared writing sessions begin with demonstration or modelling by the teacher. The teacher demonstrates how to write a text – how to use a particular feature or compose a text type – while maintaining a clear focus on the objective(s). She or he thinks the process through aloud, rehearsing each sentence before writing, sometimes revising the construction and/ or explaining why one word choice is better than another. The teacher writes the sentence, rereads it and changes it again if necessary. She or he demonstrates at least two sentences. The teacher does not take contributions from the children at this point, but will expect the children to offer opinions on her/his choice of words or construction. Every so often, shared writing is used to orchestrate a number of different objectives, calling upon all that has been learned so far. The length of time spent on demonstration will depend on the type of writing, the objective and the attention span of the children. It is important not to try to pack in too much teaching in these sessions, but to move on to the children having a go themselves.

Teacher scribing

The pupils now make contributions, building upon the teacher's initial demonstration. The teacher focuses and limits the pupils' contributions to the objective(s), e.g. previous sentence level work, reading of similar texts, word level work, prompt sheets, writing frameworks or planning sheets. The teacher challenges pupils' contributions in order to refine their understanding and compositional skills.

Children can offer their contributions by raising their hands but more considered contributions, and fuller class participation, can be achieved by asking the children, individually or in pairs, to note down their ideas, e.g. words, clauses, sentences. When the teacher receives a contribution from the children, she/he will explain its merits or ask the children to do so. The teacher may ask for a number of contributions before making and explaining her choice. If the children use wipe boards and thick-nibbed pens, they can hold them up. The teacher can then decide either to choose a contribution that will move the lesson on quickly, or a contribution which will stimulate discussion and offer the opportunity to make a teaching point.

Supported composition

The focus here is on the children's compositions. Children might use wipe boards or notebooks to write in pairs, or individually, a limited amount of text, sharply focused upon a specific objective. This needs to be swift, and once sentences are complete, they should be held up so that the teacher can make an immediate assessment. Successful examples can be reviewed with the class, whilst misconceptions are identified and corrected. The aim is to practise a number of times until the large majority, if not all, of the class has mastered the objective to the point where they can apply it when they write. Progress should be visible and swift.

In Chapter 9, I will unpick the ten most effective devices in writing, the BOOMTASTICs, to teach pupils in primary schools as they begin to explore the wealth of literary devices at their disposal.

Sentence sums

We need to view children as 'writing apprentices', learning how to craft writing using a range of linguistic strategies. During the process of writing, all three zones are being juggled at sentence level:

Ideas:

▶ The main purpose of the communication.

▶ Development of these ideas through words and the textual content we choose to include as a writer.

Tools:

▶ The indispensable parts of writing and commonly agreed ways that word classes combine to make phrases, clauses and sentences.

▶ The structures and patterns in and across sentences.

Techniques:

▶ The poetic and literary techniques at our disposal to bring form to our ideas and increased 'writerly' control.

▶ The rhythm and imagery we can bring to the reader's mind.

Teaching writing isn't about being skilled at one of these zones, but instead combining the thinking (and crafting) behind great writing across all these aspects. Teaching must connect ideas to grammar and to stylistic devices. This truly is a holistic approach to

The Techniques of Writing

Voice
Style
Techniques
Formality
Poetic Structures

Literary Devices

A System for Success

THE BOOMTASTICs

teaching writing, rather than a 'piecemeal' approach (where aspects are separated and drilled down into but are then never reconstructed back into a complete whole). There is a clever interplay in language between the essential meaning of our writing, the grammar we choose to include and the style of the writing design.

Sentence design

Sentence sums are an excellent way to engage pupils with the idea that all of these aspects can be explored and utilised as part of the sentence-designing process.

A sentence can come to life easily by focusing on vocabulary choices to build an idea. For example:

Idea: A sad woman pushing a pram up the street.

The sentence: Everyday, I see the slouched silhouette of a mum pushing that pram to nowhere.

A sentence can be carved up by having a grammar focus.

Tool: Fronted adverbial, followed by a comma.

The sentence: Walking down the street, I always noticed the regulars: the ones you could set your watch to.

Literary Technique: Simile

The sentence: The dishevelled mum pushed the pram like a heavy weight of regret.

Revealing to pupils that there can be combinations of intent with writing helps them begin to understand the power of choice they have in how meaning is conveyed. Sentences can be shaped through one aspect – as the above examples show – or through combinations of two or three of these aspects.

Idea + Tool =

Idea + Technique =

Idea + Tool + Technique =

Once a writer has an idea, the grammar and literary techniques are design tools that are used to shape the nuances and meaning of writing. We have to remind ourselves that meaning cannot be disconnected from grammar. For example:

Idea + Tool =

What a playground looks like at night + complex sentence with an embedded clause.

The sentence: Tom, who already knew this was a bad idea, looked through the gloom to see a solitary swing creaking on its hinges.

Idea + Technique =

Describe other playground equipment + personification.

The sentence: The climbing frame twitched and stretched its metal bones as the wind whipped around its rusty body.

Idea + Tool + Technique =

Tom runs to the gate + precise verb + alliteration.

The sentence: He darted and dodged through the trees, the playground gate sharply focused in his eyeline as he dashed.

Writing is never going to be easy to teach. A systematic approach gives us, as teachers, control over all the tools, devices and meaning-making strategies we have available as part of our writer's toolkit. Explicit teaching across all of these writing zones will ensure that pupils have the linguistic chunks they need closest to them when they write.

Create a BOOMTASTICs pouch display to collect great examples of authors using these techniques in their writing.

Consider

The talents of the writers in your school. What are the four and five-year-olds good at? Are their writing talents different from the ten and eleven-year-olds? Does the emphasis through the zones change as they get older?

School Impact Points

Make time for a staff meeting to explore the current emphasis within the teaching of writing in your school.

① Share research and the impact of this research on individual teaching within classes.

② Talk to colleagues in a real and honest way about aspects of the job they find challenging and share strategies most likely to have an impact on standards.

"Knowing there are three ways to write means you know what you are doing."

Ella, Year 4

What is the FANTASTIC System?

Ideas are like bees; on their own they are not productive. Together, when they live in harmony, they make honey for us all.

Chapter 7
Summary

☑ Pupils often struggle with ideas for writing. Many have untapped reservoirs of memories, with the potential to be expanded and exploited, but flounder when asked to transfer these perceptions to paper.

☑ The FANTASTICs allow pupils to explore their perceptions through nine different lenses (Noticing, Touching, Smelling, Tasting, Checking, Asking, Feeling, Imagining & Action). These lenses sharpen children's skills - scaffolding their attempts at descriptive writing and introducing them gently to the wide gamut of human thoughts, feelings, behaviours and motivations.

☑ The FANTASTICs not only help young writers to 'stop the clock' and look more closely at the world around them, they also provide a reassuring support framework for their emergent creative (and non-fiction) writing.

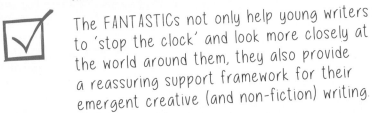

THE WRITE STUFF

What is the FANTASTIC System?

Children often really struggle with ideas. They find it tricky to come up with content for their stories and non-fiction writing. Much current teaching provides very close models for children to follow, so they don't get stuck trying to compose an original plotline or framework for their information texts.

Ultimately, if we recognise that the final destination for children's writing is independent pieces (that are complete and contain original content), then we need to work out how to foster the development of ideas. Before a genre shape emerges, or a child's wonderful writing voice speaks to the reader, we have the critical, initial problem that children essentially do not know what to write about. Individual young minds can fall anywhere on a continuum from feeling overloaded with what they would define as 'brilliant' ideas and not being able to choose between them, to a vacuous sense of 'not knowing' what to write about, let alone where to begin.

Cries of "I don't know what to write" are a teacher's worst nightmare, and the conclusion - easily jumped to - is that pupils haven't been engaged/listening. In reality, they are simply blank and do not know where to start.

Children need so much support with their ideas and teachers can end up confusing pupils, especially in English, by exposing them to endless possibilities. In reality, when generating ideas, children need a clear scaffold to ensure either the paring down of a crowded mind or the shaping up of an original idea. This is where I want to explain in detail a formula to support the generation of ideas. Essentially, writing ideas can be carved up into nine domains, and if children know about these, it will guarantee success in their writing ability.

What are the nine domains of writing?

The nine lenses have been introduced to thousands of primary schools in the UK and provide a practical hook for pupils to shape the content of their specific sentences. The following acronym is used to make the nine domains accessible for pupils, so their familiarity with them ensures breadth of ideas within writing.

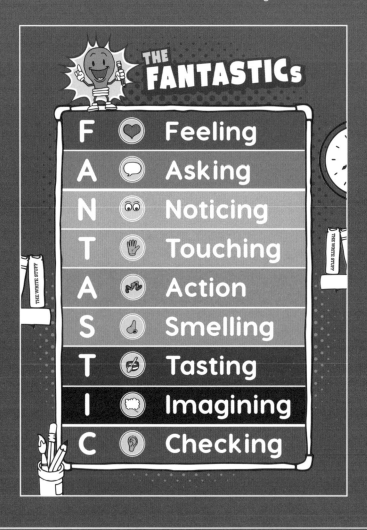

The FANTASTICs function at a far higher level than a mnemonic and mustn't be interpreted as merely a remembering tool. By categorising writing ideas across nine key areas, they offer a much-needed systematic approach for the teaching of writing. Regardless of whether a writer is designing a story or a non-fiction piece, they will lean on some, if not all, of these nine lenses.

In his book, *How Fiction Works*, critic James Wood describes writing as a 'necklace of noticings'. In other words, the writer has to help the reader see outwardly and inwardly at any given point, drawing their thinking to the relevant detail of the piece. James Wood goes on to say:

"Literature makes us better noticers of life; we get to practise on life itself; which in turn makes us better readers of detail in literature; which in turn makes us better readers in life. And so on and on. You have only to teach literature to realise that most young readers are poor noticers."

Narrative – all sub-categories of this type of writing, e.g. adventure story, fairy tale and science fiction, will be enhanced by the use of the nine FANTASTIC lenses. At certain points in the plots, some of the lenses will be more relevant than others. For example, when Goldilocks breaks into the three bears' house and eats their porridge, the lens of taste will be most relevant, as the writer will want to reference why she chose baby bear's porridge. Well, it was 'just right' of course!

Analyse the story overleaf and text mark with the FANTASTIC symbols to identify the idea lens that the writer is exploring:

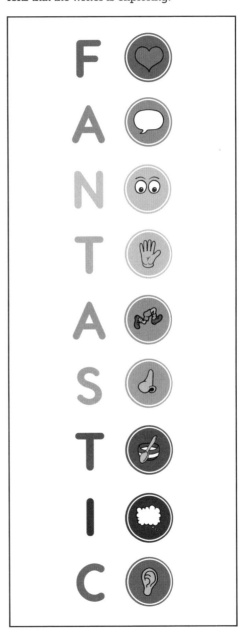

Little Red Riding Hood
by B.B. Wolfe

Once upon a far away place lived a little girl who was given a very special present from her Grandmother for her eighth birthday. This present was opened with great enthusiasm and excitement by the little girl and she tore at the wrapping paper wildly. It was quickly revealed that the wonderful gift was a coat designed in a cape-like shape in the most dynamic, remarkable colour the girl had ever seen. This coat was red, a bright, beautiful red and was soft and warm to the touch. In one bold manoeuvre, the girl swept the coat up and threw it across her back and pulled the hood up over her chocolate locks. I don't think anyone can remember a time before the coat, but certainly since the coat, Jessica was always known as Little Red Riding Hood.

Spring had grown slowly back into their lives and birdsong filled the silences in the air. The sky had found its brightness, grey had turned into blue. Mother was outside in a battle with the wind trying to encourage the washing to dance on the clothes line. Her eyes watered facing the blustery day; Little Red Riding Hood could feel that something was troubling her. Mother collected the spare pegs and was blown back indoors. Her skirt whipped up into a windswept tent. Little Red Riding Hood caught her blurry stare, "Mother, are you all right?"

"Err, yes, well, no," she garbled. "Your Grandmother is unwell." Little Red Riding Hood looked at her coat and touched it gently and felt sadness deep in her stomach. She looked back at her Mother whose eyes had given way. She threw her arms around her, kissed her hot cheek and tasted the salt of her tears. "I'll go and see her and take her some flowers and fruit."

Little Red Riding Hood's idea excited her and she pelted around the house scooping up items she could bring in her basket. Mother was relieved that Little Red Riding Hood was responding in such a practical way and began to join her daughter in gathering gifts for the visit: two chocolate cakes, three books, handkerchiefs.

At last, Little Red Riding Hood felt sufficiently laden to embark on her journey and waved her mother goodbye with a smile and a swing of her cape. She skipped energetically through the dense undergrowth of the woodland. Small snowdrops waved at Little Red Riding Hood and tides of yellow daffodils danced in the subtle shafts of sunlight. Little Red Riding Hood bent down to pick a few for Grandma and a shudder of fear prickled down her back. She gasped and quickly looked over her shoulder; she felt that someone or something was watching her.

Who could it be?

Hastily, she gathered up the flowers; the fresh scent of daffodils invaded her space. She breathed. She breathed more slowly.

The sound of a twig snapping alerted her and she was sure she saw a shadow flit in between some trees in the distance. "I need to hurry to Grandma's," she thought to herself. As she moved on, she could see the comforting familiarity of Grandma's house on the horizon settled in a clearing of the woods. Little Red Riding Hood saw some blackberries tangled in the fauna by some low lying trees and knew these would definitely make Grandma feel better.

She decided to collect some and crouched low to get a closer glimpse of the ripest ones, she tasted a few. The burst of fruitiness was tart with a sweet aftermath and she was very pleased with her find. Grandma's door was now in sight. Little Red Riding Hood sung her favourite song and the woodland creatures pricked up their ears. There was a nearby whistle melodiously akin to her song. She looked up: a woodcutter had joined in with her singing. He waved. She smiled and skipped on. Strangely, Grandma's door was ajar; Little Red Riding Hood pushed at it tentatively! The creak of the hinges left a hollow resonance in the air. Little Red Riding Hood was waiting expectantly to smell the familiar lavender wafts of Grandma but the aroma didn't hit her. "That's strange!" she thought as she crept towards her bedroom. Entering cautiously, she could see Grandma tucked up in bed but she certainly didn't look like her normal self. "You must be feeling poorly!" Little Red Riding Hood remarked. Grandma nodded. Little Red Riding Hood shuffled closer to her bedside and peered into her eyes. "What big eyes you have Grandma!" She couldn't hide the fact that she felt unnerved and a little puzzled about how awful she actually did look. She couldn't believe that only ten days ago she'd seemed so full of vitality and her cheeks had glowed a rosy pink under her crocheted blanket. Grandma coughed, her breath a sickly musty stench. "All the better to see you with my dear!"

Little Red Riding Hood was taken aback: Grandma was acting strangely and very unlike her normal self. "What big ears you have Grandma!"

"All the better to hear you with!" she replied. For a moment, Little Red Riding Hood thought about commenting on her out-of-control facial hair but reconsidered as she thought Grandma would take offence. Little Red Riding Hood knew Grandma had been having problems with her false set of teeth but didn't remember them being this over-sized: they hardly fit into her mouth. However, she felt compelled to ask her about them. "What big teeth you have Grandma!" she said.

"All the better to eat you with!" was the vicious reply. Without warning, Grandma leaped up from her bed (except Little Red Riding Hood could now see she was the wolf in disguise) and lunged violently at her with jaws wide open and displayed two sharpened fangs. "Help!" Her screams echoed far into the dark depths of the woodland. Suddenly, with an almighty crash, the woodcutter burst through Grandma's doorway and prized Little Red Riding Hood from the wolf's deadly grip. With one hefty swipe of his axe, the wolf was gone.

Silence.

Everyone stopped to listen. There was a muffled whisper coming from the wardrobe. "I'm here," was the faint retort. Little Red Riding Hood's eyes darted towards the wardrobe and she flung open the doors with both hands. It was Grandma! The lavender scent wafted into the room and the delighted young girl threw her arms around her and helped her onto the bed. The three of them, Grandma, Little Red Riding Hood and the woodcutter sat huddled together a little dazed, munching on blackberries. "What big berries you have!" announced the woodcutter.

Little Red Riding Hood and Grandma laughed.

Little Red Riding Hood
by B.B. Wolfe

Once upon a far away place lived a little girl who was given a very special present from her Grandmother for her eighth birthday. This present was opened with great enthusiasm and excitement by the little girl and she tore at the wrapping paper wildly. It was quickly revealed that the wonderful gift was a coat designed in a cape-like shape in the most dynamic, remarkable colour the girl had ever seen. This coat was red, a bright, beautiful red and was soft and warm to the touch. In one bold manoeuvre, the girl swept the coat up and threw it across her back and pulled the hood up over her chocolate locks. I don't think anyone can remember a time before the coat, but certainly since the coat, Jessica was always known as Little Red Riding Hood.

Spring had grown slowly back into their lives and birdsong filled the silences in the air. The sky had found its brightness, grey had turned into blue. Mother was outside in a battle with the wind trying to encourage the washing to dance on the clothes line. Her eyes watered facing the blustery day; Little Red Riding Hood could feel that something was troubling her. Mother collected the spare pegs and was blown back indoors. Her skirt whipped up into a windswept tent. Little Red Riding Hood caught her blurry stare, "Mother, are you all right?"

"Err, yes, well, no," she garbled. "Your Grandmother is unwell." Little Red Riding Hood looked at her coat and touched it gently and felt sadness deep in her stomach. She looked back at her Mother whose eyes had given way. She threw her arms around her, kissed her hot cheek and tasted the salt of her tears. "I'll go and see her and take her some flowers and fruit."

Little Red Riding Hood's idea excited her and she pelted around the house scooping up items she could bring in her basket. Mother was relieved that Little Red Riding Hood was responding in such a practical way and began to join her daughter in gathering gifts for the visit: two chocolate cakes, three books, handkerchiefs.

At last, Little Red Riding Hood felt sufficiently laden to embark on her journey and waved her mother goodbye with a smile and a swing of her cape. She skipped energetically through the dense undergrowth of the woodland. Small snowdrops waved at Little Red Riding Hood and tides of yellow daffodils danced in the subtle shafts of sunlight. Little Red Riding Hood bent down to pick a few for Grandma and a shudder of fear prickled down her back. She gasped and quickly looked over her shoulder; she felt that someone or something was watching her.

Who could it be?

Hastily, she gathered up the flowers; the fresh scent of daffodils invaded her space. She breathed. She breathed more slowly.

The sound of a twig snapping alerted her and she was sure she saw a shadow flit in between some trees in the distance. "I need to hurry to Grandma's," she thought to herself. As she moved on, she could see the comforting familiarity of Grandma's house on the horizon settled in a clearing of the woods. Little Red Riding Hood saw some blackberries tangled in the fauna by some low lying trees and knew these would definitely make Grandma feel better.

She decided to collect some and crouched low to get a closer glimpse of the ripest ones, she tasted a few. The burst of fruitiness was tart with a sweet aftermath and she was very pleased with her find. Grandma's door was now in sight. Little Red Riding Hood sung her favourite song and the woodland creatures pricked up their ears. There was a nearby whistle melodiously akin to her song. She looked up: a woodcutter had joined in with her singing. He waved. She smiled and skipped on. Strangely, Grandma's door was ajar; Little Red Riding Hood pushed at it tentatively! The creak of the hinges left a hollow resonance in the air. Little Red Riding Hood was waiting expectantly to smell the familiar lavender wafts of Grandma but the aroma didn't hit her. "That's strange!" she thought as she crept towards her bedroom. Entering cautiously, she could see Grandma tucked up in bed but she certainly didn't look like her normal self. "You must be feeling poorly!" Little Red Riding Hood remarked. Grandma nodded. Little Red Riding Hood shuffled closer to her bedside and peered into her eyes. "What big eyes you have Grandma!" She couldn't hide the fact that she felt unnerved and a little puzzled about how awful she actually did look. She couldn't believe that only ten days ago she'd seemed so full of vitality and her cheeks had glowed a rosy pink under her crocheted blanket. Grandma coughed, her breath a sickly musty stench. "All the better to see you with my dear!"

Little Red Riding Hood was taken aback, Grandma was acting strangely and very unlike her normal self. "What big ears you have Grandma!"

"All the better to hear you with!" she replied. For a moment, Little Red Riding Hood thought about commenting on her out-of-control facial hair but reconsidered as she thought Grandma would take offence. Little Red Riding Hood knew Grandma had been having problems with her false set of teeth but didn't remember them being this over-sized, they hardly fit into her mouth. However, she felt compelled to ask her about them. "What big teeth you have Grandma!" she said.

"All the better to eat you with!" was the vicious reply. Without warning, Grandma leaped up from her bed (except Little Red Riding Hood could now see she was the wolf in disguise) and lunged violently at her with jaws wide open and displayed two sharpened fangs. "Help!" Her screams echoed far into the dark depths of the woodland. Suddenly, with an almighty crash, the woodcutter burst through Grandma's doorway and prized Little Red Riding Hood from the wolf's deadly grip. With one hefty swipe of his axe, the wolf was gone.

Silence.

Everyone stopped to listen. There was a muffled whisper coming from the wardrobe. "I'm here," was the faint retort. Little Red Riding Hood's eyes darted towards the wardrobe and she flung open the doors with both hands. It was Grandma! The lavender scent wafted into the room and the delighted young girl threw her arms around her and helped her onto the bed. The three of them, Grandma, Little Red Riding Hood and the woodcutter sat huddled together a little dazed, munching on blackberries. "What big berries you have!" announced the woodcutter.

Little Red Riding Hood and Grandma laughed.

Non-fiction – the lens type will depend on the dominant content ideas.

Instructions – organised into a list-like structure with imperative verbs as a core sentence level aspect.

▶ This means that 'Action' will be the dominant lens.

▶ For some statements, what the observer can 'Notice/see' will be required, e.g. Stir the milk into the mixture and notice it bubble under the heat.

Explanation – a process-based text type that explains natural and social phenomena or how things work.

▶ As the writer builds logical steps and makes causal and time links between them, the most relevant lenses will be 'Notice/see' and 'Action', e.g. Water vapour high in the atmosphere forms into clouds through condensation. Eventually, the water returns to earth through precipitation. As a result of this, it seeps into the ground. Some is taken up by the plants; the rest returns to rivers.

▶ 'Smelling', 'Checking' and 'Tasting' may be relevant, depending on the explanation e.g. During Autumn, many birds fly south and migrate towards France. While this is a largely unseen dead-of-night migration, it is not a silent one.

▶ 'Feeling', 'Asking', 'Imagining' probably not relevant for this text type.

Recount – the purpose is to retell events in chronological order. All of the lenses will be relevant here as we focus on the individual using personal pronoun 'I' or reference to group participants 'we' to recount our experiences.

e.g. At the museum, we saw a range of Roman artifacts. The tour guide told us about life in this era and we touched original Roman swords. It made me think about life as a soldier and the battles they took part in.

Non-chronological report – information on a subject area that can be broken down into specific parts or classifications with more detail added at each stage. All lenses will be potentially relevant and those that are required more will depend on the topic being explored. If the topic was Mayan life in Mexico, then all lenses would be needed to give a rounded view of this ancient civilisation.

Persuasion – the purpose of this text-type is to sell or convince a reader of one point of view. All lenses will be relevant; advertisers will want to provide a full multi-sensory perception of a product or place that may include testimonials.

e.g. Paddle on Whitby beach as the smell of the sea air awakens your senses. Have tasty picnics on the sand dunes and relax in the sun. Listen to the night-time wildlife on the evening nature trail at Blackheath Nature Centre.

In more formal persuasive writing, the full nine lenses will be needed to form points

Pupils retelling their imaginary journey on the pirate ship: what they smelt, what they did, what they thought and what they felt.

and provide elaboration and reiteration of important arguments through different perspectives.

Balanced argument – arguments and information are compiled from two differing viewpoints and are set against each other to reinforce the broad perspective around one issue. Arguments for and against are supported by evidence. All lenses are potentially relevant, with dominant ones coming through depending on the subject matter.

e.g. Additionally, animals are physically and mentally healthier in the wild than in zoos. They are able to have more exercise as they can run around and hunt in larger land spaces in the wilderness. Zoos do not have such large spaces. Caged animals do not know what it is to naturally hunt their food or to explore their environment and select a mate.

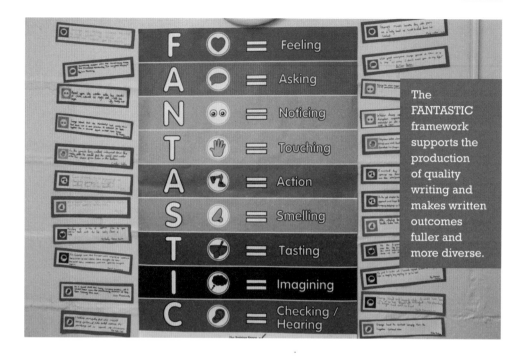

The FANTASTIC framework supports the production of quality writing and makes written outcomes fuller and more diverse.

A system of nine choices: ideas in writing

As pupils struggle with ideas for writing, the nine FANTASTIC lenses help them prepare language and organise it under nine clear headings. As a writer, there are only nine ways through which a text can be extrapolated and budding child writers need the very words, phrases and clauses, and good sentence examples, that reflect each of the lenses. The FANTASTICs provide a framework for pupils who have that sense of void at the point of writing. This model teaches children that rather than the possibilities being endless, they can begin to target their thinking around one of the nine areas. All writing can be grouped and categorised back to this system. This is why the FANTASTICs is also the ideal analysis tool for reading and exploring the content of books.

As we support children's writing to be fuller and more diverse, they need guidance about the structures and functions of written language. One of the most powerful ways to help children connect with the possibilities of their writerly choices is to collect words, phrases, clauses and sentences in reading and sort them into the FANTASTIC categories. The concept of the FANTASTICs means that children can begin to group ideas related to each of the senses. This structure enables them to sort language found in reading and use it to maximum effect in their writing.

This sentence, found in *The Green Children* by Kevin Crossley-Holland could be filed as a **'Noticing'** sentence.

"When my brother and I opened our eyes, we saw faces peering down on us."

 These sentences in *The Midnight Fox* by Betsy Byars would be filed in the **'Imagining/Thinking'** section.

"Sometimes at night when the rain is beating against the windows of my room, I think about that summer on the farm. It has been five years, but when I close my eyes I am once again by the creek watching the black fox come leaping over the green, green grass."

  There are also aspects of **action** in here: 'beating against the window...' 'leaping over the green, green, grass' and **noticing** language in 'watching'.

The FANTASTIC framework is a unique way for children to formulate their thoughts for themselves and provides a hook for them to reflect on what they mean. Their ideas can be 'shaped up' and developed through the nine lenses - empowering them in the transfer of thoughts/ideas to quality writing on a page. The sifting and sorting of language in this organised way supports children to be effective meaning makers.

Long Buckby Junior School FANTASTIC display: successful sentences are shared for other pupils to manipulate.

FANT...

F — Feeling

A — Asking

N — Noticing

T — Touching

GRAMM...

G — Adverbs and Adverbial Phrases

R — Basics

A — Sentence Structures

M — Dialogue and Contracted For...

"I'll do it!"

BOOM...

B — Onomatopoeia — Buzz

O — Alliteration — 'ph' 'f'

O — Rhyme

M — Repetitio...

...d on an...
...d on and on...
...and on and ...
...d on and on...
...nd on and ...

The Training Space

Writi...

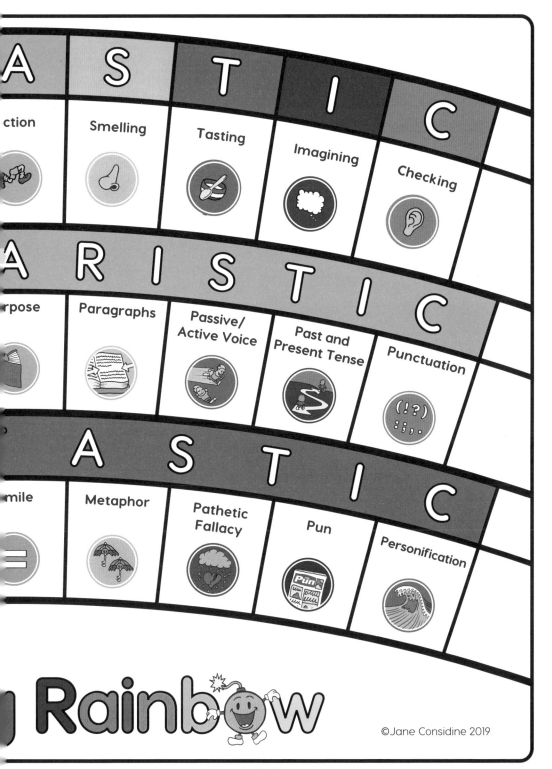

ASTIC

| ...ction | Smelling | Tasting | Imagining | Checking |

ARISTIC

| ...rpose | Paragraphs | Passive/ Active Voice | Past and Present Tense | Punctuation |

ASTIC

| ...mile | Metaphor | Pathetic Fallacy | Pun | Personification |

Rainbow

©Jane Considine 2019

FANTASTIC is an acronym that represents the nine aspects.

F — Feeling

A — Asking

N — Noticing

T — Touching

A — Action

S — Smelling

T — Tasting

I — Imagining

C — Checking

Shades of meaning

A thesaurus organises language into six main areas: abstract relations, space, matter, intellect, volition and affections. Each area is then given a detailed sub-classification and these categories organise language semantically.

Pupils need to build a repertoire of language and, through exposure to a range of words, begin to strengthen their own vocabularies. Synonyms are an important part of building children's word banks.

However, more importantly than just collecting alternatives to 'see', children need to understand the subtle nuances of different word choices. If you take these three alternatives to see: **glimpse**, **look**, **glare**, you can see they are ordered into low to high intensity words.

For example:

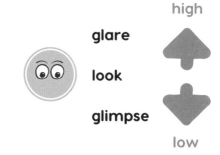

Pupils sort words into degrees of meaning. They discuss the intensity and shades of different synonyms on scales.

Pupils find visual representations of these shades of meaning helpful. The strongest, most intense word on the top and the mildest, least intense word on the bottom. It is crucial that children don't fall into the trap of just using ambitious words for the sake of it. The art of great writing is to select the just-right shade of meaning word for the required effect.

Within these intensity scales, the English language also allows us to categorise words according to their positive or negative connotations. It is easiest to understand this on a quadrant model:

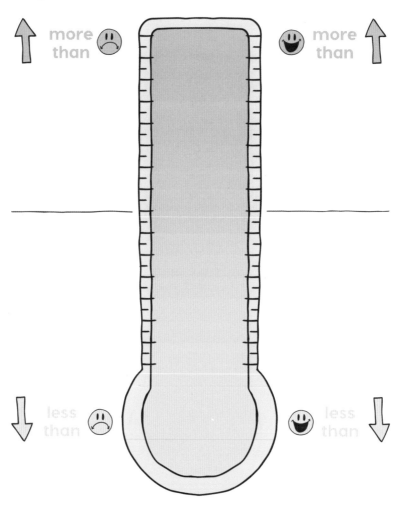

with 14
...ng'. This
...ding to

The subsequent illustration shows how extra additions of language can be used to bring positive or negative twists.

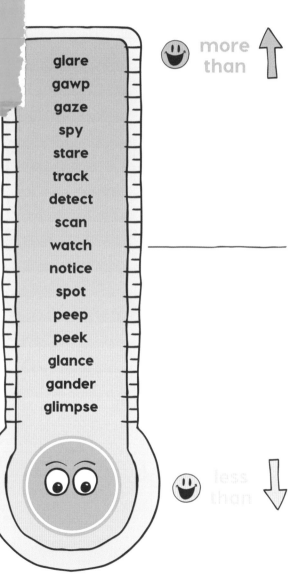

more than ⬆

glare
gawp
gaze
spy
stare
track
detect
scan
watch
notice
spot
peep
peek
glance
gander
glimpse

⬇ less than

less than ⬇

Noticing

Look

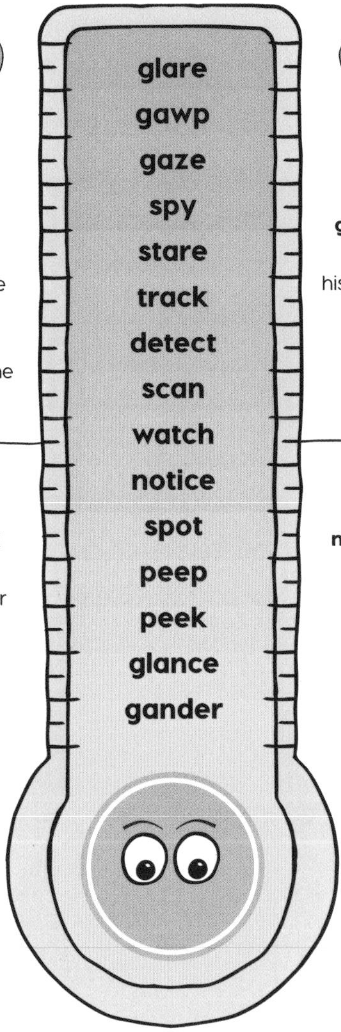
glare
gawp
gaze
spy
stare
track
detect
scan
watch
notice
spot
peep
peek
glance
gander

more than

HIGH negative

a **stare** that paralysed her
a sinister **gaze**

gawping inappropriately at the twisted wreckage

petrified, she rigidly **scanned** the deserted room

LOW negative

noticing their very late arrival

nervously **spotting** the teacher

apprehensively **glancing**

peeking slyly

less than

more than

HIGH positive

glare teasingly
gaze at the warm, peach sunset

his adoring eyes **tracked** her every move

awestruck, he **stared** at the enchanting view

LOW positive

noticing her dazzling, hazel eyes

a momentary **glimpse**

smiling as she **spotted** the delicious treats

peeping excitedly

less than

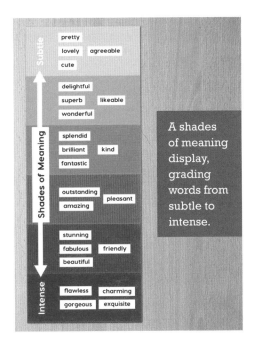

A shades of meaning display, grading words from subtle to intense.

> **As pupils struggle with ideas for their writing, the nine FANTASTIC lenses help them prepare language and organise it under these nine headings**

A KS1 teacher at Lings Primary School sorts language into high and low intensity words for 'looking'. Adjectives and adverbs are added to give positive or negative connotations.

Consider

Making a set of nine FANTASTIC symbols and displaying them in your classroom. Use them as a focal point during:

① Drama: the nine symbols can be deployed during particular conventions. For example: Freeze-frame a moment in a story and use the nine lenses to draw out feelings, thoughts, dialogue, sounds, etc.

② Speaking and listening: ask your pupils to 'talk' sentences through the nine lenses. Can they tell you what the Big Bad Wolf looks like or smells like?

③ Reading: during a shared reading session, ask pupils to identify thinking sentences, sound sentences or action sentences. The best ones can be displayed and act as 'sentence models' to inspire other children and boost their confidence and versatility around language use.

④ Writing: use one of the FANTASTIC symbols to drive an idea and show pupils how it can be used to craft more palpable, intriguing or believable sentences. Use examples - such as this one from Beatrix Potter - to convey how description enhances word pictures in the reader's mind.

"The tailor began to make a coat - a coat with cherry-coloured corded silk and embroidered with pansies and roses."
The Tailor of Gloucester

School Impact Points

Choose one of the FANTASTIC lenses as a focal point, e.g. action.

Different year groups across the school write action sentences related to their narrative and fiction work. These are shared as a discussion point across the staff team. Consider how well pupils have grasped the concept.

Kyle, Year 6

What is the Grammar of Sentence Building?

Rules are made to be broken. With grammar, you must know them well before you choose to ignore them.

Chapter 8

Summary

☑ Language is organised by a system of grammar. Many pupils have extensive inherent grammatical knowledge as it is an integral part of learning to speak.

☑ Writing can be improved further if pupils understand how grammar relates to language. Good grammatical knowledge opens up choice and freedom to manipulate language to create particular effects.

☑ The GRAMMARISTICs provide a basic and more complex targeted system, which will have a direct impact on pupils' sentence construction skills. By structuring and restructuring ideas, children develop their competence as writers.

THE WRITE STUFF

What is the Grammar of Sentence Building?

Grammar is one of the Three Zones of Writing. Mastery of the fundamentals of grammar is vital for fledgling writers, who need to understand the basics before they can begin to manipulate sentence constructions for effect. The reality is that poor grammar creates poor sentences. Children need to understand the structures of writing. Both reading practice and writing practice will co-support the quality of engagement with texts and the quality of their own writing.

Grammar is learned unconsciously at a young age. Ask any five-year-old, and he will tell you that, "I eat" and "you eat", but his "dog eats". Nouns and verbs are two indispensable word classes in the English language. Children in Year 1 and upwards can take a lot of enjoyment and comfort from the fact that once a noun is joined with a verb, a sentence lives. Young children have a fascination with language and almost no inhibitions about using it.

Nouns		Verbs
I	pronoun	wait
Jack	proper noun	sneaks
glass	common noun	shatters
boys	common noun	jump
mud	common noun	splatters
rain	common noun	pours
birds	common noun	fly
teachers	common noun	scowl
stars	common noun	glimmer
trees	common noun	sway

Adults, on the other hand, can feel very stressed by grammar, even teachers who have linguistic and English language degrees. As teachers, we cannot let the enormity of the subject weigh us down. Instead, we need to find teachable ways to explain, so as to improve children's writing. Teaching grammar can be heavy-going as it is drenched in terminology and prescriptive rules. Nevertheless, we need to view grammar as an enabler and help children to see the possibilities it opens up for their writing success.

The *Grammar Rainbow* captures, for teachers, the broad spectrum of coverage for the whole of the primary curriculum.

At this point, I want to explore the ABCD of grammar captured on the *Grammar Rainbow*. These are the most crucial aspects to ensure coverage of the curriculum, as well as to counteract weaknesses in teaching of this aspect of the English curriculum.

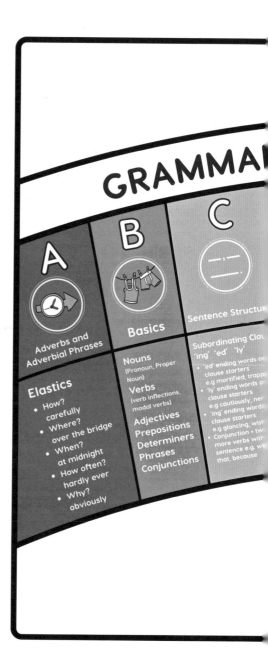

GRAMMA

A

Adverbs and Adverbial Phrases

Elastics

- How?
  carefully
- Where?
  over the bridge
- When?
  at midnight
- How often?
  hardly ever
- Why?
  obviously

B

Basics

Nouns
(Pronoun, Proper Noun)

Verbs
(verb inflections, modal verbs)

Adjectives
Prepositions
Determiners
Phrases
Conjunctions

C

Sentence Structu

Subordinating Clau
'ing' 'ed' 'ly'
- 'ed' ending words as
  clause starters
  e.g mortified, trapp
- 'ly' ending words a
  clause starters
  e.g cautiously, ner
- 'ing' ending words
  clause starters
  e.g glancing, wist
- Conjunction - tw
  more verbs with
  sentence e.g. w
  that, because

STRUCTURE AND STYLE

ogue and
cted Forms

oker's original
n inverted
s to mark
ng and end
ch
- the story on
- intrigue/
st
- about a
acter
5 contracted
contractions to
ht through direct
as informal)

P

Purpose

Engagement Devices
- Questions
- Data
- Impact Line

Stucture
- Headings
- Sub-Headings
- Fact splats

P

Paragraphs

Change of
- time
- place
- event
- person

Block Method
- cohesion within paragraph
- linking phrases, clauses, sentences.

P

Passive or Active Voice

Active
Subject + verb + rest of idea
e.g Charlie broke the window.

Passive
Verb acts on subject
e.g The window was broken.

P

Past and Present Tense

Verbs
Consistent use of present tense vs past tense

Identify verb chains -
past progressive e.g. was doing.
present perfect e.g. has wanted.

P

Punctuation

All punctuation types
e.g
- inverted commas
- possessive apostrophe
- contractions
- semi-colon, colon, dash
- bullet points
- hyphens

Grammar Rainbow

© Jane Considine 2019

Build sentences on a washing line. This example from Thomas Fulham School shows how different word classes can be replaced with alternatives e.g. instead of 'winding' insert 'meandering', instead of 'magical' insert 'dense'.

Adverbs/Adverbial Phrases

Adverbs and adverbial phrases give extra information to a verbs, adjectives, other adverbs and whole clauses. Many adverbs are formed by adding _ly to an adjective. For example, *slowly, sneakily, strangely*. However, there are adverbs that do not end in _ly. In many cases, adverbs tell us:

how (manner)
quickly, excitedly, nervously, carefully

where (place)
here, there, away, home

when (time)
now, yesterday, tomorrow, Saturday

how often (frequency)
often, regularly, intermittently

Adverbs can also function to show degrees of intensity, e.g. *really, very,* and *fairly* or the attitude of the speaker/writer to what they are saying/writing e.g. *obviously, perhaps, fortunately*

An adverbial phrase can be grouped under the same broad categories of how, where, when and how often. You will notice there is a crossover here with prepositional phrases (the broader grammatical category label for these phrases).

How - adverbial phrase - *with gritted teeth*

Where – adverbial phrase - *in the city*
When – adverbial phrase - *at dawn*
How often – adverbial phrase – *every single night*

On the *Grammar Rainbow*, these are green in colour, for the sole purpose of indicating that they are 'on the go', like the green of traffic lights. The reason for this is that adverbs and adverbial phrases are highly mobile components in a sentence and can be moved about within and around a simple noun and verb construct. For example:

Jack jumped

Add in a where?
Jack jumped in the playground.

Add in a when?
Jack jumped in the playground late at night.

Add in a how?
Jack jumped wildly in the playground late at night.

Adverbs and adverbial phrases can be moved around within the sentence. Pupils enjoy playing with these mobile components of writing. They also open up possibilities for pupils to suggest alternatives. For example:

Late at night, **Jack** wildly **jumped** in the playground.

In the playground, late at night **Jack jumped** wildly.

Wildly, late at night **Jack jumped** in the playground.

Adverb and Adverbial Phrase Word Banks

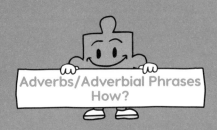

Adverbs/Adverbial Phrases
How?

A = Adverbs - How?			
angrily	anxiously	boastfully	boldly
bravely	busily	calmly	carefully
carelessly	cautiously	cheerfully	courageously
cruelly	eagerly	enthusiastically	excitedly
greedily	happily	hastily	hungrily
hurriedly	impatiently	irritably	joyously
kindly	lazily	merrily	miserably
nervously	reluctantly	proudly	sadly
selfishly	shyly	sleepily	solemnly
sternly	suspiciously	viciously	wearily
badly	quietly	recently	suddenly
easily	gently	slowly	tearfully

Once an adverb or adverbial phrase is in first position within a sentence (fronted adverbial), it is followed by a comma. It is important that this is taught well from Year 2 upwards as it features in the Key Stage 2 SPaG test.

A = Adverbial Phrases – How?			
with bated breath	in a low register	with great trepidation	like a soft breeze
in a civilised way	with great regret	in silence	in dismay
in a huff	with much consideration	with a nostalgic tone	without a care

A = Adverbs – Where? N.B. The words below are prepositions but can be used in adverbial phrases and prepositional phrases.			
near	back	on	under
here	up	through	beside
over	there	behind	next
at	in	out	over
down	around	underneath	beneath

A = Adverbs – Where? N.B. These can also be used as prepositions.		
	Used as a 'where' adverb (modifying verb)	Used as a prepositional phrase
around:	The small ball rolled around in my hand.	I am wearing a bracelet around my wrist.
behind:	Quick! You are getting behind.	Let's hide behind the curtains.
down:	Jack fell down.	Jack made his way cautiously down the mountain-side.
in:	We thought we would drop in on Jane.	I dropped the milk in the street.
off:	Let's get off to this party.	The wind blew the tiles off the roof.
on:	We rode on for days.	Put the bag on the hook.
over:	Ella turned over and went back to sleep.	I will hang the picture over my desk.

A = Adverbial phrase - Where? N.B. Prepositional phrase used as an adverbial			
across the field	in the attic	near the traffic	through the gate
over the bridge	in the playground	round the streets	at the corner of the street
through the head teacher's office	in the corridor	among the crowds	by the riverbank
up in the sky	down the lane	in between the trees	on the desk
high in the tower	over the hill	outside the tall tower	under the chair
at the Olympic Stadium	across the river	beneath the dark archway	behind the curtain
on the sea	near the lake	inside the spooky caves	in the alleyway
under the ground	in the middle of the forest	over the road	opposite the office
through the woods	above the rooftops	between the houses	underneath the shared stars
at school	beside the sea	next to the shop	below the staircase

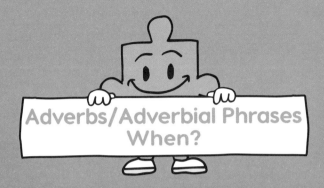

Adverbs/Adverbial Phrases
When?

If you need to use more than one adverb of time in a sentence, use them in this order:

1. how long
2. how often
3. when

e.g. She worked in a hospital for two days, every week, last year.

A = Adverbs – When?			
soon	later	tomorrow	early
now	then	today	last
tonight	yesterday	yet	first
at sunset	as dawn broke	during the summer	last Saturday

A = Adverbial Phrases - When?			
at midnight	in the dark of night	last week	as the clock struck one
later on in the day	early	in 1870	next week
that evening	at sunrise	tomorrow	next Friday
at sunset	after the game	during the summer	last Saturday
in the morning	during the night	before next week	at daybreak
late in the afternoon	at twilight	any time	in an hour
yesterday	at midday	at the break of day	at noon
on Thursday	during sundown	that morning	at dusk
in a minute	at high noon	one day	that afternoon
at 6 o'clock	in the middle of the day	later that night	at nightfall

A = Adverb – How Often?			
weekly	nightly	annually	fortnightly
monthly	quarterly	daily	hourly
yearly	frequently	regularly	often

Basics

The new national curriculum requires that children are familiar with basic terminology and its meanings, as well as being able to use this broad knowledge in context.

Noun: A noun is a word that denotes somebody or something.

Singular nouns: *problem, party, girl, book, desk.*

Plural nouns: *problems, parties, girls, books, desks.*

Collective nouns: *crowd, flock, team, gang, herd.*

Proper nouns: names of people, places, organisations and brands e.g. *Susan, Birmingham, Microsoft, Cadbury.*

Personal pronouns: *I, me, you, he, him, she, her, we, us, they, them, it.*

Verb: A verb is a word that expresses an action, a happening, a process or a state. It can be thought of as a 'doing' or 'being' word. Sometimes, two or more words make up a verb – it is useful to call these verb chains. Clauses include verbs and phrases do not.

A verb can be past or present tense.

Present tense verb e.g. Jack waits for the cab.

Past tense verb e.g. Jack waited for the cab.

Auxiliary verb: These are verbs that are used together with the other verbs. The most common auxiliary verbs are: *be, have* and *do.*

e.g. Jack had been waiting for the cab for ages.

Had and *been* are both auxiliary verbs.

Adjective: An adjective is a word that describes somebody or something, e.g. decrepit, large, tatty, fresh. Adjectives either come before a noun, e.g. *the large lady or after verbs, e.g. the lady seemed large.*

Adverb: Adverbs give extra meaning to verbs and can be combined with verbs, adjectives, other adverbs or whole sentences.

Preposition: A preposition is a word that indicates time, position or direction. There is an overlap here with adverbial phrases, which are a sub-section of prepositional phrases when they address when and where.

Indicate time: *at midnight, on Saturday.*

Indicate position: *at the school, in a warehouse.*

Indicate direction: *over the fence, under the bridge.*

Article: An article is a type of determiner. 'A' and 'an' are indefinite articles and 'the' is a definite article.

Noun phrase: Noun phrases are groups of words that function in the same way as nouns in sentences.

e.g. *a lot of sweets, my big brother, the blue car, the greatest team in the world*

Conjunction: It is paramount that pupils are taught the difference between coordinating and subordinating conjunctions as this will feed into their building of compound and complex sentences.

Coordinating conjunctions: *and, but, or, so.* These are placed between two clauses of equal weight.

e.g. I like coffee *but* I love tea.

Subordinating conjunctions: *when, while, before, after, since, until, if, because, although, that etc.*

A subordinating conjunction is placed before a subordinating clause.

e.g. We were tired *because* we had been walking all day.

e.g. *Although* I was tired, I wanted to see my mum.

A Year 6 teacher helps pupils to build an intriguing exclamation for their persuasive holiday brochures.

A pupil talks about his contribution to a sentence-stacked model. The teacher discusses edits for improvement.

On a spy-themed experience day, pupils at Boothville Primary School discuss grammar choices for their newspaper report.

Sentence Structures

To understand complex sentences, children must first understand simple and compound sentences. Interrelated understanding also cuts across into coordinating and subordinating conjunctions, as well as using commas to separate clauses.

▶ In Year 2, children will be taught the word 'clause'.

▶ In Years 3 and 4, children are expected to begin extending the range of their sentences by using more than one clause in their writing.

▶ In Years 5 and 6, children will be using a range of sentence types in their writing.

Before children can be taught about complex sentences, they need to be taught the component parts of a sentence. Sentences are made up from:

Clauses: Main clauses that stand alone can function as simple sentences and are comprised of one verb or verb chain. A verb chain is a useful term when an auxiliary verb is used with a verb, e.g. *was going*. Clauses include phrases.

Subordinate clauses: These cannot stand alone, and support a main clause in a sentence. They also contain one verb or verb chain. A complex sentence can include one or more subordinate clauses.

Phrases: Phrases are chunks of meaning that function with a dominant word.

e.g. noun phrases: *my younger sister* or *her new car*

Phrases do not include verbs. This is an important learning aspect of grammar and has featured in previous SPaG tests for Year 6 pupils.

Words: These are the individual building blocks of sentences. There are different word classes, e.g. nouns, verbs, adjectives, adverbs etc.

Sentences can be simple, compound or complex.

Simple sentence: A simple sentence consists of one clause.

e.g. Jane was late.

Compound sentence: A compound sentence consists of two or more clauses joined by coordinating conjunctions such as: *and, or, but, so.*

e.g. Jane was late but she was glad.

There is a sense of equal weight in these sentences and both the clauses can stand on their own. If the 'but' was removed, they would make two simple sentences.

e.g. Jane was late. She was glad.

Complex sentence: A complex sentence consists of a main clause, as well as one or more subordinating clauses that cannot make sense on their own.

There are five main ways we can teach children to construct complex sentences:

1. Subordinating conjunctions

Examples of subordinating conjunctions:

although	as
wherever	since
even though	after
when	until
whenever	once
that	if
while	despite
unless	because

Subordinating conjunctions make complex sentences, whether they are used at the beginning of sentences or in the middle. In the examples below, main clauses are in bold, subordinating conjunctions in green and, you will notice, no comma is required.

e.g. **Jane left early** because Jack had arrived wearing her jumper.

e.g. **Keep your hand on the cut** until the nurse asks you to remove it.

Once the subordinating conjunction is used in front position, a comma is required.

e.g. Although it is raining, **I am going to play outside.**

e.g. Even though I am upset, **I will still go to the party.**

2. Embedded clause

An embedded clause includes a verb and is used in the middle of a main clause. The embedded clause cannot stand alone and is inserted in between two commas.

e.g. Simple sentence:

The house had changed so much.

Add in an embedded clause:

e.g. **The house**, where I grew up, **had changed so much.**

e.g. **Mrs Parker**, who was the class teacher, **stared angrily at Jack.**

Embedded clauses tend to start with words such as: *that, where, for, who, which, when, whose.*

3. Starting with a verb ending in _ed

This strategy relies on front positioning a verb early into a clause that cannot stand alone, then dropping a comma and finishing with a main clause.

Examples of _ed ending verbs

mortified	trapped
strangled	delighted
terrified	gripped
daunted	adored
horrified	punched
overjoyed	drenched

e.g. Mortified by what had happened, Jessica raced out of class.

4. Starting with a verb ending in _ing.

This strategy is very similar to the strategy above and relies on a front-positioned verb.

Build the subordinating clause, then write a main clause after the comma.

Examples of verbs ending in __ing.

racing	skipping
pounding	creeping
leaping	jumping
stomping	shouting

darting	pelting
reaching	crying

N.B. Many of these words can also function as adjectives, e.g. The crying girl was lost in the city. Here 'crying' functions as an adjective.

e.g. Darting into the ball, Cinderella breathed deeply when she saw Prince Charming's face.

5. Starting with an adverb followed by a verb at the beginning of a sentence.

Once again, relying on front-loaded 'verbiness' at the beginning of a sentence to build the subordinate clause, followed by a comma and then the main clause.

Examples of adverbs ending in 'ly'

carefully	rationally
erratically	gruffly
quietly	cautiously
finally	angrily
hesitantly	triumphantly
excitedly	rapidly

e.g. Carefully unwrapping the present, John guessed it was what he had been waiting for.

Dialogue and Contracted Forms

As teachers, we are loathe to teach speech. Why? Because, as with any new tool learned by children, they over-apply it before they are able to use it deliberately and with precision. Inverted commas (speech marks) are first mentioned in the national curriculum in Year 3 and are very difficult for children to get right, mainly because of all the surrounding smaller rules about the layout of dialogue. It has its own unique rules for punctuation and there are many micro-rules surrounding it.

The rules for dialogue are:

1. Dialogue begins with a capital letter. This even applies to interrupted dialogue in writing.

2. Only direct speech requires inverted commas, not reported speech.

3. The entire piece of dialogue (if it stands alone) is surrounded by inverted commas. This includes the punctuation, whether that be a full stop, an exclamation mark, question mark or ellipsis, e.g. "I'm not going."

4. If the speech is followed by a dialogue tag (e.g. she said), then a comma needs to finish the dialogue but live inside the inverted comma, e.g. "I'm not going," she said.

5. If the dialogue tag comes before the spoken word(s), a comma is still included but lives outside the direct speech, e.g. She said, "I'm not going."

6. Write on a new line when a new speaker speaks, e.g. "I'm not going," she said. "Alice, I really want you to...please," he said, looking at her dress.

Dialogue is so difficult to teach. Paired with pupils trying to introduce characters that the central character has conversations with, it becomes every teacher's worst nightmare. It is now every Year 3 teacher's worst nightmare. It is in Year 3 that direct speech and inverted commas are the designated grammar components that need teaching. However, the current curriculum places a big contradiction and challenge on us – the issue of contracted forms. In Year 2, pupils need to learn about apostrophes to mark where letters are missing, but contractions are not as easy to teach as we might think. It is difficult to find a universal rule once you start looking at examples.

was not = wasn't – two words pushed together, with the apostrophe showing the omission of one letter in the second word.

they have = they've – two words pushed together, with the apostrophe showing the omission of two letters in the second word.

shall not = shan't – two words pushed together, with the apostrophe, showing the omission of one letter from the second word. Interestingly, the dropped 'll' is not marked with an apostrophe, otherwise this contracted form would include two apostrophes.

am not = ain't – a letter removed and replaced with a different letter and an apostrophe to show the omission of one letter in the second word.

will not = won't – three letters dropped from the first word and an apostrophe to show the omission of one letter in the second word.

None of the five contracted forms above shares a rule, making this very challenging indeed for Year 2 pupils. The other thing about contractions is that they are dominant in spoken English and they are an informal construction. It seems logical, therefore, to teach contracted forms hand in hand when teaching dialogue. Examples of questions on Year 2 SPaG papers show contracted forms within the context of speech. Equally, as a teacher, I would want to make a point of teaching them within lessons about dialogue – mainly because I wouldn't want pupils to litter their more formal writing with this short form. This needs an internal discussion within the school to perhaps start the early inroads of dialogue with Year 2 as a means of introducing contracted forms (to mitigate their usage in their formal writing).

Even though this is not an exhaustive list, the 75 common contractions of the English language are outlined on the following page.

Sentence Maker Kits are a great way for children to practise constructing sentences from the three zones of writing. They can choose different aspects to talk and write about. Go to *www.thetrainingspace.co.uk* to look at detailed copies.

75 Common Contractions of the English Language

1. ain't*	am not/are not/is not/ has not/have not	26. let's	let us	51. we've	we have
		27. mightn't	might not	52. weren't	were not
		28. might've	might have	53. what'll	what shall/ what will
2. aren't	are not/am not	29. mustn't	must not		
3. can't	cannot	30. must've	must have	54. what're	what are
4. could've	could have	31. needn't	need not	55. what's	what has/what is
5. couldn't	could not	32. not've*	not have	56. what've	what have
6. didn't	did not	33. shan't	shall not	57. when's	when has/ when is
7. doesn't	does not	34. she'd	she would		
8. don't	do not	35. she'll	she shall/ she will	58. where'd	where did
9. hadn't	had not			59. where's	where has/ where is
10. hasn't	has not	36. she's	she has/she is		
11. haven't	have not	37. should've	should have	60. where've	where have
12. he'd	he had/he would	38. shouldn't	should not	61. who'd	who would/ who had
		39. that's	that has/ that is		
13. he'll	he shall/he will			62. who'll	who shall/ who will
		40. there'd*	there had/ there would		
14. he's	he has/he is			63. who're	who are
15. how'd	how did/ how would	41. there're*	there are	64. who's	who has/who is
		42. there's	there has/ there is	65. who've	who have
16. how'll	how will			66. why'll*	why will
17. how's	how has/how is/how does	43. they'd	they had/ they would	67. why're	why are
				68. why's	why has/why is
18. I'd	I had/I would	44. they'll	they shall/ they will	69. won't	will not
19. I'll	I shall/I will			70. would've	would have
20. I'm	I am	45. they're	they are	71. wouldn't	would not
21. I've	I have	46. they've	they have	72. you'd	you had/ you would
22. isn't	is not	47. wasn't	was not		
23. it'd*	it had/it would	48. we'd	we had/ we would	73. you'll	you shall/ you will
24. it'll	it shall/it will				
25. it's	it has/it is	49. we'll	we will	74. you're	you are
		50. we're	we are	75. you've	you have

* Some are considered more informal than others

The GRAMMARISTICs

Although grammar is technically an accurate system, and provides shared terminology for analysing sentences, as teachers we want to promote it through building relevant sentences for the genres and text types being worked on in our classes. The GRAMMARISTICs are an invaluable tool, as they outline and cover national curriculum requirements, as well as providing a broad hook so pupils can deliver sentences that apply one of the grammar strands. The GRAMMARISTICs have been organised into Key Stage 1 and Key Stage 2 sections and they reflect the current emphasis on good grammar knowledge in our education system. Pupils will need to understand the different grammar aspects then use and apply these in the context of their real writing within their lessons.

Many teachers use *Sentence Maker Kits* that replicate the three zones of writing with their associated child-friendly hooks. The three zones of writing each have a related physical bag of cards, so teachers and pupils can pull out different aspects to focus on.

Red bag – **The Ideas Zone**: This includes a set of FANTASTIC symbols on individual cards: *Feeling, Asking, Noticing, Touching, Action, Smelling, Tasting, Imagining, Checking*.

Green bag – The Tools Zone: This includes the GRAMMARISTICs cards separately. Teachers use the bank that is appropriate to their class once they (the children that is) understand the grammar concept.

Blue bag – The Techniques Zone: This includes ten literary and poetic devices called the BOOMTASTICs that will be explored further in *Chapter 9: How can we teach personal style?*

Ultimately, grammar is about knowing enough about the various structures to be able to deploy them in skilled and interesting ways. Once children get to grips with the basics, they can then manipulate language and take control of a wide range of effects and intents. Good writing is about making good decisions with the tools you choose to work with. Children need to understand the wealth of tools at their disposal and move beyond the perception that good writing is defined only by interesting adjectives and ambitious words.

Taking a playful approach to grammar enables children to see that it isn't too fixed and that alternatives and amendments are possible. A sentence washing line, that can be used to word-build on, is handy for any teacher of primary-aged children and serves to show children about the mobility and changeability of word choices and phrases.

Key Stage 2 GRAMMARISTICs Poster

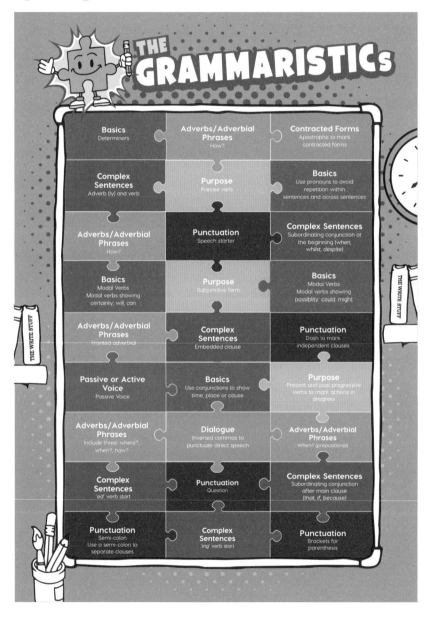

See *www.thetrainingspace.co.uk* to view the Key Stage 1 GRAMMARISTICs poster.

A range of different sentence formula...
Key Stage 1

1. Use 'when' within a sentence, e.g. The puppy wagged its tail when the waiter tickled it.

2. Use 'if' within a sentence, e.g. That puppy is cheeky if people let him get away with it.

3. Use 'that' within a sentence, e.g. The puppy realised that this was his first proper cuddle.

4. Use 'because' within a sentence, e.g. I like cherries because they are fruity and delicious.

5. Use 'when' at beginning of a sentence, e.g. When they arrived home, there was a big, wrapped present on the table.

6. Use 'if' at beginning of a sentence, e.g. If they carry on arguing, then they will have to move class.

7. Include a double adjective noun phrase in a sentence, e.g. The big, blue butterfly landed on the flower.

8. Include a coordinating conjunction, e.g. *but, or, yet, so, and* e.g. Jessica drank her juice and ran outside in the sunshine.

9. Include a plural of a noun in a sentence, e.g. The butterflies flew gracefully across the field.

10. Include a question in a sentence, e.g. What shall we do now?

A range of different sentence formula...

Key Stage 1

11. Include an exclamation beginning with 'how' or 'what', e.g. How intriguing!

12. Include a comparative in a sentence, e.g. I chose the bigger vase for my mum.

13. Include a superlative in a sentence, e.g. I ate the biggest ice-cream.

14. Include a contracted form in a sentence, e.g. I can't wait for the party.

15. Write a present tense sentence, e.g. Jack walks and notices two birds singing in the trees.

16. Write a past tense sentence, e.g. Jack walked for hours through the streets.

17. Write a command, e.g. Please put away the glue sticks.

A range of different sentence formula...

Key Stage 2

1. Begin with a subordinating clause, e.g. As the rain pelted down, Jane ran through the streets.

2. Begin with an 'ed' ending verb, e.g Mortified by what the teacher did, Alice left the class.

3. Begin with an 'ing' ending verb, e.g. Leaping out of the window, Jack's life flashed before him.

4. Begin with an 'ly' adverb followed by a verb, e.g. Cautiously creeping into the woods, Harry thought about the note.

5. Add in a relative clause using a relative pronoun (embedded), e.g. *who*, *what*, *where*, *why*, or *whose*.

   Mandy, who was extremely angry, rang the doorbell.

6. Complex sentence, using 'if' and 'then' (power of three), e.g. If they had kept to the bargain, if they had been honest, if they had paid the Piper, then their children would still be with them.

7. Include two independent clauses joined by a semi-colon, e.g. My grandmother refuses to go to bed early; she is afraid she is going to miss something.

8. Include two independent clauses joined by a coordinating conjunction, e.g My grandmother refuses to go to bed early but she will lie in on a Sunday.

A range of different sentence formula...

Key Stage 2

9. Use a subordinate clause at the end of a sentence, e.g. Jane put up her umbrella while it was raining.

10. Use dialogue with the correct punctuation, e.g. "Wait!" David screamed across the playground.

11. Include 'how' adverb in a sentence, e.g. Suddenly the sky changed and the boys felt it was dangerous.

12. Include 'when' adverbial phrase/prepositional phrase in a sentence, e.g. Next day, the coach party headed off to the zoo.

13. Include 'where' adverbial phrase/prepositional phrase in a sentence, e.g. All the children scattered across the fields.

14. Use a fronted adverbial in a sentence followed by a comma, e.g. Later that day, I heard the bad news.

15. Include a precise/powerful verb in a sentence, e.g. The lanky gentleman squeezed into the Jaguar and winked at the assistant.

16. Include a modal verb in a sentence, e.g. This might be the last time she visits Mr. Blake.

17. Use brackets, dashes or commas to indicate parenthesis in a sentence, e.g. I ate the whole box of cakes (I can't believe it!).

A range of different sentence formula...
Key Stage 2 .

18. Write a passive voice sentence, e.g. The window in the greenhouse was broken.

19. Write an active voice sentence, e.g. Jack broke the greenhouse window.

20. Include an expanded noun phrase in a sentence, e.g. The frightened boy with a bulky rucksack jumped over the fence.

21. Use a question tag in a sentence, e.g. They will always be friends, won't they?

22. Write a command, e.g. Spread butter thinly on a slice of bread.

23. Include an exclamation, e.g. How ridiculous!

24. Write in the subjunctive form, e.g. The train will probably arrive late.

25. Include past progressive verb form in a sentence, e.g. Jack was doing his work.

26. Include present perfect verb form in a sentence, e.g. Jane had wanted to go to the cinema.

Consider

Through one of your favourite books, that you share with your class, analyse the grammar deployed by the author. Later, swap the text with another teacher in school. Explore the different choices the writer has made to achieve the purpose, e.g. verb choices, use of pronouns, complex sentences.

Share findings with partner teacher. Did you notice different aspects? How did the grammar contribute to the overall impact on the reader? Why was <u>this</u> the right verb in the perfect place? Why did <u>this</u> adjective seal <u>this</u> sentence with mathematical finality?

School Impact Points

(1) Make the 'Grammar Rainbow' a focal point during a staff meeting to explore strengths and weaknesses in teaching around grammar.

(2) Talk about the <u>quality</u> of texts used with pupils to explore authors' grammatical choices. Which texts are the most inspiring to emerging writers?

"I like you holding my hand when I write. You give us half a sentence – the easy bit – and we do the hard bit (thinking of adjectives). It feels different to me. My writing is now slower and I like writing."

Evie, Year 2

How Can We Teach Personal Style?

Fear of failure, timidity and uncertainty locks children into a constrained writing style. The key to opening up their authentic voices is unlocking these shackles.

Chapter 9

Summary

☑ Writing style can be taught and practised.

☑ Over-use and cliché are common errors during the early acquisition of literary devices.

☑ A hierarchy of techniques can be learned from successful writers.

☑ A well-developed 'sense of a reader' will enable budding writers to build more meaningful sentences.

☑ Children should be taught to keep the reader in mind whenever they write.

THE WRITE STUFF

HB

How Can We Teach Personal Style?

In this era of a grammar-laden national curriculum, we need to be aware that if we focus too much on the technicalities of writing, we might put pupils off writing altogether. Literary devices are a way to make the familiar seem new and a powerful descriptive tool to lift writing off the page.

In a study in 2002, Colston and Kuiper analysed thousands of non-fiction and narrative texts targeted at children both over and under the age of eight. They discovered that, on average, there were 70 metaphors per 1,000 words in stories. Even more surprisingly, there were 37 metaphors per 1,000 words in non-fiction books. Figurative language and poetic devices are an important part of literature for children and require high-level comprehension skills to ensure accurate understanding of them. Nationally, the UK's reading results for 2014 and 2015, at level 6, stood at below 1%, which equated to approximately 850 pupils year on year who had developed mastery of reading.

"The very existence of different amounts of metaphorical language across different genre points out that literature has a complex relation with children's language comprehension abilities and should not be overlooked in our attempts to understand language comprehension development."
Colston and Kuiper (2002)

Areas that children find difficult include the subtleties of meaning, and poetic referencing used by writers to create particular images. Teaching them about the various literary devices is paramount in order to have a direct impact on reading comprehension. This needs to be taught well – so pupils can recognise clichés and lazy constructions, as well as attempts that are ineffective or plain gibberish.

Authors often paint word pictures of their impressions of a scene, object or person. They try to use vivid and precise words and phrases that appeal to the senses. Pupils need to be encouraged to use their imaginations to form 'mental images' from authors' work so they can, in turn, replicate these devices in their own writing. When children understand the repertoire of devices at their disposal, and are able to use them in a skilled way, everyone wins – the teacher, the pupils and the school (in terms of improved results).

Beware the two pitfalls

1. Cliché

Encourage children to reach beyond overused similes and be creative. Children often make more intriguing comparisons than adults when encouraged to take risks. They tend to have less fixed mindsets about the conventions surrounding English and can often surprise us with the unusual. However, the moment a child reaches for 'as white as snow' is the moment that the teacher moves in to demonstrate the more effective 'as white as a newly-bleached shirt'.

2. Overuse

As children become familiar with figurative language and other literary devices, they will begin to use them in different forms of writing. Now is the time to teach restraint. Overusing figurative language can overwhelm the reader, whereas a sprinkling of these devices adds depth and maturity to a piece of writing. Skilled writers know when to use them and when to hold back.

The BOOMTASTICs

The BOOMTASTICs are a hierarchical ten-point system for introducing the devices that will help children's writing explode off the page. They have been organised in this way to allow a whole-school approach to teaching devices, and progression to be accounted for according to the complexity of the device. It is particularly noticeable with the techniques of writing that the teacher, as a performer, comes into play. This is where reading aloud is critical, and volume and pace can be used to our advantage to draw pupils into wonderful moments of language. Together with our classes, we can get excited and delight in the word and phrase choices of a talented writer. The BOOMTASTICs give us the structure to explore a varied range of techniques used by writers that add flair and personal style to their work.

The BOOMTASTICs are organised hierarchically so pupils can add new techniques to their writing toolkits - step by step - as they become more adept at discovering techniques (through reading) and applying them in their own writing.

Key Stage 1: Years 1-2

To be explored through reading and applied through writing in the following order:

- ▶ Onomatopoeia
- ▶ Alliteration
- ▶ Rhyme
- ▶ Repetition
- ▶ Simile

Each of the devices should be explained in turn, with teachers outlining how they can benefit pupils as they start to take control of their own writing. The following reference guide will assist you in further explaining the meaning and intent of these devices.

Onomatopoeia

An onomatopoeic word is a word that phonetically imitates, resembles or suggests the source of the sound it describes. Common occurrences of onomatopoeic words include animal noises such as *"oink"*, *"miaow"* (or *"meow"*), "roar" or *"chirp"*.

Some other very common English language examples include: *"hiccup"*, *"zoom"*, *"bang"*, *"beep"*, *"moo"* and *"splash"*. Machines and their sounds are also often described with onomatopoeia, as in *"honk"* or *"beep-beep"* for the horn of a car, and *"vroom"* or *"brum"* for the engine.

Children's earliest picture books are filled with onomatopoeic words. Sometimes they take over a whole page, like the "splash" finale in *The Wide-Mouthed Frog* after the line:

"You don't see many of those around, do you?"

Children love to hear the sounds that things make in books – not only animal sounds but the *"whoosh"* of the wind and the *"pfffft"* of the flower pushing up through the ground. Children meet onomatopoeia from a young age in books like *Mmm, Cookies!*, which is full of sounds bringing foods to life. Sugar is sprinkled with a *"chik, chik, chik, chik, chik"* and washed out of the character's mouth with a *"burble,*

burble, splat, splicht, bwahhh". In *The Perfect Nest* by Catherine Friend, there is a *"CRACK!"* and *"Crackety-Snap!"* and *"Crackety-Crackety-Boom!"* to describe the sounds of baby animals bursting out of their eggs. Sometimes, the simplest of sounds evokes the reality of an event, such as the moment in Mary Quigley's book *Granddad's Fishing Buddy* when the 'plop' of the fishing line going into the water quickly puts us in the scene.

Teaching pupils to be on the lookout for this device will enhance their own writing. It is certainly a way to get noticed by the reader and is often associated with a change in font, capitalisation or an exclamation mark to draw attention to it. Onomatopoeia is a way to add a dimension to writing that is more sensory and can create interest by breaking up lengthy prose.

Onomatopoeia - examples

"Crunch, crunch, crunch, his feet sank into the snow..."
The Snowy Day by Ezra John Keats

"Splash, splosh! Splash, splosh! Splash, splosh! Splash, splosh!..."
We're Going on a Bear Hunt by Michael Rosen

"And ere three shrill notes the pipe uttered,
You heard as if an army muttered;
And the muttering grew to a grumbling;
And the grumbling grew to a mighty rumbling;
And out of the houses the rats came tumbling..."
The Pied Piper of Hamelin by Robert Browning

"Bear gnarls and he snarls. Bear roars and he rumbles! Bear jumps and he stomps. Bear growls and he grumbles!"
Bear Snores On by Karma Wilson

"Our feet crunched over the crisp snow…"
Owl Moon by Jane Yolen

"Whap. Inches from my toes, the umbrella landed in the sand like a giant dart…"
Crenshaw by Katherine Applegate

"The child was a cross little thing, always crying and refusing her food, but Lalchand built a cradle for her in the corner of the workshop, where she could see the sparks play and listen to the fizz and crackle of the gunpowder…"
The Firework-Maker's Daughter by Philip Pullman

Alliteration

Alliteration is a stylistic device in which a number of words, having the same first consonant sound, occur close together in a series. This popular literary device doesn't depend on letters, but on sounds, and is often used for emphasis in writing. A prime example is this tongue-twister, which heightens intrigue of language when read aloud:

"Peter Piper picked a peck of pickled peppers,
A peck of pickled peppers Peter Piper picked.

If Peter Piper picked a peck of pickled peppers,
Where's the peck of pickled peppers Peter Piper picked?"

Alliteration is an effective literary tool for adding drama and emphasis. It is also useful for creating mood. In *Jabberwocky*, by Lewis Carroll, many of the words in the poem are made up, but the poet's use of alliteration is so effective that a reader can still apply meaning, even without knowing the definition of the words. As a reader, we can almost hear the terrible Jabberwock come stomping and snorting to meet his death, with the repetition of harsh and jarring sounds such as:

"gyre and gimble"

"the claws that catch"

"The vorpal blade went snicker-snack!"

Alliterative phrases also help to create rhythm — and pupils are drawn to the rhythmic parts of language. Many picture books are drenched in rich onomatopoeic and alliterative language and reading these stories aloud will bolster and extend pupils' vocabularies. Children meet these phrases in their favourite books such as *Winnie-the-Pooh* by A.A. Milne:

"Here is Edward Bear, coming down the stairs now, bump, bump, bump, on the back of his head, behind Christopher Robin."

Research conducted in 2015 by Dominic Massaro, a psychology professor at the University of California in Santa Cruz, confirmed that the more challenging,

Pupils have gathered real examples from reading and captured them on post-it notes as great examples from their favourite books.

formal and poetic language of books boosted children's own language more extensively than just talk alone.

Reading aloud was the best way to help children develop word mastery and grammatical understanding, said Massaro, who specialises in language acquisition and literacy. He found that picture books were two to three times as likely as parent/child conversations to include a word that was not among the 5,000 most common English words.

Picture books also included more uncommon words than conversations among adults, he said.

"We talk with a lazy tongue," Massaro said. "We tend to point at something or use a pronoun and the context tells you what it is. We talk at a basic level."

He pointed out that writing was always more formal than the spoken word, even in children's books.

"Reading takes you beyond the easy way to communicate. It takes you to another world and challenges you."

Reading picture books to babies and toddlers is important because the earlier children acquire language, the more likely they are to master it.

"You are stretching them in vocabulary and grammar at an early age. You are preparing them to be expert language users, and indirectly you are going to facilitate their learning to read."

Whether it is to create mood, rhythm or humour, pupils enjoy experimenting with alliteration to take control of writerly effects.

Alliteration - examples

"Alice's fat aunt ate apples and acorns around August..."
Alice in Wonderland by Lewis Carroll

"Great Aunt Nellie and Brent Bernard who watch with wild wonder at the wide window as the beautiful birds begin to bite into the bountiful birdseed..."
Thank you for the Thistle by Dorie Thurston

"And terrible teeth in his terrible jaws. He has knobbly knees, and turned-out toes..."
The Gruffalo by Julia Donaldson

"Then there was trouble, a horrible squabble, a row, a racket, a rumpus in the old white cabin..."
Pumpkin Soup by Helen Cooper

"I heard something scratching in one of the corners, and something scuttling about, then it all stopped and it was just dead quiet in there..."
Skellig by David Almond

"The house was all alight within, and the joyous hubbub of its activity contrasted with the sombre sighing of the wind and the hideous howling of the wolves without..."
The Wolves of Willoughby Chase by Joan Aiken

"They have grumbling lions with gleaming teeth..."
The One and Only Ivan by Katherine Applegate

"He was lying there in the darkness behind the tea chests, in the dust and dirt..."
Skellig by David Almond

Rhyme

Reading well-written rhyme should be an effortless pleasure. The words should flow easily, enhancing the read-aloud enjoyment. A child's book without rhyme would be like a world without music.

The Gruffalo by Julia Donaldson is a popular story in Key Stage 1, used by teachers as a model for pupils to create their own unique stories. The far-reaching appeal of this narrative can be attributed to a literary device often seen in poetry: the end rhyme, where the end word of every line rhymes.

"A mouse took a stroll through the deep dark wood. A fox saw the mouse and the mouse looked good. Where are you going to, little brown mouse? Come and have lunch in my underground house."

Pupils having fun trying to say alliterative tongue twisters in Year 3.

However, this is not the only way to lean on rhyme in story and non-fiction as it can also be embedded within sentences and paragraphs to enhance flow and interest. Good rhyme is fun to read out loud. Good rhyme is enjoyable to listen to and can make the piece lively or clever. Rhyme is unfashionable at the moment, but done well, it is delicious. My favourite line of all time is one that includes rhyme in a children's picture book by Neil Gaiman, *The Wolves in the Walls* (this is both a simile and rhyme with 'quick' and 'flick' making it great to read aloud):

"Quick as the flick of the wing of a bat, Lucy slipped into the wall."

The Cat in the Hat by Dr. Seuss has embedded rhyme and repetition in its opening line for effect.

"The sun did not shine, it was too wet to play, so we sat in the house all that cold, cold wet day. I sat there with Sally. We sat here we two, and we said 'How we wish we had something to do'."

The word 'sat' is repeated three times to emphasise how bored and fed-up the children are on this rainy day. Alongside this, there is rhyme between 'play' and 'day' as well as 'two' and 'do'.

Meanwhile, *Madeline* by Ludwig Bemelmans uses a rhyme dropped internally within the sentence to add intrigue and make it wonderful to read aloud:

"In an old house in Paris that was covered with vines, lived twelve little girls in two straight lines."

Rhyme - examples

"How we love to crash cans,
Mash and smash and bash cans..."
Racoon Tune by Nancy E. Shaw

"Quick as the flick of the wing of a bat, Lucy
slipped into the wall..."
The Wolves in the Walls by Neil Gaiman

"Yes to Herbert's surprise from Miss Annabel's
eyes came the sudden appearance of tears..."
The Ghost of Miss Annabel Spoon by
Aaron Blabey

"The chickens flounced, trounced and body
bounced. The dogs pounced. Drooling
muzzles dribbled. Frightened yard birds
quibbled. Sharp teeth crashed. Pointed
beaks smashed. Snouts snapped. Wings
flapped. Until..."
Big Chickens Fly the Coop by Leslie
Helakoski

"A fleet of spaceships heads this way,
They're fifty zillion miles away
But getting closer every day
The aliens are coming..."
Here Come the Aliens by Colin
McNaughton

"Splats, hats and lots of rats!"
Horrible Histories - The Measly Middle
Ages by Terry Deary

"She then gave a swift demonstration with
backflips and butterfly kicks. The wolf
looked quite shaken, but hollered, 'Yo,
Bacon! I'm not scared of your tricks'..."
The Three Ninja Pigs by Corey Rosen
Schwartz

"A mouse took a stroll through the deep
dark wood. A fox saw the mouse and the
mouse looked good..."
The Gruffalo by Julia Donaldson

Repetition

Repetition is the simple repeating of a word or phrase within a sentence in order to secure emphasis. Notice how repetition of the word 'away' sharpens our empathy as the reader and makes the central character's need to run away more poignant:

"I'm going away from this place. Away
from the angry teacher, away from the
lonely playground and away from the
staring eyes."

As pupils experiment with a wider range of techniques, they use the power of repetition to strengthen the non-fiction and the emotion in a narrative.

Books they will meet from an early age include *Funnybones* by Janet and Allan Ahlberg. This is a clever tale that builds up suspense using 'dark' as an adjective twice before all nouns in the story. Children enjoy finding this pattern and replicating it in their own writing:

"This is how the story begins. On a dark,
dark hill, there was a dark, dark town."

Sometimes, the repeated part does not have to be that significant to impress on a reader. Here in *The Wolves of Willoughby Chase* by Joan Aiken the reusing of the word 'dusk' with the added 'winter' as an adjective helps us visualise how cold and dark this dusk is:

"It was dusk, winter-dusk."

Repetition is not just applied to moments of suspense or times when texts need to be slowed down but also to create humour and rhythm. A great example of this is in the opening of *Fantastic Mr. Fox* by Roald Dahl. The text repeats 'farms', 'men' and 'nasty' and reveals one new bit of information as the opening builds. The humour is further reinforced by the silly alliterative names of the farmers:

"Down in the valley there were three farms. The owners of these farms had done well. They were rich men. They were also nasty men. All three of them were about as nasty and mean as any men you could meet. Their names were Farmer Boggis, Farmer Bunce and Farmer Bean."

In *Tom's Midnight Garden* by Philippa Pearce, we can see a more poetic use of repetition, and the fact that the word 'tears' is repeated, impresses on us the importance of them for Tom and the sentiment behind them:

"If, standing alone on the back doorstep, Tom allowed himself to weep tears, they were tears of anger."

What is particularly interesting about the following two extracts is that they both repeat the word 'nobody' but with two very different outcomes. *The True Story of the Three Little Pigs* by Jon Scieszka makes the reader believe they are being entrusted with a little-known secret about what really happened in the age-old fairytale. The word 'nobody' emphasises the exclusivity of the information we are about to receive:

"Everybody knows the story of The Three Little Pigs. Or at least they think they do. But I'll let you in on a little secret. Nobody knows the real story, because nobody has ever heard my side of the story. I'm the Wolf."

Alternatively, the repeated use of 'Nobody knows' in *The Iron Man* by Ted Hughes functions like a piece of poetry. What starts out as ordinary language quickly develops a poetic quality which marks it out as literary and special:

"The Iron Man came to the top of the cliff. How far had he walked? Nobody knows. Where had he come from? Nobody knows. Taller than a house, the Iron Man stood at the top of the cliff, on the very brink, in the darkness."

Reading is essential to show explicitly to children that book language operates to different rules than spoken language. As teachers, we need to transparently show writers' techniques so pupils have clear expectations about how language is structured.

Repetition - examples

"It rapped. It grated. It snarled. It scarpered. It shrieked. It growled..."
The Witches by Roald Dahl

"Sparks fly. Flames leap. Oil boils. Rats howl. Skin shrivels..."
The Witches by Roald Dahl

"Pa shrugged and I shrugged. I was not disappointed..."
Owl Moon by Jane Yolen

"Behind him there were other figures, even more shadowy than he was, even more silent..."
The Amber Spyglass by Philip Pullman

"They hunt frantically, stalking, pushing, grumbling. Then they leave, clutching bags filled with things - bright things, soft things, big things - but no matter how full the bags, they always come back for more..."
The One and Only Ivan by **Katherine Applegate**

"And then she's in the road and then and then a car a squeal of brakes a scream, a SCREAM silence..."
Vicky Angel by Jacqueline Wilson

"And it doesn't hurt the way I thought it would. It's not sharp all the time. It's dull, dull, dull. I want it to hurt more..."
Vicky Angel by Jacqueline Wilson

Simile

A simile directly compares two things through the explicit use of connecting words such as 'like', 'as', 'so' and 'than'.

> ## " Reading is essential to show explicitly to children that book language operates to different rules than spoken language "

Of Mice and Men by John Steinbeck has a memorable, highly evocative simile that compares a man to a dying fish. The use of alliteration strengthens the simile:

"Curley was flopping like a fish on a line."

My Dog is as Smelly as Dirty Socks by Hanoch Piven is a fabulous book to use with Key Stage 1 pupils, as a starting point when teaching similes. The girl in the book uses household objects to capture her family members. Her dad is represented by a collage picture and has string for a mouth because he is:

"as stubborn as a knot in a rope."

Once pupils are shown how to identify similes, they are able to find them quite easily in their writing. *My Family and Other Animals* by Gerald Durrell is a good example of how the initial simile is further strengthened by the subsequent verb that personifies the wind:

"July had been blown out like a candle by a biting wind that ushered in a leaden August sky..."

Simile - examples

"Somewhere behind us, a train whistle blew, long and low like a sad, sad song,
"The trees stood still as giant statues,
"And when their voices faded away it was as quiet as a dream..."
Owl Moon by Jane Yolen

"Amber lived on a mountain so high, it poked through the clouds like a needle stuck in down..."
Amber on the Mountain by Tony Johnston

"She had small piggy eyes, a sunken mouth and one of those white flabby faces that looked exactly as though it had been boiled. She was like a great white, soggy overboiled cabbage..."
James and the Giant Peach by Roald Dahl

"She would roll it round and round her mouth like a piece of hot pork crackling before spitting it out..."
The Witches by Roald Dahl

"Dark clouds raced across it like wild horses..."
A Letter to Amy by Ezra Jack Keats

"'Welcome to borstal,' she added, spraying bits of crisps out of her mouth like snowflakes..."
Matilda by Roald Dahl

"My Dad is like a gorilla because he is powerful, fierce-looking and gentle..."
Gorillas and my Dad by Anthony Browne

"If you have good thoughts, they will shine out of your face like sunbeams..."
The Twits by Roald Dahl

"Nothing like the smell of new turned earth. A cold metal smell it is, but clean and good like the first breath of life..."
War Horse by Michael Morpurgo

"A giant of a man was standing in the doorway. His face was almost completely hidden by a long, shaggy mane of hair and a wild, tangled beard, but you could make out his eyes glinting like black beetles under all the hair..."
Harry Potter and the Philosopher's Stone by J.K. Rowling

"Her skin was a rich black that would have peeled like a plum snagged, but then no one would have thought of getting close enough to Mrs. Flowers to ruffle her dress, let alone snag her skin..."
I Know Why the Caged Bird Sings by Maya Angelou

Key Stage 2: Years 3-4

All of the above as well as...

Metaphor

A metaphor's function is to make an even stronger image in the reader's head by describing a place, subject or object as something unlikely.

"The teacher was a witch."

"A sea of chaos."

"Drowning in self pity."

Often, two nouns are compared and contrasted to each other, with the verbs 'is', 'are' and 'was' being dominant.

"I am a storm."

"Her eyes are glistening jewels."

Metaphor - examples

"The world's a stage..."
As You Like It by **William Shakespeare**

"Mrs Dursley was thin and blonde and had nearly twice the usual amount of neck, which came in very useful as she spent so much time craning it over garden fences, spying on the neighbours..."*
Harry Potter and the Philosopher's Stone by **J.K. Rowling**

"He got so angry that his anger became a stormcloud exploding thunder and lightning and hailstones..."
Angry Arthur by **Hiawyn Oram**

"That night he was almost too happy to sleep and so much love stirred in his little sawdust heart that it almost burst. And into his boot-button eyes that had long ago lost their polish, there came a look of wisdom and beauty..."
The Velveteen Rabbit by **Margery Williams**

A Year 5 pupil, dressed as a spy, builds a simile to use in their suspense writing based on Stormbreaker by Anthony Horowitz.

"Fire burns away all our illusions. The world itself is all illusion. Everything that exists flickers like a flame for a moment, and then vanishes. The only thing that lasts is change itself..."
The Firework-Maker's Daughter by **Philip Pullman**

"Each piece was sweet and light to the very centre and Edmund had never tasted anything more delicious. He was quite warm now and very comfortable..."
The Lion, the Witch and the Wardrobe by **C.S. Lewis**

"It took me some time to recognise all those human sounds, to weave words into things. But I was patient..."
The One and Only Ivan by **Katherine Applegate**

"The blackbird flew off his shoulder and vanished in midair and there was the angel again, sulking in the halflight. Before they went back through, Will looked all around, sniffing the air, taking the measure of the world where Lyra was captive..."
The Amber Spyglass by **Philip Pullman**

"Tears scorching her cheeks, she hurled herself across the room and beat him fiercely with her fists..."
Madame Doubtfire by **Anne Fine**

"The lamps of Piccadilly, stringing away beside the trees of the park, were becoming pale and moth-like..."
The Rainbow by **D.H. Lawrence**

Pathetic Fallacy

The phrase *pathetic fallacy* is a literary term for the attributing of human emotion and conduct to all aspects within nature. It is a kind of personification that is found in narrative writing when, for example, *"clouds seem sullen"*, *"trees tremble"*, or *"when rocks seem indifferent"*. It gives human emotions to inanimate objects of nature – for example, referring to weather features reflecting a mood.

This device is used to strengthen a match between a central character's emotion and the weather, or something in nature or the physical environment that correlates, to amplify this feeling. Pathetic fallacy is fascinating because it offers human beings a different way to begin to understand and comprehend the natural world. By projecting human thoughts and behaviours onto elements of our environment, we make understanding it more accessible; we are comparing it to something we already know and understand.

The film of *Holes* (2003), based on the children's novel (published in 1998) by American writer Louis Sachar, also provides a good live action example of pathetic fallacy. The part of the film (based on Chapter 29) that begins "there was a change in the weather. For the worse" shows the tension at Camp Green Lake slowly building as the weather becomes hotter and hotter. It's not until the tension is broken that the rain comes.

Pathetic fallacy can really set the atmosphere of a scene and help to bring out themes and motivations. In particular, effective pathetic fallacy can draw you into the central character's dilemma.

The Borribles by Michael de Larrabeiti is a good example of nature mirroring the mood of the story:

"The swirling rain-clouds rushed on revealing the bright moon, and the two Borribles dodged behind the bushes and kept as quiet as they could."

Equally, Judith Kerr's *When Hitler Stole Pink Rabbit* shows how the *"sad, greying heaps"* come to represent the main character's existence during the war:

"Anna was walking home from school with Elsbeth, a girl in her class. A lot of snow had fallen in Berlin that winter. It did not melt, so the street cleaners had swept it to the edge of the pavement, and there it had lain for weeks in sad, greying heaps."

Pathetic Fallacy - examples

"Nobody noticed that she was missing. They were all too busy thinking of the journey ahead. As the geese disappeared into the grey sky, tears trickled down Borka's beak..."
Borka **by John Burningham**

"Thunder crashed against the corners of the world and lightning split the sky as we reached the road, but we did not stop. We dared not. We had to reach Papa..."
Roll of Thunder, Hear my Cry **by Mildred D. Taylor**

"He lurks in his Lerkim, cold under the roof, where he makes his own clothes out of miff-muffered moof. And on special dark midnights in August, he peeks out of the shutters and sometimes he speaks..."
The Lorax **by Dr Seuss**

"Once upon a time, a tiny striped caterpillar burst from the egg which had been home for so long. 'Hello world,' he said. 'It sure is bright out here in the sun'..."
Hope for the Flowers **by Trina Paulus**

"Behind him, just beyond the point where the sunlight reached, Mrs. Coulter was heating some water in a small pan over a naphtha stove. Her daemon uttered a warning murmur, and Mrs. Coulter looked up..."
The Amber Spyglass **by Philip Pullman**

"It was dusk, winter-dusk. Snow lay piled on the dark road across Willoughby Wold, but from dawn, men had been clearing it with brooms and shovels. There were hundreds of them at work, wrapped in sacking because of the bitter cold and keeping together in groups for fear of the wolves, grown savage and reckless from hunger..."
The Wolves of Willoughby Chase **by Joan Aitken**

"Mrs. Coulter took Ama's hand as they went back to the cave entrance and saw the girl's father watching anxiously from

below...Father and daughter bowed once more to the cave and then set off, to vanish among the gloom of the heavy rhododendrons..."
The Amber Spyglass by **Philip Pullman**

"Will jumped over the fence into the next door garden, down the passage beside the house, over the next garden wall, across the dew wet lawn, through the hedge and into the tangle of shrubs and trees between the housing estate and the main road. There he crawled under a bush and lay panting and trembling..."
The Subtle Knife by **Philip Pullman**

Key Stage 2: Years 5-6

All of the above as well as...

▶ Pun

▶ Personification

▶ Symbolism

Pun

Pun relies on the double function of language. 'Sweet' and 'hard' can refer to the physical properties of things but also to the psychological properties of people.

Puns are an extremely high-order skill and require a mastery of language and a clear understanding of the functionality of homophones.

A sentence can be weighted in meaning with the deliberate use of a pun. Consider this sentence that provides information:

"The boy wore a blue jumper: he was sad."

If the same essence of meaning is captured but a pun is used, playing on the duality of meaning of the word 'blue', the sentence suddenly gains more presence and showcases the writer's skill:

"The boy's mood was like his jumper, blue."

Pun - examples

"Knight bus"
"Don't count your owls before they are delivered"
"Knockturn Alley"
"Don't cry over spilt potion"
"Grimauld Place..."
Harry Potter and the Philosopher's Stone by **J.K. Rowling**

"How do you know when Santa is in the room? You can feel his presents..."
100 Best Jokes for Kids

"Not I, believe me. You have dancing shoes with nimble soles: I have a soul of lead so stakes me to the ground I cannot move..."
Romeo and Juliet by **William Shakespeare**

Gathering ideas in Key Stage 2 to write a pathetic fallacy sentence, where there is a match between a frightened character and frightening weather.

"Dear Deer,
I now live at the Zoo.
Wait until you hear what goes on over here.
Love Aunt Ant..."
Dear Deer by Gene Barretta

"When we were little...We went to school in the sea. The master was an old Turtle - we used to call him Tortoise – 'Why did you call him Tortoise if he wasn't one?' Alice asked. 'We called him Tortoise because he taught us'..."
Alice in Wonderland by Lewis Carroll

"When he was in school, he longed to be out and when he was out, he longed to be in. On the way, he thought about coming home, and coming home, he thought about going. Wherever he was, he wished he were somewhere else, and when he got there, he wondered why he bothered. Nothing really interested him - least of all things that should have..."
The Phantom Tollbooth by Norton Juster

Personification

Personification is a type of figurative language where inanimate objects are given human characteristics (emotions, sensations, speech, physical movements):

"The cruel waves screamed and swallowed the boat."

Here, the writer describes the waves using human attributes, 'cruel' and 'screamed'. The waves are also given a human physical process, 'swallowing', when waves cannot literally swallow something.

Personification - examples

"In the space of thirty seconds, the atmosphere in the tiny room had changed completely and now it was vibrating with awkwardness and secrets..."
Matilda by **Roald Dahl**

"Adrift on eight pond pillows, pink cheeked blossoms rest..."
One Leaf Rides the Wind by **Celeste Mannis**

"...trees are scratching at the sky..."
Who Took my Hairy Toe? by **Shutta Crum**

"The Moon made his face into a silver mask..."
Owl Moon by **Jane Yolen**

"The tree awakened earlier than usual one morning and stretched her arms toward the horizon as if to invite the early rays of dawn into her world. She shivered with delight, wiggling her roots in the muddy earth, which had only recently yielded its frozen hardness..."
The Tree that Survived the Winter by **Mary Fahy**

"Once she was out of her cradle, she toddled around the workshop laughing as the fire flared and the sparks danced..."
The Firework-Maker's Daughter by **Philip Pullman**

"The fog comes on little cat feet.
It sits looking over harbour and city on silent haunches and then moves on..."
The Fog by **Carl Sandburg**

"The night was creeping on the ground! She crept and did not make a sound..."
Check by **James Stevens**

"I heard a plane threading the clouds high above us and let my oars drag, neck craning up, arrested by a vision of our little armada from such a height: this world I had chosen and everything I had in it, all of our precious, peculiar lives, contained in three splinters of wood adrift upon the vast, unblinking eye of the sea..."
Hollow City: The Second Novel of Miss Peregrine's Children by **Ransom Riggs**

"The day waves yellow with all its crops..."
The Waves by **Virginia Woolf**

Extended Metaphor

"It is that ability to summarise and encapsulate that makes symbolism so interesting, useful, and – when used well - arresting. You could argue that it's really just another kind of figurative language. Symbolism exists to adorn and enrich, not to create a sense of artificial profundity. It can serve as a focusing device for both you and the reader, helping to create a more unified and pleasing work."
Stephen King 2000

Extended Metaphor is based on taking one idea and extending it across a whole piece of writing. For example, if a pupil was writing a persuasive holiday brochure to promote Mauritius, and a reference was made to it being *"the jewel of the Indian ocean"*, a metaphor would have been established linking the island to precious stones and jewellery. This could then be a starting point for an ongoing symbol to be established. If a mind map of ideas was to be generated around the central idea of jewellery, the following extended ideas might emerge:

"a necklace of cliffs surround the emerald green ocean..."

"the dazzling sands are like a precious lost treasure yet to be discovered..."

"marvel at the nightlife that glints with the promise of a pleasurable escape..."

Extended Metaphor - examples

An extended metaphor that is continually referenced through a text to provide a textual glue through a themed idea:

▶ Prison

▶ Dance

▶ Jewellery

▶ Beach

▶ Carnival

▶ Space

▶ Water

▶ Fire

▶ Sky

▶ Forest

▶ Weapons

▶ Storm

This is a technique that sustains a metaphor over time. The author exploits one analogy to make multiple links throughout the writing.

"Bobby Holloway says my imagination is a three-hundred-ring circus. Currently I was in ring two hundred and ninety-nine, with elephants dancing and clowns cartwheeling and tigers leaping through rings of fire. The time had come to step back, leave the main tent, go buy some popcorn and a Coke, bliss out, cool down..."
Seize the Night - Dean Koontz

Extended Metaphor:

Creating a mind map supports written work to build an extended metaphor

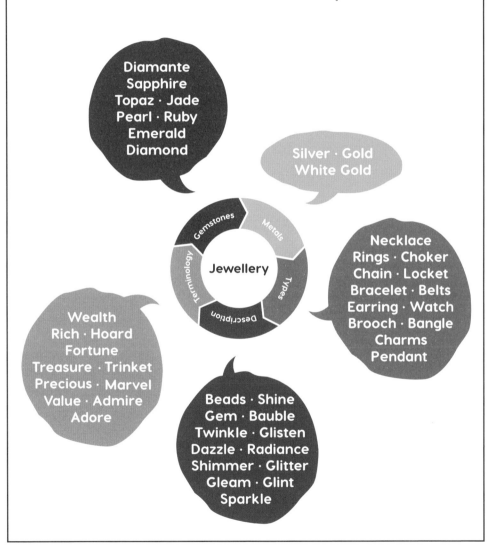

THE WRITE STUFF
Personification
THE BOOM
Pun
Pathetic Fallacy
Metaphor

Sense of a reader

The internalised 'sense of a reader' supports a pupil to make appropriate and powerful choices. A text is shaped by a writer and they need to continually assess the impact of their work. Alongside this, they need to be crucially aware of their audience and purpose throughout the writing process. Pupils cannot be expected to be good at this instinctively, but D.W. Harding coined two phrases in 1963 that are still applicable today. These phrases, 'read like writers' and 'write like readers' demonstrate how both skills co-support each other. With this in mind, teachers should show the impact of the written word on us as readers and how reading can make us consciously connect with language choices and shapes.

Read like writers

As a reader, constantly asking yourself:

▶ What works?
▶ How are you affected?
▶ Why did the writer do that?
▶ How do you feel now?
▶ Is this effective?
▶ Can you relate to this part?
▶ How connected or disconnected are you to the writing?

Write like readers

As a writer, constantly ask yourself:

▶ Is this what I am trying to say?
▶ Is this the most effective image?
▶ Am I bored?
▶ Is this clear enough?
▶ Do I know what is happening?
▶ Is the pace right?
▶ Is this the best way to explain this moment?

The experienced writer is able to craft texts with the reader in mind and to reflect critically on their own writing.

Myra Barrs and Valerie Cork give power to the teacher as a 'reader performer' as they see the act of reading dramatically as the ultimate teacher duty to breathe life, urgency, danger and love into a text. It is through our performances of texts that pupils can begin to 'see' the devices deployed by the writer and the intentions of the author:

"The giving of voice and breadth to a text, instead of leaving it inertly as marks on a page, is an essential way of communicating the full range of its force and meaning."

Pupils exploring the different techniques and discussing examples they like and those they've created themselves.

Consider

Constructing an area in the staffroom to collect sparkling, magical, dark or intriguing sentences. This can be a way of putting in place an ongoing system to support one another. Real examples from quality texts make the job of explaining the ten BOOMTASTIC strategies easier and more transparent.

School Impact Points

Adopt a whole-school approach to teaching writing techniques.

Collect examples of the BOOMTASTICs from age-appropriate books and texts so that pupils are clear about the quality and function of these literary devices.

Showcase the BOOMTASTICs through teacher demonstration of written sentences. The process of constructing the sentences is voiced aloud, so specific language choices (and their functions) are explained in detail.

"My teacher makes each part interesting and challenges us to use things that will make better sentences."

LiLi, Year 6

How Can We Assess Writing?

Good writing should be judged by reliable and valid yardsticks. To capture what writing quality means, these measures should be more inclusive than standard practice.

Chapter 10

Summary

- ☑ Schools have been asked to design their own assessment tools.

- ☑ Assessment needs to be manageable and fit for purpose.

- ☑ The 'Performance of Writing' tool is a set of discrete statements linked to the national curriculum to support judgements of pupils' writing capabilities against age expectations.

- ☑ Assessment processes need to support teaching and learning and assist the teacher in making meaningful judgements, as well as setting ambitious targets for pupils.

THE WRITE STUFF

How Can We Assess Writing?

The NAHT produced its *Assessment Commission Report* in February 2014, with a set of guiding principles for schools about assessment. While primaries at this time knew what the national curriculum's remodelled content included, assessment was in a state of flux because levels were being removed and it was an era when enormous pressure was placed on schools to produce individualised, tailored assessment tools.

Assessment needs to be fit for purpose and the principles shaped by the working party at NAHT are a powerful place to start when evaluating your own assessment systems and processes.

Assessment – Guiding Principles

1. Assessment is at the heart of teaching and learning.

2. Assessment is fair.

3. Assessment is honest.

4. Assessment is ambitious.

5. Assessment is appropriate.

6. Assessment is consistent.

7. Assessment outcomes provide meaningful and understandable information for:

   a. pupils in developing their learning;

   b. parents in supporting children with learning;

   c. teachers in planning teaching and learning. Assessment must provide information that justifies the time spent;

   d. school leaders and governors in planning and allocating resources; and

   e. government and agents of government.

8. Assessment feedback should inspire greater effort and a belief that through

hard work and practice more can be achieved.

The *Performance of Writing (POW)* framework provides a reliable and valid assessment tool. It is ambitious and detailed and is cross-referenced closely to the national curriculum, as well as building in extra and explicit smaller steps to move pupils from one stage to the next. Discrete and tangible statements have been developed that are appropriate for each year group.

POW has been designed with two components: one aspect is the teacher tool, with descriptive statements that aid the assessment of writing, and the other aspect is a pupil progress plan that supports the sharing of targets and managing guidance for pupils to continually improve. The statements are colour-coded in both the teacher assessment tool and the pupil targets, so there is a clear correlation between them. The POW framework supports the diagnosis of pupil progress and is layered into four judgement areas against specific age-related expectation criteria.

P	Progressing towards	Emerging Developing	A pupil who is working to grasp the key skills and competencies of that age expectation
O	On track	Secure Confident	A pupil who is working securely at expected level for their age
W	Way ahead	Exceeded Excelled	A pupil who demonstrates competence that is excellent for their age
D+	Greater depth	Depth Breadth Higher attaining	A pupil who is able to demonstrate depth and breadth of understanding of skills acquired by applying them in a range of cross curricular writing.

Performance of Writing assessment tool

The structure is numerically banded and benchmarked so there are clear cut-off points when pupils move from one phase within an age expectation to the next. This tool has been trialled in over 50 schools and development and feedback has ensured that it is a challenging tool that matches closely to the national curriculum higher expectations.

The POW framework runs from Foundation Stage to Year 6 and supports consistency

in assessment from Early Years to Year 6. Every attempt has been made to make it streamlined and easy to use.

What is the POW Framework?

The Performance of Writing approach is a comprehensive resource that enables teachers to track pupil progress in writing, related to age expectations. It is organised

Discussions are most useful when comparing work from same-age pupils. This comparative information is useful to gauge expectations.

for age expectation from the end of Foundation Stage all the way up to Year 6. The scale is easy to use and very manageable. It provides clear, accessible information about key aspects of writing that need to be targeted in relation to pupils' current writing achievements. Most importantly, the scale is designed to provide a positive assessment judgement for both pupils and parents. To achieve the highest attainment for pupils, the POW Framework must be used in conjunction with Writing Progress Plans.

How are judgements reached?

Pupils will be assessed against the relevant age expectations for writing. According to evidence in relation to specific targets, their final quantity achieved will yield an assessment. This assessment will be age-related and easily transferred into numerical data such as percentage scores or other 'out of 100' quotients. The judgement will be meaningful for teachers, parents and pupils. Outlined below is the language of the POW framework: positive and engaging for everyone:

P = Progressing towards

O = On track

W = Way ahead

Performance of Writing - Expected Standard at end of Foundation Stage POW!

	Aut 1	Aut 2	Spr 1	Spr 2	Sum 1	Sum 2
In some writing, usually with support						
Purpose and Impact						
Write in an interesting, engaging or thoughtful way.						
Talk about the part of the story/event that is interesting.						
Add detail orally to a story or an event or an experienced event.						
Arrange writing going from left to right, top to bottom.						
Produce texts which are appropriate to reader and purpose.						
Attempt writing for different purposes e.g. label, list.						
Invent own compositions but writing might need mediation.						
Structure and Shape						
Organise and present writing.						
Include character names in narrative and basic topic words in non-fiction.						
Write phrases about areas of interest.						
Group main ideas together through repeated nouns/pronouns.						
Sentence Structure						
Vary sentences for clarity, purpose and effect.						
Use pictures to yield more meaning to words.						
Write simple words and phrases.						
Conjunctions						
Add in joining words like 'and' when reading back writing.						
Writerly Techniques						
Deploy poetic style to engage the reader.						
Add onomatopoeic sounds to pictures e.g. Wheeeeeeee! Crash!						
Vocabulary						
Select appropriate and effective vocabulary.						
Use some 'yellow' ambitious vocabulary appropriately (see yellow Writing Progress Plan).						
Punctuation						
Write with technical accuracy of punctuation.						
Use full stops at random.						
May use a capital letter at the start of writing.						
Spelling and Word Structure						
Apply spelling rules into writing.						
Use phonic knowledge to begin to write CVC words e.g. cat.						
Correctly choose initial letters and some final letters.						
Read back work to give meaning to it.						
Broadly this will not influence judgement but this is the Year 1 benchmark						
Handwriting and presentation						
Form some recognisable letters.						
Sometimes leave 'finger' spaces between groups of letters.						

The Training Space

Terminology For Pupils	Aut 1	Aut 2	Spr 1	Spr 2	Sum 1	Sum 2
Phoneme						
Grapheme						
Digraph						
Trigraph						
Word						
Sentence						
Capital Letter						
Full Stop						

Effective Examples Of Writing Ideas

F						
A						
N						
T						
A						
S						
T						
I						
C						

Expected Standard Progression Key:

Please note two of the criteria need to be from the purpose and impact section.

Individual Marks		Overall Totals
	No/Little Evidence	0 - 3
P	Progressing Towards	4 -9
O	On Track	10 -14
W	Way Ahead	15 -21
D+		22 + = Greater Depth: Apply skills and competencies through a broader range of genres through cross-curricular writing opportunities and demonstrating through stamina-based independent writing. Pupils should show security and consolidation of particular skills in a wider range of writing tasks.

The Training Space

Performance of Writing - Expected Standard at end of Year 1

	Aut 1	Aut 2	Spr 1	Spr 2	Sum 1	Sum 2
In some writing, usually with support						
Purpose and Impact						
Write whole texts that are interesting, engaging or thoughtful.						
Form short narratives/retell short recounts.						
Use relevant words that are about my topic/story.						
Produce texts which are appropriate to reader and purpose.						
Know the purpose and the forms of some simple writing (labels, message, invitation).						
Structure and Shape						
Organise and present whole texts effectively that sequence and structure information.						
Include familiar storytelling language e.g. Once upon a time, One day, The end.						
Order some events using number/time sequence indicators e.g. Then I had lunch.						
Construct a cohesive piece with logical links/ breaks.						
Repeat key words to show meaning.						
Sentence Structure						
Vary sentences for clarity, purpose and effect.						
Write in simple phrases and clauses.						
Start sentences with the pronoun, 'I'.						
Start sentences with a name.						
Start sentences in a different way, e.g. Naughty Goldilocks ate the porridge.						
Tense						
Sometimes use the correct tense and maintain it.						
Conjunctions/Complex Sentences						
Use 'and' to join two words together.						
Use 'and' to join two clauses together.						
Writerly Techniques						
Deploy poetic style to engage the reader.						
Use onomatopoeic to grab the reader's attention e.g. Splash!						
Use alliteration to make the reading interesting e.g. The dark, deep cave.						
Vocabulary						
Select appropriate and effective vocabulary.						
Use simple speech - like words.						
Use some simple descriptive words (shape, colour, size, emotions).						
Use some 'blue' ambitious vocabulary (see blue Writing Progress Plan).						
Punctuation						
Write with technical accuracy of punctuation.						
Sometimes use capital letters, full stops, question marks and exclamation marks.						
Use capital letters for names and for the personal pronoun 'I'.						
Spelling and Word Structure						
Apply spelling rules into writing.						
Have a 'go' and spell some unknown words phonetically.						
Show evidence of using suffixes __ing, __ed, __est.						
Use the spelling rule for plural adding __s, __es.						
Use prefix un__ e.g. unkind.						
Broadly this will not influence judgement but this is the year 1 benchmark.						
Handwriting and presentation						
Form capital letters.						
Form digits 0-9.						
Begin to form lower-case letters in the correct direction, starting and finishing in the right place.						

The Training Space

© Jane Considine 2015

Terminology For Pupils

	Aut 1	Aut 2	Spr 1	Spr 2	Sum 1	Sum 2
Letter						
Capital Letter						
Word						
Singular						
Plural						
Punctuation						
Full Stop						
Question mark						
Exclamation mark						

Effective Examples Of Writing Ideas

		Aut 1	Aut 2	Spr 1	Spr 2	Sum 1	Sum 2
F							
A							
N							
T							
A							
S							
T							
I							
C							

Expected Standard Progression Key:

Please note two of the criteria need to be from the purpose and impact section.

Individual Marks		Overall Totals	
	No/Little Evidence	0 – 3	
P	Progressing Towards	4 – 9	
O	On Track	10 – 14	
W	Way Ahead	15 – 21	
D+		22 + =	Greater Depth: Apply skills and competencies through a broader range of genres through cross-curricular writing opportunities and demonstrating through stamina-based independent writing. Pupils should show security and consolidation of particular skills in a wider range of writing tasks.

Performance of Writing - Expected Standard at end of Year 2

	Aut 1	Aut 2	Spr 1	Spr 2	Sum 1	Sum 2
In some writing, usually with support						
Purpose and Impact						
Write whole texts that are interesting, engaging or thoughtful.						
Ideas are mostly suitable for a narrative.						
Sometimes the viewpoint is indicated by comments.						
Ideas are relevant for non-fiction e.g. informative points in a report, memories in a recount.						
Produce texts which are appropriate to reader and purpose.						
Include the main features of a genre/text type.						
Structure and Shape						
Organise and present whole texts effectively that sequence and structure information.						
Include enough information and description to interest the reader.						
Order writing using line breaks to show new ideas in narrative or use numbers in non-fiction.						
Construct a cohesive piece with logical links/ breaks.						
Group main ideas together.						
Sentence Structure						
Vary sentences for clarity, purpose and effect.						
Use sentences with different forms: statement, question, exclamation and command.						
Ask questions to the reader.						
Write sentences with adventurous adjectives.						
Write long sentences.						
Write short sentences.						
Start sentences in different ways from a name or personal pronoun, e.g. One bright morning...						
Include expanded noun phrases for description and specification e.g. The blue butterfly.						
Tense						
Use correct verb forms e.g. present; she is drumming, past; he was shouting.						
Apply correct tense across a piece of writing including progressive form to mark actions in progress e.g. they were jumping						
Conjunctions/Complex Sentences						
Write compound sentences that include co-ordination e.g. or, and, but.						
Write complex sentences that include subordination e.g. when, if, that, because.						
Writerly Techniques						
Deploy poetic style to engage the reader.						
Use rhyme for effect e.g. He was snoring and roaring.						
Use repetition in a basic way that follows story models e.g. run, run, as fast as you can.						
Vocabulary						
Select appropriate and effective vocabulary.						
Choose words appropriate to the writing.						
Construct sentences that include adjectives, adverbs and precise verbs.						
Use some 'purple' ambitious vocabulary (see purple Writing Progress Plan).						
Adverbs/adverbial phrases						
Begin sentences with an adverb/adverbial phrase and reposition in different places within the sentence e.g. 'ly' word, quickly						
Punctuation						
Write with technical accuracy of punctuation.						
Always use full stops.						
Use commas to separate items in a list.						
Use capital letters more than 50% of the time.						
Use apostrophes to mark missing letters in contracted forms e.g. I've, We'll.						
Use exclamation marks and question marks.						
Use the apostrophe to mark singular possession e.g. the girl's bag.						
Spelling and Word Structure						
Apply spelling rules into writing.						
Use phonetically plausible strategies to spell unknown polysyllabic words.						
Use suffixes such as ___ness, ___er, to form nouns or by compounding e.g. sleepiness.						
Use adjectives ending in ___ful, ___less, ___er, ___est e.g. beautiful.						
Turn adjectives into adverbs through applying 'ly' e.g. slowly						
Broadly this will not influence judgement but this is the year 2 benchmark						
Handwriting and presentation						
Form lower case letters of the correct size in relation to other letters.						
Start using some of the diagonal and horizontal strokes to join letters.						

The Training Space

Terminology For Pupils

	Aut 1	Aut 2	Spr 1	Spr 2	Sum 1	Sum 2
Noun						
Noun Phrase						
Statement						
Question						
Exclamation						
Command						
Compound						
Suffix						
Adjective						
Adverb						
Verb						
Tense (past, present)						
Apostrophe						
Comma						

Effective Examples Of Writing Ideas

F						
A						
N						
T						
A						
S						
T						
I						
C						

Expected Standard Progression Key:

Please note two of the criteria need to be from the purpose and impact section.

Individual Marks		Overall Totals	
	No/Little Evidence	0 - 3	
P	Progressing Towards	4 - 9	
O	On Track	10 - 14	
W	Way Ahead	15 - 21	
D+		22 + =	Greater Depth: Apply skills and competencies through a broader range of genres through cross-curricular writing opportunities and demonstrating through stamina-based independent writing. Pupils should show security and consolidation of particular skills in a wider range of writing tasks.

Performance of Writing - Expected Standard at end of Year 3

	Aut 1	Aut 2	Spr 1	Spr 2	Sum 1	Sum 2
In some writing, usually with support						
Purpose and Impact						
Write whole texts that are interesting, engaging or thoughtful.						
Develop multiple ideas in a story enriched with descriptive detail.						
Develop multiple ideas in non-fiction that are factual and precise.						
Express a basic viewpoint, an opinion or promote an idea e.g. I believe...						
Produce texts which are appropriate to reader and purpose.						
Maintain the main features of a genre/text type.						
Content makes sense throughout the piece.						
Structure and Shape						
Organise and present whole texts effectively that sequence and structure information.						
Strategies used to create flow e.g. pronouns, cohesive phrases, references back to previous point.						
Begin to understand what a paragraph is and show ideas grouped together.						
Construct a cohesive piece with logical links/ breaks.						
Use headings and sub-headings to group ideas.						
Opening signalled in narrative and non-fiction e.g. Early one morning..., Whales are the largest sea creatures...						
Closing signalled in narrative and non-fiction e.g. Eventually..., Ultimately...						
Sentence Structure						
Vary sentences for clarity, purpose and effect.						
Use one word in isolation to grab the reader's attention e.g. Stop!						
Add detail into descriptions e.g. precise words, descriptive noun phrases.						
Use prepositions that position in place/environment e.g. in, on, behind, under.						
Tense						
Use the present perfect form of verbs, instead of simple past e.g. 'He has gone out to play' contrasted with 'He went out to play'.						
Conjunctions/Complex Sentences						
Experiment with a widening range of conjunctions e.g. while, so, although.						
Writerly Techniques						
Deploy poetic style to engage the reader.						
Write sentences that use repetition of key words for impact e.g. He ran and ran. He ran until his bones ached.						
Use the word 'like' to build a simile e.g. Her eyes were like deep pools.						
Vocabulary						
Select appropriate and effective vocabulary.						
Choose words because of the effect they will have on the reader.						
Use some 'red' ambitious vocabulary (see red Writing Progress Plan).						
Adverbs/adverbial phrases						
Use adverbs/adverbial phrases that position in time e.g. then next, soon, later that day, as dawn broke.						
Use adverbs/adverbial phrases that build a relationship or 'cause' e.g. therefore, as a result.						
Punctuation						
Write with technical accuracy of punctuation.						
Emerging use of inverted commas to punctuate direct speech.						
Emerging use of other direct speech punctuation e.g. punctuation inside inverted commas.						
Spelling and Word Structure						
Apply spelling rules into writing.						
Use a range of prefixes to extend repertoire of nouns e.g. super___, anti___, auto___.						
Use 'a' or 'an' correctly according to next word beginning with consonant or vowel.						
Experiment with more complicated words built from a common word e.g. dissolve, solution.						
Broadly this will not influence judgement but this is the year 3 benchmark.						
Handwriting and presentation						
Use diagonal and horizontal strokes to join letters that are adjacent and know which are best left unjoined.						
Show increased legibility and quality to handwriting.						

Terminology For Pupils

	Aut 1	Aut 2	Spr 1	Spr 2	Sum 1	Sum 2
Preposition						
Conjunction						
Word family						
Prefix						
Clause						
Subordinate clause						
Direct speech						
Consonant						
Consonant letter						
Vowel						
Vowel letter						
Adverb						
Inverted commas (or "speech marks")						

Effective Examples Of Writing Ideas

F						
A						
N						
T						
A						
S						
T						
I						
C						

Expected Standard Progression Key:

Please note two of the criteria need to be from the purpose and impact section.

Individual Marks		Overall Totals
	No/Little Evidence	0 - 3
P	Progressing Towards	4 - 9
O	On Track	10 - 14
W	Way Ahead	15 - 21
D+		22 + = Greater Depth: Apply skills and competencies through a broader range of genres through cross-curricular writing opportunities and demonstrating through stamina-based independent writing. Pupils should show security and consolidation of particular skills in a wider range of writing tasks.

The Training Space

© Jane Considine 2015

Performance of Writing - Expected Standard at end of Year 4

	Aut 1	Aut 2	Spr 1	Spr 2	Sum 1	Sum 2
In some writing, usually with support						
Purpose and Impact						
Write whole texts that are interesting, engaging or thoughtful.						
Ideas are developed in detail (e.g. stories: in-depth description, non-fiction: anecdotes, facts and reflections.)						
Point of view is maintained throughout the work.						
Produce texts which are appropriate to reader and purpose.						
Include all the features of a genre/text type appropriately and consistently.						
Create narratives that create intrigue (e.g. suspense, cliff hangers) or non-fiction that is more complicated (e.g. contrasting ideas, opinions.)						
Structure and Shape						
Organise and present whole texts effectively that sequence and structure information.						
Structure and organise writing with a clear beginning, middle and end.						
Write sentences that are developed on from previous sentences to form a group of connected/ related ideas.						
Start a new paragraph to organise ideas around a theme.						
Construct a cohesive piece with logical links/ breaks.						
Use appropriate choice of pronoun or noun within and across sentences to aid cohesion and avoid repetition.						
Openings signalled in narrative and non-fiction with content to capture reader's interest.						
Closings signalled in narrative that is dramatic or link back to opening and in non-fiction is strong/ draw conclusions.						
Sentence Structure						
Vary sentences for clarity, purpose and effect.						
Ask rhetorical questions to heighten reader engagement e.g. Can we honestly believe...?						
Use more complicated noun phrases (expanded by modifying adjectives, nouns and preposition phrases) e.g. The strict geography teacher with slick, black hair.						
Tense						
Use standard English verb inflections e.g. 'we were...' , 'I did...' (instead of local spoken forms such as 'we was ', 'I done ')						
Conjunctions/Complex Sentences						
Use a widening range of conjunctions e.g. while, so, although.						
Use more complicated conjunctions that set up contrast or relationships e.g. despite, nevertheless, consequently.						
Writerly Techniques						
Deploy poetic style to engage the reader						
Use the word 'as' to build a simile e.g. the train was as slow as a hearse.						
Use metaphor to create vivid images in the reader's mind.						
Vocabulary						
Select appropriate and effective vocabulary.						
Make language choices that are interesting and varied.						
Use some 'orange' ambitious vocabulary (see orange Writing Progress Plan).						
Adverbs/adverbial phrases						
Use 'where' adverbial phrases in fronted position in sentences e.g. At the seaside, Janice fed the seagulls.						
Use 'how' 'ly' adverbs and '___ing' adverbial phrases in fronted position in sentences e.g. Rushing against the clock, Jack knew it would be difficult.						
Punctuation						
Write with technical accuracy of punctuation.						
Correct use of inverted commas and other punctuation to indicate direct speech (comma after reporting clause; end punctuation within commas.) e.g. The teacher screamed, "Be quiet!"						
Use apostrophes to mark plural possession e.g. The boy's name, the boys' names.						
Use comma after fronted adverbial.						
Spelling and Word Structure						
Apply spelling rules into writing.						
Use knowledge of phonics, morphology and etymology to spell new and unfamiliar words.						
Distinguish between the spelling of common homophones.						
Show through ' -s' and punctuation the grammatical difference between plural and possessive.						
Broadly this will not influence judgement but this is the year 4 benchmark.						
Handwriting and presentation						
Show consistency in style ensuring that the downstrokes of letters are parallel and equidistant.						
Avoid ascenders and descenders touching each other from one line to the next.						

Terminology For Pupils

	Aut 1	Aut 2	Spr 1	Spr 2	Sum 1	Sum 2
Determiner						
Pronoun						
Possessive pronoun						
Adverbial						

Effective Examples Of Writing Ideas

F						
A						
N						
T						
A						
S						
T						
I						
C						

Expected Standard Progression Key:

Please note two of the criteria need to be from the purpose and impact section.

Individual Marks		Overall Totals
	No/Little Evidence	0 - 3
P	Progressing Towards	4 - 9
O	On Track	10 - 14
W	Way Ahead	15 - 21
D+		22 + = Greater Depth: Apply skills and competencies through a broader range of genres through cross-curricular writing opportunities and demonstrating through stamina-based independent writing. Pupils should show security and consolidation of particular skills in a wider range of writing tasks.

Performance of Writing - Expected Standard at end of Year 5

	Aut 1	Aut 2	Spr 1	Spr 2	Sum 1	Sum 2
In some writing, usually with support						
Purpose and Impact						
Write whole texts that are interesting, engaging or thoughtful.						
Ideas are developed in narrative and in non-fiction.						
Point of view is clear and controlled with some elaboration.						
Produce texts which are appropriate to reader and purpose.						
Execute a text type/genre by including all features or adapt when required.						
Create more complicated narratives e.g. parallel plot, flashback, parody and more controlled non-fictions e.g. language choices support the purpose.						
Structure and Shape						
Organise and present whole texts effectively that sequence and structure information.						
Structure and organise writing with pace in narrative and supporting evidence in non-fiction.						
Start new paragraphs to show changes in time, place, event or person.						
Construct a cohesive piece with logical links/ breaks.						
Use devices to build cohesion within paragraphs e.g. then, after, that, this, firstly.						
Link ideas across paragraphs using a range of devices e.g. phrases that back reference previous points.						
Sentence Structure						
Vary sentences for clarity, purpose and effect.						
Create different emphasis in sentences through word order and noun phrases.						
Mix short and long sentences to change, accelerate or show pace for reader.						
Tense						
Deploy tense choices that support cohesion by making links e.g. he had seen her before.						
Use modal verbs to show something is certain, probable or possible (or not) e.g. might, should, will, must.						
Conjunctions/Complex Sentences						
Use relative clauses within complex sentences beginning with who, which, where, when, whose, that. e.g. Maisie, who was extremely tired, finished the race.						
Use verbs ending in 'ed' or 'ing' to start clauses to build complex sentences e.g. Mortified by what he saw, Harry fled the scene.						
Writerly Techniques						
Deploy poetic style to engage the reader.						
Use pathetic fallacy to mirror and extend character's emotions e.g.(aspect of nature or weather reflects feeling).						
Use pun to enhance the double meaning of language e.g. The cheetah, a predatory cheater of the jungle.						
Vocabulary						
Select appropriate and effective vocabulary.						
Some vocabulary choices are for effect or emphasis e.g. technical terminology, vivid language.						
Use some 'green' ambitious vocabulary (see green Writing Progress Plan).						
Adverbs/adverbial phrases.						
Indicate degree of possibility using adverbs e.g. perhaps, surely.						
Use a range of adverbs to link ideas: adverbs of time e.g. later, adverbs of place e.g. nearby and number e.g. secondly.						
Punctuation						
Write with technical accuracy of punctuation.						
Use brackets, dashes or commas to indicate parenthesis.						
Use commas to clarify meaning or avoid ambiguity e.g. 'Let's eat dad.' or 'Let's eat, dad.'						
Spelling and Word Structure						
Apply spelling rules into writing.						
Convert nouns or adjectives into verbs using suffixes e.g. ___ate, ___ise, ___ify.						
Apply prefixes to change intent of verbs e.g. dis___, de___, mis___, over___, re___.						
Broadly this will not influence judgement but this is the year 5 benchmark						
Handwriting and presentation						
Make quick choices whether or not to join specific letters.						
Use a style that encourages speed, legibility and fluency.						

The Training Space

Terminology For Pupils

	Aut 1	Aut 2	Spr 1	Spr 2	Sum 1	Sum 2
Modal verb						
Relative pronoun						
Relative clause						
Parenthesis						
Bracket						
Dash						
Cohesion						
Ambiguity						

Effective Examples Of Writing Ideas

F						
A						
N						
T						
A						
S						
T						
I						
C						

Expected Standard Progression Key:

Please note two of the criteria need to be from the purpose and impact section.

Individual Marks		Overall Totals
☐	No/Little Evidence	0 - 3
P	Progressing Towards	4 -9
O	On Track	10 -14
W	Way Ahead	15 -21
D+		22 + – Greater Depth: Apply skills and competencies through a broader range of genres through cross-curricular writing opportunities and demonstrating through stamina-based independent writing. Pupils should show security and consolidation of particular skills in a wider range of writing tasks.

Performance of Writing - Expected Standard at end of Year 6

	Aut 1	Aut 2	Spr 1	Spr 2	Sum 1	Sum 2
In some writing, usually with support						
Purpose and Impact						
Write whole texts that are interesting, engaging or thoughtful.						
Manipulates reader through the telling of a narrative e.g. Use of humour or controls the direction of non-fiction through a range of strategies e.g. persuasive devices.						
Convey a convincing viewpoint using the point of view of others to support or contrast writers own opinion.						
Produce texts which are appropriate to reader and purpose.						
Choose style/genre features to maintain and challenge the reader's interest e.g. elaborate detail in narrative or succinctness in police report.						
Adapt well known genres to create different effects e.g. fairytales with a twist exploring new viewpoint.						
Structure and Shape						
Organise and present whole texts effectively that sequence and structure information.						
Navigate a reader through a text in a logical, chronological way or subvert this e.g. flash forward, opposing viewpoint.						
Use a range of layout devices e.g. headings, sub-headings, columns, bullets, tables etc.						
Construct a cohesive piece with logical links/ breaks.						
Link ideas across paragraphs using a wider range of cohesive devices e.g. repetition of word or phrase, use of ellipsis as cliffhanger at end of section.						
Apply paragraphs across a whole text to support the 'ease of engagement' for the reader.						
Sentence Structure						
Vary sentences for clarity, purpose and effect.						
Write informally or formally appropriate to genre/ text type.						
Vary the types of sentences within a piece across simple, compound and complex constructions.						
Tense						
Use the subjunctive form of the verb to emphasise formality, urgency or importance e.g. The teacher insists that her pupils be on time.						
Passive Voice						
Use passive voice to affect the presentation of information in a sentence e.g. The window in the greenhouse was broken.						
Conjunctions/Complex Sentences						
Use a range of complex construction strategies to build subordinating clauses with verb starts ending in 'ing', 'ed' or adverbs 'ly' followed by verbs, relative clauses and subordinating conjunction starts.						
Writerly Techniques						
Deploy poetic style to engage the reader.						
Use personification to give human attributes to inanimate objects/things.						
Use symbolism as a recurring idea to emphasise a themed motif e.g. ongoing referencing to water.						
Vocabulary						
Select appropriate and effective vocabulary.						
Use varied and precise vocabulary to create particular stylistic effects.						
Use some 'pink' ambitious vocabulary (See Pink Writing Progress Plan)						
Adverbs/adverbial phrases.						
Use more complicated adverbial phrases to link ideas e.g. on the other hand, in contrast, as a consequence.						
Use adverbs and adverbial phrases to qualify, intensify or emphasise e.g. 'The dog is so incredibly stupid', '... an exceptional result.'						
Punctuation						
Write with technical accuracy of punctuation.						
Use semi-colon, colon and dash to mark the boundary between independent clauses e.g. It's snowing; I am delighted.						
Use of the colon to introduce a list and use of semi-colons within lists.						
Use bullet points to list information.						
Use hyphens to avoid ambiguity e.g. recover or re-cover.						
Spelling and Word Structure						
Apply spelling rules into writing.						
Use the appropriate words according to formality e.g. 'discover' or 'find out', 'ask for' or request' or 'go in' or 'enter'.						
Discover synonyms and antonyms for a word and choose the degree of meaning required for the sentence.						
Broadly this will not influence judgement but this is the year 6 benchmark						
Handwriting and presentation.						
Write speedily in a joined, legible style.						
Choose the right handwriting style according to purpose e.g. neat and joined for final version and unjoined for labelling a diagram or data.						

The Training Space

Terminology For Pupils

	Aut 1	Aut 2	Spr 1	Spr 2	Sum 1	Sum 2
Subject						
Object						
Active						
Passive						
Synonym						
Antonym						
Ellipsis						
Hyphen						
Colon						
Semi-colon						
Bullet points						

Effective Examples Of Writing Ideas

F						
A						
N						
T						
A						
S						
T						
I						
C						

Expected Standard Progression Key :

Please note two of the criteria need to be from the purpose and impact section.

Individual Marks		Overall Totals
	No / Little Evidence	0 - 3
P	Progressing Towards	4 -9
O	On Track	10 -14
W	Way Ahead	15 -21
D+		22 + = Greater Depth : Apply skills and competencies through a broader range of genres through cross-curricular writing opportunities and demonstrating through stamina based independent writing. Pupils should show security and consolidation of particular skills in a wider range of writing task.

Verbal Feedback is really powerful and pupils connect quickly with writerly advice from their teacher.

Writing progress plans for pupils

Alongside the detailed POW framework, there are related pupil Writing Progress Plans. These are excellent for children as the summary target statements are captured succinctly in one colourful place and keep pupils focused on the most important aspects to accelerate writing.

The language to be shared with parents is positively loaded, even if under-attainment is occurring. The associated Writing Progress Plans provide good information for parents and can be annotated by class teachers to show which aspects have been achieved and which aspects still need work.

Ultimately, these child-friendly pupil progress plans can be tailored to pupils' needs and will foster a culture of support and challenge, as well as providing clarity to pupils about exactly what is needed to improve.

All writing progress plans come with a recommended ambitious words list for different pupils. To purchase, please visit www.thetrainingspace.co.uk

How can writing progress be accelerated

Pupils of all ages have informally fed back to say that they have enjoyed working with the Writing Progress Plans because they show everything that needs to be done to achieve age-expectations and motivate them to 'get on with it'.

"Feedback allows them to track performance in relation to their goals so that adjustments in effort, direction and even strategy can be made as needed."
What makes great pedagogy? Nine claims from research, Chris Husbands and Jo Pearce

Once pupils have clear, assigned goals, their confidence to achieve them improves. Through 'knowing what to do next to get better', self-sufficiency improves and this enables them to independently control personal development.

The POW tool has been designed with the intent of it being as clear as possible, and care has been taken in the language used to avoid adverbs or constructions that might be ambiguous. Daisy Christodoulou, author of *Seven Myths about Education*, is against descriptive statements for assessment due to the wealth of interpretation and amount of differing responses they could elicit. One of the biggest problems with

Pupils like to know where they are in their writing and the next small steps they need to get better.

descriptive statements, she states, are the adjectives and adverbs used within them:

"adverbs are extremely vague and their meaning lies in the eye of the beholder."

Criteria, appearing to be such a clear-cut system, are in actual fact very malleable and fluid and are at risk of causing confusion or misjudgement. Daisy suggests questions of the closed variety are more likely to yield accurate judgements. As an English specialist, I stand by the belief that the nature of English means that some aspects can be tracked on a continuum and others are about the beauty of application in timely and convincing ways. Questions or statements? Statements or questions? Both formats, I believe are open to misinterpretation or a wide manner of interpretations in English written work due to its multifaceted orchestration of a range of skills applied through one genre or text type. Nonetheless, as a profession with choice at our disposal, we need something to begin to carve an assessment-without-levels pathway to making judgements. Ofsted does not expect to see any particular system of assessment. Ofsted will consider the consistency of the assessment system to make judgements about pupil progress and attainment. Within the inspectorate framework, special mention is given to both the 'accuracy' and 'impact' of assessment, in particular when it is seen to modify teaching to enable pupils to achieve their potential.

The most important component of assessment is that we have a clear view of expectations for different age groups. The heart of the matter for benchmarking is knowing how descriptors translate into real written work. Once we have a portfolio of written evidence of pupil capabilities, at different ages, then this will ultimately yield a sense of how to make judgements using a comparative scale of what is realistic for 4-year-olds to 11-year-olds to produce independently.

Writing portfolios

One of our current challenges is knowing what excellence looks like in writing for different age groups against the national curriculum requirements. Banks of pupil writing that are collated from our own schools are a great starting point. Once this evidence bank begins to build, then cross-referencing this writing with other evidence from similar schools develops discussion about the real possibilities for writing outcomes. Finally, once these are then compared with national exemplars, as a profession we can begin to have a sharper view of expectations. It is through this real compilation of work that progress can be defined and conceived in a concrete way. Portfolios of this nature will help to clarify expectations for year groups, as well as for senior managers, about the capabilities of pupils — and make high expectations a matter of course. Exemplar material is necessary to dispel uncertainty about benchmarks and provides a definition of quality for all those involved in teaching and learning. Exemplification material produced by the Department for Education is an excellent place to start to establish a communal understanding of expectations for the profession.

Foundation Stage Age Expectations for Writing

Yellow Writing Progress Plan

Conjunctions / Complex Sentences

I can add in 'and' when reading back. ☐

Writer's Techniques

I can add in sound words e.g. *Crash!* ☐

FEELING · ASKING · NOTICING
TOUCHING · ACTION · SMELLING
TASTING · IMAGINING · CHECKING

Structure and Shape

I can include character names in stories and 'I' in recount. ☐

I can write ideas about things I like. ☐

Purpose and Impact

I can talk about a story or about an event. ☐

I can add detail when I retell. ☐

I can write left to right. ☐

I can write in different ways e.g. *label, invitation.* ☐

I can invent writing ideas. ☐

Spelling

I can write some CVC words e.g. *cat, dog.* ☐

I can choose the right letters at the beginnings of words. ☐

I can read back my work. ☐

Vocabulary

I can use yellow ambitious words in my writing. ☐

Sentence Structure

I can use pictures to add meaning. ☐

I can write some words and phrases. ☐

Year One Age Expectations for Writing

Blue Writing Progress Plan

Punctuation

I try to use capital letters, full stops, question and exclamation marks. ☐

I can use capital letters for names and 'I'. ☐

Writer's Techniques

I can use onomatopoeia e.g. Splash! ☐

I can use alliteration e.g. ...big, blue bucket. ☐

Conjunctions / Complex Sentences

I can use 'and' to join two words together. ☐

I can use 'and' to join two clauses together. ☐

Vocabulary

I can use speech-like words. ☐

I can describe shape, colour, size, emotion. ☐

I can use blue ambitious words in my writing. ☐

Spelling

I can 'have a go' at spelling unknown words. ☐

I can use -ing, -ed and -est at the end of words. ☐

I can use plurals -es and -s. ☐

I can use a prefix un- e.g. unkind. ☐

Purpose and Impact

I can write stories and recounts. ☐

I can use topic words. ☐

I know why different writing is important. ☐

Structure and Shape

I can include story words e.g. Once upon a time... ☐

I can order writing using numbers, time, words, phrases. ☐

I can repeat key words. ☐

Sentence Structure

I can write simple phrases/clauses. ☐

I can start sentences with 'I'. ☐

I can start sentences with a name. ☐

I can start sentences in different ways. ☐

Tense

I can use the right tense. ☐

POW 1

© Jane Considine 2015

Year Two Age Expectations for Writing

Purple Writing Progress Plan

Punctuation
- I can use full stops.
- I can use commas in a list.
- I can use capital letters.
- I can use apostrophes in words like *can't*, *we'll*, *should've*.
- I can use exclamation and question marks.
- I can use an apostrophe to show singular belonging to e.g. *the girl's bag*.

Spelling
- I can 'have a go' at spelling polysyllabic words.
- I can use suffixes such as _ness, _er or compounds to create nouns.
- I can use adjectives ending in _ful, _less, _er, _est e.g. beautiful.
- I can turn adjectives into adverbs using 'ly' e.g. 'slow' into 'slowly'.

Purpose and Impact
- My ideas are interesting for stories.
- My ideas are factual for non-fiction.
- I sometimes include my view in writing.
- I can include key features in my writing.

Adverbs/ Adverbial Phrases
- I can use 'ly' adverbs in different positions in a sentence e.g. quickly, carefully.

Conjunctions / Complex Sentences
- I can write compound sentences that include 'or', 'and', 'but', 'so'.
- I can use 'when', 'if', 'because' and 'that' in my sentences.

Vocabulary
- I can choose appropriate words for my writing.
- I can write sentences that include adjectives and adverbs.
- I can use purple ambitious words in my writing.

Sentence Structure
- I can use statements, questions, exclamations and commands.
- I can ask the reader a question.
- I can include adventurous adjectives e.g. not colour or repetitive.
- I can write long sentences.
- I can write short sentences.
- I can start sentences in different ways e.g. One day...
- I can include noun phrases e.g. big, red.

Writer's Techniques
- I can use rhyme for effect e.g. Sally was slipping and flipping.
- I can use repetition that follows story patterns e.g. jump, jump as high as you can.

FEELING   ASKING   NOTICING

TOUCHING   ACTION   SMELLING

TASTING   IMAGINING   CHECKING

Structure and Shape
- I can include information and description to interest the reader.
- I can order my writing using line breaks and numbers.
- I can group main ideas together.

Tense
- I can use present and past tense e.g. is drumming, was shouting.
- I can show actions in progress e.g. they were jumping.

Year Three Age Expectations for Writing

Red Writing Progress Plan

Punctuation

I can begin to use inverted commas to punctuate direct speech. ☐

I can begin to include other direct speech punctuation e.g. comma, capital letter. ☐

Conjunctions / Complex Sentences

I can use a widening range of conjuctions e.g. while, so, although. ☐

Vocabulary

I can choose words because they create effect. ☐

I can use some red ambitious words in my writing. ☐

FEELING   ASKING   NOTICING
TOUCHING   ACTION   SMELLING
TASTING   IMAGINING CHECKING

Spelling

I can use prefixes accurately to build new nouns e.g. anticlimax. ☐

I can use 'an' and 'a' correctly before a word beginning with a consonant or vowel. ☐

I can experiment using more complicated words from a common word e.g. dissolve. ☐

Adverbs/ Adverbial Phrases

I can use adverbs/adverbial phrases that indicate position in time e.g. next, soon, later that day, as dusk fell. ☐

I can use adverbs/adverbial phrases that build a relationship or cause e.g. therefore, as a result. ☐

Structure and Shape

I can create flow by using pronouns, linking phrases and referencing points already made. ☐

I can group ideas together and sometimes create paragraphs. ☐

I can use headings and sub-headings. ☐

I can use openings in stories and non-fiction e.g. 'Early one morning...', 'Whales are the largest creatures.' ☐

I can use closings in stories and non-fiction e.g. Eventually..., Ultimately... ☐

Writer's Techniques

I can use repetition of key words for impact e.g. He stopped. Stopped, really still. ☐

I can use 'like' to build a simile e.g. her eyes were like deep pools. ☐

Purpose and Impact

I can write 2 to 3 story sentences on one idea. ☐

I can write 2 to 3 non-fiction sentences on one idea. ☐

I can express my viewpoint e.g. I believe... ☐

I can include the main features of a story/text type. ☐

I can ensure my writing makes sense. ☐

Sentence Structure

I can use one word in isolation to grab the reader's attention e.g. Stop! ☐

I can add increasing detail into descriptions e.g. precise verbs, descriptive noun phrases. ☐

I can use prepositions that indicate position in a place or an environment e.g. in, on, behind, under. ☐

Tense

I can use present perfect verbs e.g. He has gone to the shops. ☐

POW 3

© Jane Considine 2015

Year Four Age Expectations for Writing

Orange Writing Progress Plan

Punctuation

I can use all correct direct speech punctuation e.g. inverted commas, commas, new line etc. ☐

I can mark plural possession using an apostrophe e.g. The boys' names. ☐

I can use a comma after a fronted adverbial. ☐

Tense

I can use standard English verbs e.g. I did, we were. ☐

Vocabulary

I can make interesting and varied language choices. ☐

I can use orange ambitious words in my writing. ☐

FEELING · ASKING · NOTICING
· ACTION · SMELLING
TASTING · IMAGINING · CHECKING

Spelling

I can use a range of techniques to spell unfamiliar words. ☐

I can spell homophones correctly according to use e.g. their, there, too, to. ☐

I can show the difference in writing between plural and possessive with _s punctuation. ☐

Adverbs/ Adverbial Phrases

I can use fronted 'where/when' adverbial phrases e.g. As dawn broke, the scarecrow cried. ☐

I can use 'how' adverbs and adverbial phrases in fronted positions e.g. Worrying about the crash, Roger raced home. ☐

Structure and Shape

I can organise my writing with a clear beginning, middle and end. ☐

I can write sentences that lead on from a previous sentence. ☐

I can start a new paragraph organising ideas around a theme. ☐

I can use pronouns and nouns within and across sentences to aid readability. ☐

I can use exciting openings to capture the reader's attention. ☐

I can use dramatic endings in stories and strong conclusions in non-fiction. ☐

Writer's Techniques

I can use 'as' to build a simile e.g. The train was as slow as a hearse. ☐

I can use metaphors to create vivid images. ☐

Purpose and Impact

I can add detail to my ideas. ☐

I can maintain a point of view. ☐

I can include all the features of a genre/text type appropriately. ☐

I can create intriguing narratives and more complicated non-fictions e.g. persuasive leaflet. ☐

Sentence Structure

I can ask rhetorical questions to involve the reader. ☐

I can use more complicated noun phrases e.g. The beautiful lady with the yellow bun. ☐

Conjunctions / Complex Sentences

I can use a larger range of conjunctions accurately e.g. while, although. ☐

I can use conjunctions to set up contrasts or relationships e.g. despite, nevertheless, consequently. ☐

POW 4

© Jane Considine 2015

Year Five Age Expectations for Writing

Green Writing Progress Plan

Punctuation
I can use brackets, dashes or commas to indicate parenthesis.

I can use commas to clarify meaning or avoid ambiguity e.g. 'Let's eat Grandad.' or 'Let's eat, Grandad.'.

Vocabulary
I can use particular vocabulary for effect or emphasis e.g. technical terminology, vivid language.

I can use green ambitious words in my writing.

Tense
I can use tense choices to support cohesion e.g. He had seen her before.

I can use modal verbs e.g. might, should, will, must.

Purpose and Impact
I can develop imaginative and logical ideas.

I can make a clear point of view and elaborate.

I can include all genre features or adapt deliberately.

I can create complicated narratives and non-fictions.

Spelling
I can use suffixes to convert nouns and adjectives into verbs e.g. _ate, _ise, _ify.

I can use prefixes to change intent of verb e.g. dis_, de_, mis_, over_ and re_.

Structure and Shape
I can organise my writing so it reflects different paces in story or evidence in non-fiction.

I can start a new paragraph to show change in time, place, event or person.

I can use words and phrases to build links within paragraphs e.g. then, after, that, this.

I can link ideas across paragraphs by making references back to original points.

Writer's Techniques
I can use pathetic fallacy to mirror a character's emotions in nature/weather e.g. She shook under the heavy covers as the fog suffocated the garden.

I can use puns to create humour and intrigue in my writing.

FEELING   ASKING   NOTICING
TOUCHING   ACTION   SMELLING
TASTING   IMAGINING   CHECKING

Adverbs/ Adverbial Phrases
I can use degree of possibility adverbs e.g. perhaps, surely.

I can use adverbs of time e.g. later, adverbs of place e.g. nearby and number e.g. secondly.

Conjunctions / Complex Sentences
I can use relative clauses beginning with 'who', 'which', 'where', 'when', 'whose', 'that' e.g. John, who was sad, dragged his feet.

I can use verbs ending in _ed or _ing to start clauses to build complex sentences.

Sentence Structure
I can create different emphasis through the word order and choice in sentences.

I can mix short and long sentences to change the pace for the reader.

POW 5

© Jane Considine 2015

Year Six Age Expectations for Writing

Pink Writing Progress Plan

Punctuation

I can use semi-colon, colon and dash to show independent clauses.

I can use a colon to introduce a list and a semi-colon within a list.

I can use bullet points to list information.

I can use hyphens to avoid ambiguity e.g. recover or re-cover.

Adverbs/ Adverbial Phrases

I can use adverbial phrases to link ideas e.g. on the other hand, in contrast.

I can use adverbs and adverbial phrases to qualify, intensify or emphasise e.g. incredibly, exceptional.

FEELING   ASKING   NOTICING

ACTION   SMELLING

TASTING   IMAGINING   CHECKING

Conjunctions / Complex Sentences

I can use all five main ways of creating a complex sentence.

1. _ed verb start subordinate clause.

2. _ing verb start subordinate clause.

3. _ly adverb followed by verb subordinate clause.

4. Embedded relative clause.

5. Subordinating conjunction at start or middle e.g. despite, nevertheless.

Vocabulary

I can use precise vocabulary for desired effects.

I can use pink ambitious vocabulary in my writing.

Purpose and Impact

I can tell a story with imaginative flair and with control and direction in non-fiction.

I can convey a convincing viewpoint using another's point of view to support or contrast my own.

I can challenge the reader's interest through style and feature choices.

I can manipulate well-known genres for different effects.

Writer's Techniques

I can use personification e.g. The trees trembled with fear as the furious fog descended.

I can use a recurring symbol e.g. ongoing comparison / referring to jewellery.

Tense

I can use the subjunctive form e.g. The teacher insists that you are on time.

Structure and Shape

I can navigate a reader through a text in a logical way or change this deliberately e.g. flashforward or opposing viewpoints.

I can use a range of layout devices e.g. columns, bullets, tables etc.

I can consistently use paragraphs across the whole text.

I can link ideas across paragraphs using a wide range of devices e.g. repetition of words, ellipsis at the end of a section.

Passive Voice

I can use passive voice to hide the 'doer' of the action e.g. The gun was removed from the cabinet.

Spelling

I can use appropriate formal synonyms for informal words. e.g. 'find out', 'to discover'.

I can choose the correct shade of meaning word from a range of antonyms and synonyms.

Sentence Structure

I can choose whether to be formal or informal in my writing.

I can use a range of simple, compound and complex sentences.

Consider

Assessing a piece of writing using the Performance of Writing Framework. This will enable you to look closely at what a pupil can or can't do in terms of their writing competency. The results will reveal aspects of the writing process that are weak and need more targeted support for teaching.

Personalised targets for pupils can be carved up from the Performance of Writing Framework and identified for them using the associated Writing Progress Plans.

School Impact Points

Reflect on the current assessment tool you use for writing:

① Does it give enough information to you, as a teacher, about providing the next steps of development for the pupils?

② Does your current assessment tool reflect the Three Zones of Writing? Many assessment tools in schools are too grammar-focused and do not give enough recognition to the flair and ideas of writing.

Zeb, Year 6

Appendix

Examples of pupil work from Long Buckby Junior School show the impact of teaching the Three Zones of Writing.

Independent writing

Year 3

An example of writing from a Year 3 pupil before being taught the Three Zones of Writing

'The Clocktower' (page 331)

An example of writing from the same Year 3 pupil after being taught the Three Zones of Writing.

'Escape from Pompeii' (page 332)

Years 5 and 6

An example of writing from a Year 5 pupil before being taught the Three Zones of Writing.

'A letter from the trenches' (page 333)

An example of writing from the same pupil, now in 6, after being taught the Three Zones of Writing.

'A letter from Beowulf' (page 334)

Thank you to Lynn Newbery for sharing the progress made by these pupils in their writing.

Year 3

Friday 11 September

The clock tower

Once upon a time there was a girl who was dancing and twirling around, to time colur. One day she went to the window and opened it. She looks out there and reached for a grey balloon.

When she went outside the time and colur stoped she walked thurther up and touched a balloon. Everything was black and white. She probaly felt sad and annoyyed, so she went back in the clock tower.

When she got back she got back in she probaly felt locked up. It was the same Augisn every day. Then she started twirling and dancing again.

Pupil work before being introduced to the Three Zones of Writing.

Long Buckby Junior School. Year 3: September.

Thursday 10th December

Escape from Pompeii

Once on a sunny day in Pompeii, there was a tiny rumble. The ground shook and most of the windows clattered. NoWone knew what was going on. "Oh dont worry," shouted Franio. "Its just that silly old volcano," he said. Everyone carried on because it had happened before. The animals panicked a little bit but still carried on.

18 hours later they heard an angrier grumble like a motercycle. Bang! A humungous rock came rolling down the volcano and smashed on the floor. There were Lava Lakes pouring down the side of the volcano. The volcano was spitting Lava out Like Fireworks. Crash! Boulders were hitting the buildings. It was striking with a terrible rage. It covered the city by minute. They Lava disolved everything in there sight. Ash was floating around in the air like stars. Half of the volcano was blown of. Everything in sight was destroyed.

Impact of The Write Stuff System
Pupil work after being taught through The Three Zones of Writing.

Long Buckby Junior School. Year 3: December.

<u>Thursday 11th September</u>

<u>A letter from the trenches</u>

Dearest Connie,

I write to you in a much happier frame of mind because something wonderful has just happened that I must tell you about at once.

All these years i've been in the war fighting for our country and I have good news...... I'm coming home! Me and the gang are in our tank and we are on are way. Hopefully the Germans have decided not to create another world war but on the other hand I am still alive, so I should be home soon. I am sure you are very pleased that I am still alive.

Love you lots

Jim

Pupil work before being introduced to the Three Zones of Writing.

Long Buckby Junior School. Year 5: September.

Friday 27th November

A letter from Beowulf

My Dearest King Hrothgar,

It is I, the almighty Beowulf, writing to inform you that I stand and victorious against the monster well known as Grendel. I'm sure you want to hear what happened and I'm happy to share it.

What happened in Heorot is hard to explain to the but I'll do my best to. We all slept as we waited for Grendel to come. I could hear him swiftly swiftly sprinting throug the moores, readying himself for another terror raid. So he thought! Although Grendel burst through the doors, not one of us even flinched. Poor Handscio was his first victim. Grendel simply grinded each limb x, sucked on his rib-cage and sucked on his skull until his brain was in Grendel's putrid jaw. Handscio was like a brother to me in a way. I assumed he thought this raid would be easy but no. I was next. Before Grendel Grendel could even touch me, I locked onto his arm. & I gripped onto the x dirty, scaly arm as much as I could, twisting and turning until the bone joints burst, the shoulder muscles split apart, the tendons snapped and Grendel's arm was torn off. Blood was drained draining rapidly from his body as he let out a cacophonus like screech Grendel ran back to his lair where he would eventually die

Because I have banished this demon, you and the queen may return to the kingdom in safety. I have restored

Impact of The Write Stuff System.
Pupil work after being taught through The Three Zones of Writing.

Long Buckby Junior School. Year 6: November.

peace and happiness in your kingdom. I ❤ hope I see you again in matter that when you return to your kingdom I will be home again.

Your faithful companion,
Beowulf

Impact of The Write Stuff System.
Pupil work after being taught through The Three Zones of Writing.

Long Buckby Junior School. Year 6: November.

Examples of Year 6 pupil work from Wollaston Community Primary School in Northamptonshire. The unit of work was based on the Disney film 'Paperman'.

Independent writing

Three narratives are included here from:

▶ Jasmine

▶ Anais

▶ Luke

The standards are high and there is evidence that these three pupils are working at greater depth at Key Stage 2.

Thank you to Alison Pullin for sharing pupil work taught through a sentence-stacking approach, targeting the "Three Zones of Writing'.

Jasmine

Motionless Malcom stood still. Bored out of his mind he waited on the dusty old train platform. Whoosh! Went the trains behind malcom. Clutching hold to his precious, organised files. Malcom looked blank. Dressed in his coal black suit and his blood red tie he prepared himself to board the next train. Sighing deeply Malcom looked down at his shiny shoes sighing once again. Now looking at his files Malcom began to think about a white cloud floating across a summers sky. He had only just realised the world was flashing by his eyes. Sadness was in malcom's heart and it was filling it quickly.

In the distance Malcom could hear the ear bleeding screech of the train's wheels coming to a squeaky stop on the track. Then suddenly he heard a faint rhythmic tap of a woman coming towards him. Malcom turned to see an astounding lady infront of him. His jaw dropped, his eyes popped and then his heart skipped a beat. Swept off his feet Malcom asked himself. Am I in love? Everything was silent Malcom could smell a waft of the lady's perfume. He now knew for sure he was in love, her blue dress was beautiful, her heels were amazing and her eyes twinkled in the summer day light.

Rapidly a green train rushed along the rusty old track. Malcom turned around on his heels. He once again saw the gorgeous girl standing infront of him. Suddenly a tornado filled with fear struck against Malcom. Clenching hold to his files he shut his eyes expecting the worst. Sneakily a piece of paper slithered out of the file Malcom was holding, h had never felt so embarassed (but yet in a way he felt slightly happy Malcom's cheeks went rose red he began to feel tense. one by one Malcom opened his eyes. Shock hit his eyes but a small smile crept along his face. Slowly moving over to the lady Malcom stopped. Standing still If this was his chance he had defiently blown it.

Based on Paperman film by Disney.
Wollaston Primary School.
Year 6: Pupil writing outcomes from sentence-stacking lessons.

Finally the paper had landed right in the middle of the lady's face. Thoughts were running wild in Malcom's mind, he felt completely broken shattered like glass. Malcom began to think if he should run or try and fix this mess he had just made. Should I apologise? Butterflies were dancing delicately in Malcom's curious stomach. He leant in. Reaching carefully over to the woman, Malcom peeled the piece of paper off of the lady's face. Suddenly Malcom saw the lady's bright red lipstick marked on his paper, quickly pulling a goofy smile Malcom tryed to laugh, the lady tucked her hair behind her ear. Looking down Malcom pulled a smile.

Malcom turned his head to the woman once more, but to his surprise she was gone...

Malcom walked down the busy street. The skyscrapers stood tall. The building Malcom worked in seemed to be the most unhappy place on Earth. Turning round and round the revolving doors looked like a place where dreams were crushed. Suddenly something struck Malcom's pounding heart something was happening, Malcom could feel it in his bones.

Thump! went the stack of papers on Malcom's desk (They had landed right in the middle of it.) With a deep breath Malcom sighed. He wondered. Will I ever be loved? and will I ever be done? Malcom began to dream of a cold winter day as he felt his heart freeze.

Malcom then felt a chill down his back. Walking to the drinks Malcom picked up a nice warm coffee suddenly frowning it smelt vile, he poured it down the drain. Thud, clomp, clack as Malcom went up the stairs squeak! Malcom always forgot about the squeaky step. I wish I didn't work here. Malcom Mumbled.

The train zoomed by Malcom on the old, rickety tracks. Malcom stood still on the platform, mezmerised by the gloomy, grey world around him. Motionless Malcom sighed every morning he reluctantly walked to the shady train station and waited for the train. He held white files against his black blazer, the two boring colours clashed like Malcom's grey eyes against the bright world everyone thinks it is. Malcom wore a white marble shirt under his blazer and a sooty black tie. The winter sky was dark but today seemed the darkest. Malcom's emotionless face didn't change as another train sped by, it didn't seem to bother him.

Malcom could suddenly hear a delicate tap of a shoe. He turned his head, surprised by a gush of wind but when he opered his eyes he saw a girl who he thought was an angel. Malcom's eyes were fixed on her. The sudden burst of wind as the train went by brought him back to reality. What was she called? Malcom had so many questions to ask. She was standing next to him Malcom just wanted to squel. The lady brought joy to Malcom's face and for the in forever he smiled.

Suddenly a train zoomed by the love birds messing up Malcom's hair. The cold took Malcom's breath away. It made him close his eyes and lose grip of his files. A piece of rogue paper escaped Malcom's loosered grip. When Malcom opened his eyes and sighed at the sight he saw, the marble white had blown into the lady's face. Malcom's arms had gone stiss, his face had gone red and the fluffy, white clouds were now rough and grey. Drizzle drizzle drop drop went the icy rain.

Malcom couldn't feel more scared. What if she shouted at him? even worse attacked him?! The dreadful time had come to peel the snowy, white file from her gorgeous face. Malcom took a deep breath and slowly removed the paper, but she was still an ange not a tomato. The lady sniggered at something on the paper. Malcom was very confused but after a quick look at the paper he understood. A bright pink pair of lips had appeared. Malcom didn't find it funny but the lady did so he faked a laugh and closed his eyes. When he opened them she was gone.

Malcom's world was crushed. Would he ever see her again? He stepped into the busy street and strolled across the road, through the spinning doors. He clambered up stairs and into the office. Every face seemed soulless, their eyes grey and their dry cracked lips were just like Malcom's. Thud! Malcom's boss slammed down a giant pile of papers in front of him. Malcom hated his boss and his job, he couldn't be more sad. The love of his life had gone and now he had to fill out hundreds of files. He'd rather be locked up in an empty room rather than being at work. The other workers probably felt the same thought Malcom but they hadn't experienced what he had.

The office was dull and grey. There were patches of water on the ceiling. The smell of fresh bread and cakes wafted up Malcom's nose. Malcom took a sip of his caramel latté and imagined if he was the boss he would make Jeromy (his nemisis) do even more work than anyone could imagine and buy everyone cakes from Tim's bakery. Unfortunately this was not the case. Malcom just kept on dreaming.

Suddenly a fire truck sped by the bystanders below. It was the ear piercing sound of the siren that caught his attention. He got up and looked out the window to see what the fuss was all about.

Jeremy stood silently as the speedy train sped along the rusty, maroon tracks. The pale face of Jeremy told his life story. He was lonely, he had no friends, all he had was his trusty files to work through on a daily basis. Jeremy hated his job, he'd rather go on the London eye. (He's afraid of heights.) The black suit/tuxedo made him look very important, but he wasn't, he was just ordinary person at the train station.

The station master shouted "ALL ABOARD" as though his dull, boring life depended on it. Jeremy could hear the deep, annoying sound of the blank bell every time a train stopped in front of him. The flowers twirled and turned as the train sped by. The acrobatic air sizzled as it clicked Jeremy's ears, it flew past the girl next to him like Usain Bolt on a running track. Jeremy couldn't believe that this gorgeous girl was... actually... standing next to him. The luxurious lady flicked her hair as she turned. Everything stopped, the flowers, the train, everything, as though this was Jeremy's moment to introduce himself, but he didn't. He just carried on standing, looking at the gloomy world that stood before him.

He could hear another bell, he knew a train must be near, he looked carefully left, he looked cautiously right. Then he looked down in shame, the rumbling rain pounded his head as though twenty bold bricks had just fallen on the ground. Suddenly a huge train ran past them both at top speed and knocked a piece of paper onto the lady's face. Jeremy was embarrassed, praying that this day wouldn't get any worse. Evil was having it's first day of freedom. He couldn't help but to look at the other individuals and think if their day was going any better than his. Clickety clack, clickety clack. The station master was walking over, not to him though, to the big train that had just stopped at the train station, the bell was still ringing...

His heart twisting Jeremy felt hugely humiliated. He started to desperately but slowly peel the snow, white piece of paper off the gorgeous lady's face. The train had now left the anxious station. The lady started becoming visible again, Jeremy took one more look at the terrific sight in front of him, before he started to feel nervous by the beautiful lady that stood before him. He turned his rosy, red face towards the paper and finally realised what had happened, the perky, pink lipstick had stained th perfect paper. Jeremy couldn't stop himself but he had to laugh. The lady had made Jeremy feel tired, his frantic frown had been turned upside down! He felt like he had a third eye seeing unreal things. The lady was confused as the next train passed by. Jeremy realised the bell had stopped ringing. By now the lady and Jeremy were silent, they were too shy to even say 'hello'. Shockingly Jeremy had not said a word. He was love struck. The sight was too good to be true!

Jeremy stood silently on the train station's platform, the lady had got on the troubled train and was now half a mile away. Tediously Jeremy crept through the solid, stable, spinnings doors. POOF! A bunch of dust punched him in the face when the paperboring, precious paper had been slammed down on the table. Jeremy looked around for anyway out of this monotonous place, he didn't see an exit, he started to roll his eyes as his boss started walking away trying as hard as he could not to look suspicious, he had failed miserably. Jeremy wanted to die, he couldn't bare his job. Jeremy had hardly noticed everyone was staring at him, he looked at the time, he was mega late. Jeremy stood embarresed wondering. He couldn't think of a way to say 'please don't fire me' without saying it in that exact way. His boss was still walking, failing every step...

Jeremy slowly started realising that his heart was cracking, he heard a bang! On the window, it was just the curtains flapping around like mad. He got up to close the window, when the wind turned his head to the building opposite to him. His heavy heart re-formed itself from the cruel crack a few minutes ago. Jeremy could see the gorgeous, golden, stupendous star.

Department for Education Guidance
Working at greater depth within the expected standard: KS2

Piece B: Description

As part of a focus on autobiography, pupils researched accounts of key moments in the lives of performers such as Olympic athletes and musicians. They then selected a particular performance or competition and described in detail the opening moments of their chosen event.

Frankie's writing analysed through the 'The Writing Rainbow'

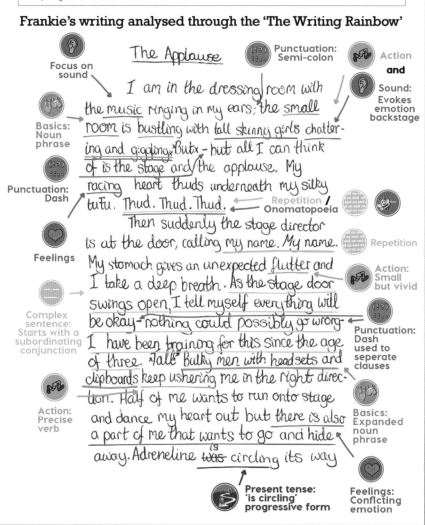

Focus on sound

Basics: Noun phrase

Punctuation: Dash

Feelings

Complex sentence: Starts with a subordinating conjunction

Action: Precise verb

The Applause

Punctuation: Semi-colon

Action **and**

Sound: Evokes emotion backstage

Repetition / Onomatopoeia

Repetition

Action: Small but vivid

Punctuation: Dash used to seperate clauses

Basics: Expanded noun phrase

I am in the dressing room with the music ringing in my ears; the small room is bustling with tall skinny girls chattering and giggling. Butx – but all I can think of is the stage and the applause. My racing heart thuds underneath my silky tutu. Thud. Thud. Thud. Then suddenly the stage director is at the door, calling my name. My name. My stomach gives an unexpected flutter and I take a deep breath. As the stage door swings open, I tell myself everything will be okay—nothing could possibly go wrong. I have been training for this since the age of three. Tall Bulky men with headsets and clipboards keep ushering me in the right direction. Half of me wants to run onto stage and dance my heart out but there is also a part of me that wants to go and hide away. Adreneline was is circling its way

Present tense: 'is circling' progressive form

Feelings: Conflicting emotion

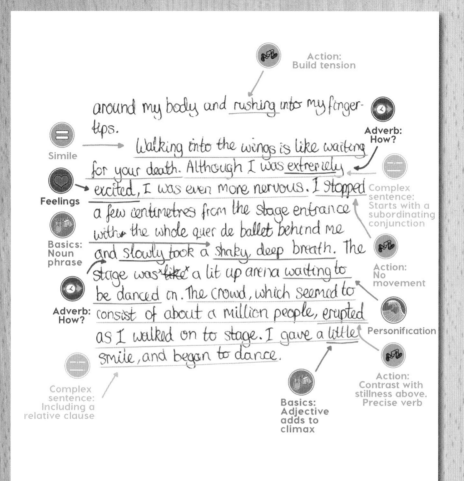

Action: Build tension

around my body and rushing into my finger-tips.

Adverb: How?

Walking into the wings is like waiting for your death. Although I was extremely excited, I was even more nervous. I stopped a few centimetres from the stage entrance with the whole quer de ballet behind me and slowly took a shaky, deep breath. The stage was like a lit up arena waiting to be danced on. The crowd, which seemed to consist of about a million people, erupted as I walked on to stage. I gave a little smile, and began to dance.

Simile

Feelings

Basics: Noun phrase

Adverb: How?

Complex sentence: Starts with a subordinating conjunction

Action: No movement

Personification

Action: Contrast with stillness above. Precise verb

Complex sentence: Including a relative clause

Basics: Adjective adds to climax

Analysis through the 'The Writing Rainbow' shows that writing at greater depth is robust across techniques, ideas and grammar.

Case Study 1

Kippax Ash Tree Primary School

Kippax Ash Tree Primary School in Leeds is much larger than the average-sized primary school. The proportion of pupils known to be eligible for free school meals is a little above average. Most pupils are White British. The proportion of pupils supported by School Action Plus or with a statement of Special Educational Needs is above average. The school meets the current floor standards, which set the government's minimum expectations for attainment and progress.

Kippax Ash Tree was a 'good' school but wanted to intensively focus on writing and consider new ways to raise standards. Jane Considine started working in the school in 2012/13 and introduced the FANTASTICs, a sharpened emphasis on grammar and maps for writing (for both narrative and non-fiction).

This case study will provide a brief overview of how Jane's models to improve writing were deployed in the classroom, and the subsequent impact on results. The journey will be tracked from Year 1 to Year 6.

Further interesting data:

Writing: 30.8 APS - this is 3.0 APS increase from last year
SPaG: 30.6 APS - this is 4.1 APS increase from last year

Our value added scores are:

Writing: 102.6 for all pupils, but we are really celebrating the boys' score of 102.0. FSM is 103.1

In Writing and SPaG we 'closed the gap' for all groups of learners in writing.

Writing	KS2 Results	Following Year KS2 Results	Increase
Working Towards Writing	91%	95%	4%
Expected Standard Writing	20%	44%	24%
Greater Depth Writing	0%	12%	12%

Impact at different year groups

Year 1

In Year 1, there was a strong focus on the concept of a sentence. Teachers worked hard to exemplify what constituted a sentence, and sentence washing lines were used to highlight the mobility of language and the function of particular words as well as the 'knowing it makes sense' aspects of writing. Pupils found the explicit demonstration of sentences on large paper clear, which helped support their thinking when constructing their own sentences.

Year 2

In Year 2, there was a huge emphasis on mapping out stories physically, so children could 'walk and talk' down entire shapes of stories, cognitively offloading their ideas.

The teachers provided large shapes with footstep visuals, so pupils could see the plot pathways. Using both a map on a working wall, as well as massive maps on the classroom floor, pupils were able to plot the bare bones of stories they knew well.

As pupils became more familiar with stories and retelling them orally using pictures, they captured the sequence using words. Using shared composition strategies, teachers then outlined other stories with similar journey patterns.

Year 3

In Year 3, there was a heavy emphasis on non-fiction. The non-fiction massive maps were used.

The children regularly 'walked down' the maps, articulating relevant non-fiction sentences. Alongside this, they would make jottings on laminated whiteboards, paper and Post-its to add vocabulary and sentences.

Not only did Year 3 have shared working maps, they also worked on mini maps in groups in a differentiated way. As part of a larger teaching sequence on each text type, the pupils worked on a basic non-fiction map, adding their ideas so they could see the individual parts of their writing as well as the whole.

Year 4

Year 4 pupils enjoyed adding the FANTASTIC layer to massive and mini maps. They worked extensively at considering positive and negative aspects of a story from the main character's perspective. The position of a 'high' or 'low' on a large visual map developed rich discussion and facilitated their thinking to enable more empathetic writing. Narrative became more focused and engaging and became a broader sensory reader experience.

Years 5 and 6

The teachers in Years 5 and 6 focused on incorporating grammar in context. The emphasis was on creating sentences that included particular grammar tools.

Balanced argument on a mini map. Notes and key sentences prepared prior to final writing.

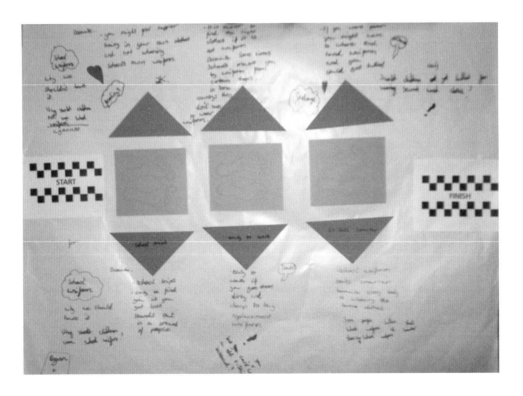

"We have just been notified by the Minister for Schools, David Laws MP, that we have won the DfE Award for our fantastic Key Stage 2 results in writing."
Amanda Campbell – Head Teacher, Kippax Ash Tree

Discursive text. Planning opposing arguments in two halves. Individual ideas captured on new shapes.

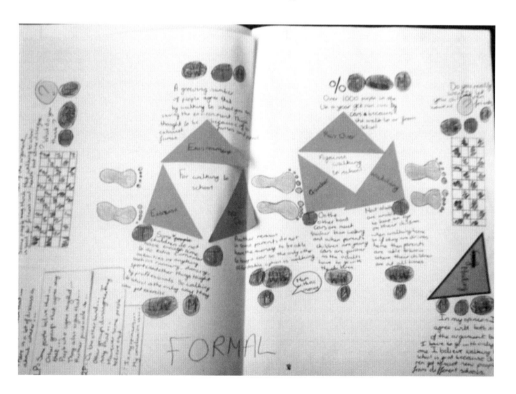

Case Study 2

Boothville Primary School

Before the Three Zones of Writing...

The teaching of English was set-based and planned around texts and topics. Rich and varied activities were planned and provided for children but disappointingly, outcomes did not reflect this. Much of the children's writing took place in isolation, with links implied rather than made explicit as to how each lesson built towards a final piece of writing.

Assessment, both in year groups and at the end of Key Stages, highlighted poor sentence structure and lack of textual cohesion. Many children in different year groups were not securely and consistently using sentence punctuation across a range of writing genres. SPaG was taught separately, with few references to the text-based work taking place in writing sessions.

The demands of the 2014 curriculum had highlighted the need for teacher subject knowledge to be quickly updated. Coupled with this, there was no subject leader for English and the role was split between senior managers. Although our data showed some considerable improvement, there were still inconsistencies at age expectation in Year 3 and Year 5. There was a need for solid foundations to be built and meaningful opportunities for children to develop and embed their writing skills.

Why the Three Zones of Writing?

As a whole school, we had introduced Book Talk and had a brief outline of The Write Stuff model. It made sense for staff and children to link the teaching of reading and writing so we decided to undertake training, planning and observations. Foundation, Key Stage 1 and 2 all participated in an initial session led by Jane. This outlined The Write Stuff model and gave an overview of how it could fit to our developing needs.

The FANTASTICs, The GRAMMARISTICs and The BOOMTASTICs

The FANTASTICs are displayed during our Book Talk sessions and all classrooms have a FANTASTICs writing stimulus display. Many classes use the smaller lens templates to aid sentence writing.
Posters are displayed, with shared vocabulary demonstrating degrees and scales of intensity.

All year groups have completed planning with Jane using the FANTASTICs. Activities are tailored around these, encouraging greater understanding of texts. It is felt that using the lenses gives a deeper focus on what we are asking the children to do and leaves less to chance – everyone can write a successful sentence. The children are enabled to include a range of descriptive themes and ideas with appropriate meaning in their writing.

Key Stage 2 is focused on the use of the GRAMMARISTICs. Our classrooms have displays detailing the GRAMMARISTICs and these support the teaching of SPaG and text-based grammar activities. Key Stage 1 teachers are using these alongside the FANTASTICs and identifying meaningful opportunities to teach grammar requirements.

The use of writing progress plans is underway, with staff and children using these to highlight grammar expectations for each year group.

In creating genre/unit plans with Jane, the BOOMTASTICs were already in our planning. Posters are displayed and children and staff are learning how these can be used to enhance writing. We are now focused on ensuring that they are transferred to each sequence plan and series of sentence-stacking lessons.

Impact so far...

We are in the initial stages of using The Write Stuff approach and there are many observations. We have seen:

▶ Improved pace in lessons

▶ Raised expectations of children in composing quality sentences

▶ A sense of confidence growth for many different groups of children (middle to lower ability, SEN, EAL)

▶ Sentence stacking leaves nothing to chance and there are positive outcomes at the end of each lesson for every child. Success is 'in-built'.

▶ Our expectations of children have developed more clarity and focus

▶ Inspirational elements remain but we are now making these more relevant and pertinent to the writing outcomes that follow

▶ There is greater purpose in writing sessions. Children are able to use success criteria and therefore self and peer assess more effectively

▶ Sentence stacking encourages refinement of experience and ideas

▶ Following the introduction of sentence stacking, EAL pupils are viewing high frequency words, simple and complex sentences and sentence punctuation. They are being immersed in quality language intensively and showing improved progress

▶ SEN children are making greater effort and feel supported as they attempt to create their own ideas

▶ There is a focused and explicit emphasis on modelling quality sentences

▶ There is a noticeable effect on our marking and the visibility of marking in children's books

Key Stages 1 and 2

There is some impact observed in children's books at both Key Stages. These include the quality of language use, the use of correct grammar and sentence punctuation.

Planning

Each year group is using the effective sequence-planning model to provide a broad overview of lessons and experiences related to each text/unit/genre. Sessions have been undertaken with Jane for each team to turn genre/unit plans into a sequence of work and into weekly sentence-stacking lessons using the Initiate, Model and Enable structure.

There is an improved pace of teaching and the structure of lessons has changed. Meaningful and inspirational ideas are leading to the effective modelling of quality sentences. There is a shift to shared ownership of learning in the classroom: it is not teacher teaching then child doing. We feel a sense of working together in sharing and learning. There is a sharper focus in teacher input and subject knowledge is increasing where it needed to.

By planning in this way, texts are being used with increased purpose and being utilised to best meet the needs of the English curriculum and the needs of the children.

Case Study 3

St John's C of E Primary School, Dorking

Type of school: Primary
School category: Academy sponsor-led
Age range of pupils: 3–11
Gender of pupils: Mixed
Number of pupils on the school roll: 206

- Just under half the pupils at the school are eligible for the pupil premium. This is much higher than other schools across the country.

- The percentage of pupils who have special educational needs and/or disabilities is also very high at over a third.

Source: Ofsted report

"Over the past two years, our school has fully embedded 'The Write Stuff' into daily practice from Reception to year 6. As a result, progress scores were in the top 4% of all schools nationally for writing. Our work with Jane Considine has been fundamental in our school's progress and our children's outcomes, helping the school's Ofsted rating go from Inadequate to GOOD in 3 years. Thank you!"

Mark Richards, Headteacher

Writing progress score for St John's Church of England Primary School

This school's writing progress score is

5.0

Confidence interval **2.1** to **7.9**

Well below average | Below average | Average | Above average | **Well Above**

Referencing

Adams, M. J. (2006) *The promise of automatic speech recognition for fostering literacy growth in children and adults.* In M.C. McKenna, L.D. Labbo, R. D. Kieffer, & D. Reinking (Eds.), International Handbook of Literacy and Technology, Volume 2. Mahwah, NJ: Lawrence Erlbaum Associates.

Ahlberg, A., Ahlburg, J. (1999) *Funnybones.* Puffin; New Ed edition.

Aiken, J (1962) *The Wolves of Willoughby Chase.* Jonathan Cape.

Allan, J., Ellis, S., Pearson, C. (2005) *Literature Circles, Gender and Reading for Enjoyment.* Department of Childhood and Primary Studies (University of Strathclyde).

Almond, D. (1998) *Skellig.* London: Hodder Headline.

Amery, H. (2004) *The Usborne Book of Fairy Tales: "Cinderella", "The Story of Rumpelstiltskin", "Little Red Riding Hood", "Sleeping Beauty", "Goldilocks and the Three Bears", "Three Little Pigs"* (First Stories) Usborne Publishing Ltd.

Anderson, H. C. (1844) *New Fairy Tales, First Book, First Collection.* C.A. Reitzel.

Anderson, R. C., Wilson, P. T., Fielding, L. G. (1988) *Growth in reading and how children spend their time outside of school.* Reading Research Quarterly, 23, 285–303.

Andrews, R., Torgerson, C., Low, G., McGuinn, N. (2009) *Teaching argument writing to 7 - to 14 - year olds: an international review of the evidence of successful practice.* Cambridge Journal of Education, 39:3, 291-310.

Angelou, M. (1984) *I Know Why the Caged Bird Sings.* New York: Random House.

Applegate, K. (2012) *The One and Only Ivan.* New York: Harper.

Applegate, K. (2015) *Crenshaw.* Feiwel and Friends.

Artell, M. (2005) *Reaching the Reluctant Writer: Fast, Fun, Informational Writing Ideas.* Maupin House Publishing.

Barretta, G. (2010) *Dear Deer: A Book of Homophones.* New York: Square Fish.

Barrs, M., Cork, V. (2001) *The Reader in the Writer.* Centre for Language in Primary Education.

Baums, L. F. (1900) *The Wonderful Wizard of Oz*. George M. Hill Company.

Belloc, H. (1870 – 1953) Poem: *Matilda told such awful lies*.

Bemelmans, L. (1939) *Madeline*. Scholastic; 70th anniversary edition edition (5 Jan. 2009).

Bianco, M.W., Officer, R. (1996) *The Velveteen Rabbit*. New York: Barnes & Noble.

Bjork, R. A. (2011) *On the symbiosis of remembering, forgetting and learning. In Successful Remembering and Successful Forgetting*: A Festschrift in Honor of Robert A. Bjork, ed. AS Benjamin, pp. 1–22. London: Psychol. Press.

Blabey, A. (2010) *The Ghost of Miss Annabel Spoon*. Camberwell, Vic.: Penguin, 2010.

Blank, R.K., de las Alas, N. (2009). *Effects of Teacher Professional Development on Gains in Student Achievement: How Meta-Analysis Provides Scientific Evidence Useful to Education Leaders.*

Boudart, J. (1996) *The Virtue of Love; The Velveteen Rabbit.* Lincolnwood, Illinois: Publications International.

Brothers Grimm (2013) *Little Red Riding Hood (Usborne Picture Books)* Usborne Publishing Ltd.

Browne, A. (2003) *My Dad*. New York: Farrar Straus Giroux.

Browning, R. (1986) *The Pied Piper of Hamelin*. New York: Lothrop, Lee & Shepard.

Bruner, J. (1996) *The culture of education.* Cambridge, MA: Harvard University Press.

Buck, C., Lee, J. (Directors) (2013 Film) *Frozen*. Production Companies: Walt Disney Animation Studios, Walt Disney Pictures. Distributed by Walt Disney Studios Motion Picture.

Burningham, J. (1964) *Borka*. Johnathan Cape.

Byatt, A.S. (1990) *Possession*. The Folio Society; First Edition edition (2009).

Byatt, A. S. (2010) *On Histories and Stories: Selected Essays.* Cambridge, Mass, United States, Harvard University Press.

Byars, B. (1968) *The Midnight Fox*. Faber & Faber; Main edition.

Carroll, L. (1865) *Alice in Wonderland.* Ware: Wordsworth Editions.

Carroll, L. (1871) *Jabberwocky: Taken from: Through the Looking-Glass, and What Alice Found There.* Macmillan.

Casarosa, E. (Director) (2011 Film) *La Luna.* Production Companies: Pixar Animation Studios, Walt Disney Pictures. Distributed by Walt Disney Studios Motion Pictures.

Christodoulou, D. (2013) *Seven Myths about Education.* The Curriculum Centre, Routledge.

Clark, C. (2015) *Children's and Young People's Writing in 2014. Findings from the National Literacy Trust's annual survey.* London: National Literacy Trust.

Clark, C., Douglas, J. (2011) *Young People's Reading and Writing: an in-depth study focusing on enjoyment, behaviour, attitudes and attainment.* National Literacy Trust.

Clark, C., Dugdale, G. (2009) *Young People's Writing: attitudes, behaviour and the role of technology.* National Literacy Trust in collaboration with Booktrust.

Coe, R., Aloisi, C., Higgins, S., Major, L. E. (2014) *What Makes Great Teaching?* Available at: http://www.suttontrust.com/wp-content/uploads/2014/10/What-makes-great-teaching-FINAL-4.11.14.pdf (Accessed: 27 November 2015).

Collodi, C. (2008) *The Adventures of Pinocchio.* Radford: Wilder Publications.

Colston, H., Kuiper, M. (2002) *Figurative Language Development Research and Popular Children's Literature: Why We Should*

Know, "Where the Wild Things Are" Journal: Metaphor and Symbol vol. 17, no. 1, pp. 27-43.

Cook, B., Bancroft, T. (Directors) Coats, P. (Producer) (1998 Film) *Mulan.* Production Companies: Walt Disney Pictures, Walt Disney Feature Animation. Distributed by Buena Vista Pictures.

Cooper, H. (1998) *Pumpkin Soup.* Random House.

Cooper, H. (1999) *Black Notice.* London: Random House Children.

Crenshaw, J. L. (1981) *Old Testament Wisdom: An Introduction.* Atlanta: John Knox.

Crewe, W. J. (1990) *The illogic of logical connectives.* ELT Journal, 44 (4), 316-325.

Crossley-Holland, K. (1966) *The Green Children.* Oxford University Press; New edition edition (8 May 1997).

Crum, S. (2001) *Who Took my Hairy Toe.* Albert Whitman and Company.

Crystal, D. Prof. (2004) *Making Sense of Grammar.* Longman.

Crystal, D. Prof. (2005) *How Language Works.* Penguin; First Paperback Edition.

Cunningham, A.E., Stanovich, K.E. (1998) *'What Reading does for the mind'* American Educator 22.

Dahl, R (1982) *The BFG.* Johnathan Cape/ Penguin Books.

Dahl, R. (1963) *James and the Giant Peach.* Alfred A. Knopf, Inc.

Dahl, R. (1983) *The Witches.* New York: Farrar, Straus, Giroux.

Dahl, R. (1988) *Matilda.* New York, N.Y.: Viking Kestrel.

Dahl, R. (2006) *The Twits.* New York.: Scholastic/Puffin.

Dahl, R., Reid, S (1987) *Roald Dahl's Fantastic Mr Fox: A Play.* Harmondsworth: Puffin.

Daldry, S. (Director) Brenman, G., Finn, J. (Producers) (2000 Film) *Billy Elliot.* Production Companies: BBC Films, Tiger Aspects Pictures, StuidoCanal, Working Title Films. Distributed by Universal Pictures, Focus Features.

Daly, C. (2003) *Literature search on improving boys' writing.* Published by Ofsted.

De Larrabeiti, M. *The Borribles.* Macmillan.

De Sica, V. (Director) (1948 Film) Studio: Arrow Films in Reading.

Deans for Learning, (2015) *The Science of Learning.*

Deary, T. (1997) *Horrible Histories: The Measly Middle Ages.* New York: Scholastic.

Department for Education, (2012) *What Is The Research Evidence On Writing?* Available at: https://www.gov.uk/government/uploads/system/uploads/attachment_data/file/183399/DFE-RR238.pdf (Accessed: 25 November 2015).

Department for Education (2013) *The national curriculum in England Key stages 1 and 2 framework document.* Available at: https://www.gov.uk/government/uploads/system/uploads/attachment_data/file/425601/PRIMARY_national_curriculum.pdf (Accessed: 22 November 2015).

Department for Education (2014) Reforming assessment and accountability for primary schools. Available at: https://www.gov.uk/government/uploads/system/uploads/attachment_data/file/297595/Primary_Accountability_and_Assessment_Consultation_Response.pdf (Accessed: 22 November 2015).

Department for Education (2014) Common inspection framework: education, skills and early years from September 2015. Available at: https://www.gov.uk/government/publications/common-inspection-framework-education-skills-and-early-years-from-september-2015 (Accessed: 26 February 2016).

Department for Education (2012) *What is the research evidence on writing?* Education Standards Research Team, Department for Education Ref: DFE-RR238

Department for Education (2012) *The research evidence on "writing"* Education Standards Research team Education Standards Analysis & Research Division.

DfES (2007) *Gender and education: the evidence of pupils in England.*

Dickens, C. (2008) *A Christmas Carol (Templar Classics).* Templar New Edition.

Donaldson, J. (1999) *The Gruffalo.* UK: Macmillan.

Downey, F. (1942) *War Horse.* New York: Dodd, Mead and Co.

Durrell, G. (2006) *My Family And Other Animals.* 1st Edition. Puffin.

Education Endowment Foundation (2014) *Improving Writing Quality, Evaluation Report and Executive Summary.* Available at: https://v1.educationendowmentfoundation.org.uk/uploads/pdf/EEF_Evaluation_Report_-_Improving_Writing_Quality_-_May_2014.pdf (Accessed 26 February 2016).

Erdrich, L. (1954 – Present) *"When we are young, the words are scattered all around us. As they are assembled by experience, so also are we, sentence by sentence, until the story takes shape."*

Estyn (2008) *Closing the gap between boys' and girls' attainment in schools.*

Fahy, M. (1938) *The Tree that survived the Winter.* Paulist Press.

Falck-Ytter, T., Carlstrom, C., Johansson, M. (2015) *Eye Contact Modulates Cognitive Processing Differently in Children With Autism.*

Faulkner, W. (1897 – 1962).

Fine, A. (1995) *Madame Doubtfire.* London: Puffin.

Fleckenstein, K.S., Calendrillo, L.T., Worley, D.A. (2002) *Language and Image in the Reading – Writing Classroom.* Mahwah N.J.: Lawrence Erlbaum.

Flood, A. (2015) *National curriculum is damaging children's creative writing, say authors.* Available at: http://www.theguardian.com/books/2015/jun/23/national-curriculum-is-damaging-childrens-creative-writing-sayauthors (Accessed: 25 November 2015).

Gaiman, N. (2003) *The Wolves in the Walls.* New York: HarperCollins.

Gaiman, N. (2015) *Where do you get your ideas?* Blog www.neilgaiman.com

Gardner, P. (2011) *The Reluctant Writer in the Primary Classroom: an investigation of mind mapping and other pre-writing strategies to overcome reluctance.* Bedford: The Bedford Charity (Harpur Trust).

Ghaaemi, M. (2013) *An investigation into the use of Cohesive devices in Second Language Writings.* UK: Academy Publications.

Gillespie, A. and Graham, S. (2010) *Evidence-based practices for teaching writing.* Johns Hopkins University School of Education: New Horizon for learning. http://education.jhu.edu/newhorizons/Better/articles/Winter2011.html

Graham, B. (2001) *Let's Get a Pup!* Cambridge, Mass. Candlewick, Print.

Graham, S., Bollinger, A., Booth Olson, C., D'Aoust, C., MacArthur, C., McCutchen, D., & Olinghouse, N. (2012). *Teaching elementary school students to be effective writers: A practice guide* (NCEE 2012- 4058). Washington, DC: National Center for Education Evaluation and Regional Assistance, Insti¬tute of Education Sciences, U.S. Department of Education. Retrieved from http://ies.ed.gov/ncee/wwc/publications_reviews.aspx#pubsearch.

Halliday, M.A.K., Hasan R. (1976) *Cohesion in English* (English Language Series) Routledge; 1 edition.

Halliday, M.A.K., Hasan R. (1986) *Language, context and text: Aspects of language in a social-semiotic perspective.* Deakin University, Australia.

Helakoski, L. (2008) *Big Chickens Fly the Coop.* New York: Dutton Children's.

Hemingway, E. (1899 – 1961) *"All you have to do is write one true sentence. Write the truest sentence that you know."*

Henson, J. (1988 Film) *The Storyteller (The Soldier and Death).* Production Companies: Jim Henson Productions, TVS Television.

Hornby, N. (1998) *About a Boy.* New York: Riverhead.

Horrocks, R. D., Vallentine, J. F. (1999) *Harvested Forages.* San Diego, Academic Press.

Horowitz, A. (2002) *Alex Rider Series: Skeleton Key.* UK: Walker Books.

Hughes, T. (2015) *The Iron Man.* Faber & Faber; Main edition.

Husbands, C., & Pearce, J. (2012). *What is great pedagogy: A literature review for the National College of School Leadership.* National College for School Leadership. Ings, R. (n.d.) Writing is Primary. UK: Esmee Fairbairn Foundation.

Jacobs, J. (2013) *Jack and the Beanstalk* (Illustrated). The Planet.

Jeffers, O. (2005) *The Heart and the Bottle.* New York: Philomel.

Jeffers, O. (2007) *The Way Back Home.* New York: Philomel.

Johnston, T. (1994) *Amber on the Mountain.* New York: Dial for Young Readers.

Jones, K. (Producer) Doran, L., Bevan, T., Fellner, E. (Producers) (2005 Film) *Nanny McPhee.* Production Companies: StudioCanal, Metro-Goldwyn-Mayer, Working Title Films, Three Strange Angels, Nanny McPhee Productions. Distributed by Universal Pictures.

Juster, N. (1961) *The Phantom Tollbooth.* New York: Epstein & Carroll.

Kahrs, J. (Director) Reed, K. (Producer) (2012 Film) *Paperman.* Production Companies: Walt Disney Animation Studios, Walt Disney Pictures. Distributed by Walt Disney Studios Motion Pictures.

Keats, E. J. (1962) *The Snowy Day.* Viking Press.

Keats, E. J. (1968) *A Letter to Amy.* New York: Harper & Row.

Keer, J. (2016) *When Hitler Stole Pink Rabbit* (Essential Modern Classics) HarperCollinsChildren'sBooks; New edition edition (1 July 2008).

King, S. (2000) *On Writing. A Memoir of the Craft.* Hodder & Stoughton.

Kirschner, P.A., Sweller, J., Clark, R.E. (2006) *Why Minimal Guidance During Instruction Does Not Work: An Analysis of the Failure of Constructivist, Discovery, Problem-Based, Experiential, and Inquiry-Based Teaching.* EDUCATIONAL PSYCHOLOGIST, 41(2), 75–86 Lawrence Erlbaum Associates, Inc.

Kitamura, S. (2008) *The Stone Aged Boy.* Walker.

Kolln, M. (2006) *Rhetorical Grammar: Grammatical Choices, Rhetorical Effects.* Longman; 5th edition

Koontz, D. R. (1999) *Seize the Night.* UK: Bantam Books.

Lawrence, D. H. (1915) *The Rainbow.* Modern Library.

Lee, I. (2002). *Teaching coherence to EAL students: A classroom inquiry.* Journal of Second Language Writing, 11, 135-159.

Lewis, C. S. (1994) *The Lion, the Witch, and the Wardrobe.* New York: HarperCollins.

Mannis, C. D. and Hartung, S. K. (2002) *One Leaf Rides the Wind: Counting in a Japanese Garden.* New York: Viking.

Massaro, D. (2015) *Two Different Communication Genres and Implications for Vocabulary Development and Learning to Read.* Department of Psychology University of California, Santa Cruz.

McNaughton, C. (1995) *Here Come the Aliens!* Cambridge, MA: Candlewick.

Meehan, T. (2013) *Annie.* Puffin Books; Updated edition.

Meek, M. (1991) *On Being Literate,* London: Bodley Head.

Miller, G., Morris, J., Coleman. (Directors) (2006) *Happy Feet.* Production Companies: Animal Logic, Village Roadshow Pictures. Distributed by Warner Bros.

Milne, A. A. (2004) *Winnie-the-Pooh.* New Ed Edition. Egmont Books Ltd.

Morpurgo, M. M.B.E. (2006) *War Horse.* Edition. Egmont Books (UK).

Morris, R. *Why Writers Should Read.* Interview for www.thewritepractice. com by Joe Bunting. Available at http:// thewritepractice.com/roz-morris-on- why-writers-should-read/ (Accessed 29 February 2016).

Mortimore, P., Sammons, P., Stoll, L., Lewis, D. & Ecob, R. (1988). *School Matters: The Junior Years.* Wells: Open Books.

Muijs, D., Kyriakides, L., van der Werf, G., Creemers, B., Timperley, H., Earl, L. (2014) *State of the art – teacher effectiveness and professional learning, School Effectiveness and School Improvement:* An International Journal of Research, Policy and Practice.

Myhill, F. (2010) *Rhythm and Blues: Making Textual Music with Grammar and Punctuation.* in Wyse D, Andrews R, Hoffman J (eds) The International Handbook of English, Language and Literacy Teaching, London: Routledge.

Myhill, D., Fisher, R. (2010) *Editorial: Writing development: cognitive, sociocultural, linguistic perspectives.* Journal of Research in Reading.

Myhill, D., Lines, H., Watson, D. *Making Meaning with Grammar: A Repertoire of Possibilities.* University of Exeter, UK.

NAHT (2014) *Report of the NAHT Commission on Assessment.*
Available at: www.naht.org.uk/assets/ assessment-commission-report.pdf (Accessed: 26 February 2016).

O'Brien, R. C. (1975) *Mrs Frisby and the Rats of NIMH.* Heinemann.

OECD, (2000): *PISA Programme for International Student Assessment.* OECD Publishing.

OECD (2002) *Reading for Change, Performance and Engagement across Countries. Results from PISA 2000.* OECD Publishing.

OECD (2012), *Equity and Quality in Education: Supporting Disadvantaged Students and Schools,* OECD Publishing.

Ofsted (2005b) *Informing practice in English: a review of recent research in literacy and the teaching of English.* Debra Myhill and Ros Fisher, University of Exeter (reference no: HMI 2565).

Oram, H. (2008) *Angry Arthur.* Anderson Press.

Oz, F. (Director) Geffen, D. (Producer) (1986 Film) *Little Shop of Horrors.* Production Company: The Greffen Company. Distributed by Warner Bros. Pictures.

Paulus, T. (1972) *Hope for the Flowers.* New York: Newman.

Pearce, P. (2015) *Tom's Midnight Garden.* OUP Oxford; Reissue edition

Pfister, M. (1992) *The Rainbow Fish.* New York: North-South.

Piven, H. (2012) *My Dog is as Smelly as Dirty Socks: and Other Family Portraits.* Dragonfly Books.

Potter, B. (1987) *The Tailor of Gloucester.* Middlesex, England; New York: F. Warne.

Pritchard, A. (2005) *Ways of Learning: Learning Theories and Learning Styles in the Classroom.* Routledge; 3 edition (22 Nov. 2013).

Proulx, E. A. (1935 – Present) *"You should write because you love the shape of stories and sentences and the creation of different words on a page. Writing comes from reading, and reading is the finest teacher of how to write comes."*

Provost, G. (1944 – 1995) *"This sentence has five words. Here are five more words. Five-word sentences are fine. But several together become monotonous. Listen to what is happening. The writing is getting boring. The sound of it drones. It's like a stuck record. The ear demands some variety.*
Now listen. I vary sentence length, and I create music. Music. The writing sings. It has a pleasant rhythm, a lilt, a harmony. I use short sentences. And I use sentences of medium length.
And sometimes, when I am certain the reader is rested, I will engage him with a sentence of considerable length, a sentence that burns with energy and builds with all the impetus of a crescendo, the roll of the drums, the crash of the cymbals - sounds that say listen to this, it is important."

Pullman, P. (1997) *The Subtle Knife.* New York: Alfred A. Knopf.

Pullman, P. (1999) *The Golden Compass: His Dark Materials.* New York: Ballantine Books.

Pullman, P., Gallagher, S. (1999) *The Firework-maker's Daughter.* New York: Arthur A. Levine Books.

Pullman, P (2000) *The Amber Spyglass.* Scholastic/David Fickling Books.

Quigley, M. (2007) *Granddad's Fishing Buddy.* New York: Dial for Young Readers.

Riggs, R. (2014) *Hollow City: The Second Novel of Miss Peregrine's Home for Peculiar Children.* Philadelphia: Quirk Books.

Rosen, M. and Oxenbury, H. (1989) *We're Going on a Bear Hunt.* New York: Margaret K. McElderry Books.

Rowling, J. K. (1997) *Harry Potter and the Philosopher's Stone.* London: Bloomsbury.

Sachar, L, (2015) *Holes.* Bloomsbury Childrens.

Sachar, L. (2003 Film) *Holes.* Production Company & Distributors: Walt Disney Motion Pictures.

Sandburg, C. (1916) *The Fog*

Santangelo, T. and Olinghouse, N. (2009) *Effective writing instruction for students who have writing difficulties. Focus on exceptional children.*

Scientific Learning Corporation (2008) *Adding ten minutes of reading time dramatically changes levels of print exposure.* Available at: http://www.iowaafterschoolalliance.org/documents/cms/docs/10_minutes.pdf (Accessed: 20 November 2015).

Scieszka, J. (1996) *The True Story of the Three Little Pigs.* Puffin.

Schwartz, C. R. (2012) *The Three Ninja Pigs.* New York: G.P. Putnam's Sons Books for Young Readers.

Sendak, M. (2000) *Where the Wild Things Are.* Red Fox; New Ed edition.

Seuss, Dr. (1957) *The Cat in the Hat.* Random House, Houghton Mifflin.

Seuss, Dr. (1971) *The Lorax.* Random House.

Sherrington, T. (2015) *Principles of Effective Teaching.* Blog: @headguruteacher.

Siraj, I., Taggart, B. with Melhuish, E., Sammonds, P., Sylsa, K. (2012) *Exploring Effective Pedagogy in Primary Schools: Evidence from Research.* Pearson.

Shaw, N. E. (2003) *Raccoon Tune.* New York: H. Holt.

Shakespeare, W. (1594-96) *Romeo and Juliet.* Thomas Creede/Wordsworth Classics.

Shakespeare, W. (1590 – 1597) *A Midsummer Night's Dream.* Wordsworth Editions; 1st. Edition edition (5 May 1992).

Sharratt, N. & Lindsay, E. *Socks.* Random House.

Southley, R. (1897) *Goldilocks and the Three Bears.* Usborne Publishing Ltd; New edition (1 Aug. 2012).

Spielberg, S. (Director) Spielberg, S., Kennedy, K. (Producers) (1982 Film) *E.T. The Extra-Terrestrial.* Production Company: Amblin Entertainment. Distributed by Universal Pictures.

Stanton, A. (Director) Walters, G. (Producer) (2003 Film) *Finding Nemo.* Production Companies: Walt Disney Pictures, Pixar Animation Studios. Distributed by Buena Vista Pictures.

Steinbeck, J. (1993) *Of Mice and Men.* New York: Penguin.

Stevenson, R. (Director) Disney, W., Walsh, B. (Producers) (1964 Film) *Mary Poppins.* Production Company: Walk Disney Productions. Distributed by Buena Vista Distribution.

Stewart, S. (2008) *The Gardener.* Library Binding.

Stipek, D. (2010) *Motivation to Learn.* Preparing educators to engage families (2nd edition) Thousand Oaks CA: Sage Publications.

Strunk, W. Jr. (1999) *The Elements of Style.* 4th edn. New York: Longman.

Tan, S. (2010) *The Red Tree.* Hodder Children's Books.

Taylor, M. D. (1976) *Roll of Thunder, Hear My Cry.* New York: Dial.

Tierney, R. J., Pearson, P. D. (1983) *Toward a composing model of reading.* Washington, D.C. Distributed by ERIC Clearinghouse.

Timperley, H., Wilson, A., Barrar, H., Fung, I. (2007) *Teacher professional learning and development: Best evidence synthesis iteration.* Wellington, New Zealand: Ministry of Education.

Timperley, H. (2008). *Teacher professional learning and development. International Academy of Education, International Bureau of Education,* UNESCO.

Thurston, D. (2000) *Thank You for the Thistle.* Chesterfield, VA: Dorie Books.

Tolkien, J. R. R. (2013) *The Hobbit.* HarperCollinsChildren'sBooks.

Unseld, S. (Director) (2013 Film) *The Blue Umbrella.* Production Companies: Pixar Animation Studios, Walt Disney Pictures. Distributed by Walt Disney Studios Motion Pictures.

Waddell, M. (1992) *Farmer Duck.* Cambridge, MA: Candlewick.

Walt Disney (1988) *Winnie the Pooh.* New York: Derrydale.

Wedge, C. (Director) (2002 Film) *Ice Age.* Production Company: Blue Sky Studios. Distributed by 20th Century Fox.

Wells, G. (1986) *The Meaning Makers: Children Learning Language and Using Language.*

Wheeler, W. *"Good writing is clear thinking made visible."*

Williams, M (1922) *The Velveteen Rabbit.* George H. Doran Company.

Wilson, J. (2001) *Vicky Angel.* New York: Delacorte.

Wilson, K. (2005) *Bear Snores on.* New York: Little Simon.

Wise, D. (2010) *The Routledge international handbook of English, language and literacy teaching.* London: Routledge.

Wood, J. (2008) *How Fiction Works.* New York: Farrar, Straus and Giroux.

Woolf, V. (1931) *The Waves.* Hogarth Press.

Yolen, J. (1987) *Owl Moon.* New York: Philomel Books.

Younger, M., Warrington, M. with Gray, J., Ruddock, J., McLellan, R., Bearne, E., Kershner, R., Bricheno, P. (2005) *Raising boys' achievement: a study funded by the Department for Education and Skills* (University of Cambridge, Faculty of Education). DfES RR636.

Bibliography

Adams, M. J. (2006) *The promise of automatic speech recognition for fostering literacy growth in children and adults.* In M.C. McKenna, L.D. Labbo, R. D. Kieffer, & D. Reinking (Eds.), International Handbook of Literacy and Technology, Volume 2. Mahwah, NJ: Lawrence Erlbaum Associates.

Allan, J., Ellis, S., Pearson, C. (2005) *Literature Circles, Gender and Reading for Enjoyment.* Department of Childhood and Primary Studies (University of Strathclyde).

Anderson, R. C., Hidde, J. L. (1971) *Imagery and sentence learning. Journal of Educational Psychology.*

Andrews, R., Torgerson, C., Low, G., McGuinn, N. (2009) *Teaching argument writing to 7 to 14-year olds: an international review of the evidence of successful practice,* Cambridge Journal of Education, 39:3, 291-310.

Annis, L., Davis, J. K. (1978) *Study techniques: Comparing their effectiveness.* American Biology Teacher.

Amrein-Beardsley, A. (2008) *Methodological concerns about the education value-added assessment system.* Educational Researcher.

Artell, M. (2005) *Reaching the Reluctant Writer: Fast, Fun, Informational Writing Ideas.* Maupin House Publishing.

Balch, W. R. (2006) *Encouraging distributed study: A classroom experiment on the spacing effect.* Teaching of Psychology.

Barrs, M., Cork, V. (2001) *The Reader in the writer.* Centre for Language in Primary Education.

Bearne, E., Wolstencroft H. (2007) *Visual Approaches to Teaching Writing: Multimodal Literacy 5 - 11 (Published in association with the UKLA)* SAGE Publications Ltd.

Bjork, R. A. (2011) *On the symbiosis of remembering, forgetting and learning. In Successful Remembering and Successful Forgetting:* A Festschrift in Honor of Robert A. Bjork, ed. AS Benjamin, pp. 1–22. London: Psychol. Press.

Blank, R.K., de las Alas, N. (2009) *Effects of Teacher Professional Development on Gains in Student Achievement: How Meta-Analysis Provides Scientific Evidence Useful to Education Leaders.*

Bransford, J. D., Brown, A. L., Cocking, R. R. (2000) *How People Learn: Brain, Mind, Experience, and School.* Washington, DC: National Academy Press.

Britton, J. (1983) *Writing and the story of the world.* In B. M. Kroll & C. G. Wells (Eds.), Explorations in the development of writing: Theory, research, and practice (pp. 3–30). New York, NY: Wiley.

Brown, P. C., Roediger III, H. L., McDaniel, M. A. (2014) *Make it Stick: The Science of Successful Learning.* Harvard University Press.

Bruner, J. (1996) *The culture of education.* Cambridge, MA: Harvard University Press.

Cameron, J., Banko, K. M., Pierce, W. D. (2001) *Pervasive negative effects of rewards on intrinsic motivation: The myth continues.* The Behavior Analyst.

Carey, B. (2015) *How We Learn: Throw out the rule book and unlock your brain's potential.* Macmillan; Main Market Ed. edition (4 Jun. 2015).

Catrambone, R. (1998) *The subgoal learning model: Creating better examples so that students can solve novel problems.* Journal of Experimental Psychology: General.

Christodoulou, D. (2013) *Seven Myths about Education.* The Curriculum Centre, Routledge.

Clark, C. (2015) *Children's and Young People's Writing in 2014. Findings from the National Literacy Trust's annual survey.* London: National Literacy Trust.

Clark, C., Douglas, J. (2011) *Young People's Reading and Writing: an in-depth study focusing on enjoyment, behaviour, attitudes and attainment.* National Literacy Trust.

Clark, C., Dugdale, G. (2009) *Young People's Writing: attitudes, behaviour and the role of technology.* National Literacy Trust in collaboration with Booktrust.

Coe, R., Aloisi, C., Higgins, S., Major, L. E. (2014) *What Makes Great Teaching?* Available at: http://www.suttontrust.com/wp-content/uploads/2014/10/What-makes-great-teaching-FINAL-4.11.14.pdf (Accessed: 27 November 2015).

Colston, H., Kuiper, M. (2002) *Figurative Language Development Research and Popular Children's Literature: Why We Should Know, "Where the Wild Things Are"* Journal: Metaphor and Symbol vol. 17, no. 1, pp. 27-43.

Crystal, D. Prof. (2004) *Making Sense of Grammar.* Longman.

Crystal, D. Prof. (2005) *How Language Works.* Penguin; First Paperback Edition.

Cunningham, A. E., Stanovich, K. E. (1998) *'What Reading does for the mind'* American Educator 22.

Daly, C. (2003) *Literature search on improving boys' writing.* Published by Ofsted.

Deans for Learning, (2015) *The Science of Learning.*

DfES (2007) *Gender and education: the evidence of pupils in England.*

Education Endowment Foundation (2014) *Improving Writing Quality, Evaluation Report and Executive Summary.* Available at: https://v1.educationendowmentfoundation.org.uk/uploads/pdf/EEF_Evaluation_Report_-_Improving_Writing_Quality_-_May_2014.pdf (Accessed 26 February 2016).

Elliott, E. S., Dweck, C. S. (1988) *Goals: An approach to motivation and achievement.* Journal of Personality and Social Psychology.

Estyn (2008) *Closing the gap between boys' and girls' attainment in schools.*

Fleckenstein, K.S., Calendrillo, L.T., Worley, D.A. (2002) *Language and Image in the Reading–Writing Classroom.* Mahwah N.J.: Lawrence Erlbaum.

Flood, A. (2015) *National curriculum is damaging children's creative writing, say authors.*
Available at: http://www.theguardian.com/books/2015/jun/23/national-curriculum-is-damaging-childrens-creative-writing-sayauthors (Accessed: 25 November 2015).

Gage, N.L. (1978). *The scientific basis of the art of teaching.* New York, NY: Teachers College Press.

Gardner, P. (2011) *The Reluctant Writer in the Primary Classroom: an investigation of mind mapping and other pre-writing strategies to overcome reluctance.* Bedford: The Bedford Charity (Harpur Trust).

Ghaaemi, M. (2013) *An investigation into the use of cohesive devices in Second Language .*

Gillespie, A. and Graham, S. (2010) Evidence-based practices for teaching writing. Johns Hopkins University School of Education: New Horizon for learning. http://education.jhu.edu/newhorizons/Better/articles/Winter2011.html
Writings. UK: Academy Publications.

Graham, S., Bollinger, A., Booth Olson, C., D'Aoust, C., MacArthur, C., McCutchen, D., & Olinghouse, N. (2012) *Teaching elementary school students to be effective writers: A practice guide* (NCEE 2012-4058). Washington, DC: National Center for Education Evaluation and Regional Assistance, Insti¬tute of Education Sciences, U.S. Department of Education. Retrieved from http://ies.ed.gov/ncee/ wwc/publications_reviews.aspx#pubsearch.

Halliday, M.A.K., Hasan R. (1976) *Cohesion in English (English Language Series).* Routledge; 1 edition.

Halliday, M.A.K., Hasan R. (1986) *Language, context and text: Aspects of language in a social-semiotic perspective.* Deakin University, Australia.

Husbands, C., Pearce, J. (2012) *What is great pedagogy: A literature review for the National College of School Leadership.* National College for School Leadership.

Ings, R. (n.d.) *Writing is Primary.* UK: Esmee Fairbairn Foundation.

Kaplan, H., Hooper, P., Gurven, M. (2009) *The evolutionary and ecological roots of human social organization.* Philosophical Transactions of the Royal Society 364:3289-3299.

Kolln, M. (2006) *Rhetorical Grammar: Grammatical Choices, Rhetorical Effects.* Longman; 5th edition.

Meek, M. (1991) *On Being Literate,* London: Bodley Head.

Massaro, D. (2015) *Two Different Communication Genres and Implications for Vocabulary Development and Learning to Read.* Department of Psychology University of California, Santa Cruz.

Miller, G.A. (1956) *The magical number seven, plus or minus two: some limits on our capacity for processing information.* Psychological review.

Mortimore, P., Sammons, P., Stoll, L., Lewis, D. & Ecob, R. (1988). *School Matters: The Junior Years.* Wells: Open Books.

Myhill, D. and Fisher, R. (2010) *Editorial: Writing development: cognitive, sociocultural, linguistic perspectives.* Journal of Research in Reading.

Myhill, D., Lines, H., Watson, D. (2011) *Making Meaning with Grammar: A Repertoire of Possibilities.* University of Exeter, UK.

Myhill, F. (2010) *Rhythm and Blues: Making Textual Music with Grammar and Punctuation.* in Wyse D, Andrews R, Hoffman J (eds) The International Handbook of English, Language and Literacy Teaching, London: Routledge.

NAHT (2014) *Report of the NAHT Commission on Assessment.* Available at: www.naht.org.uk/assets/assessment-commission-report.pdf (Accessed: 26 February 2016).

OECD (2002) *Reading for Change, Performance and Engagement across Countries. Results from PISA 2000.* OECD Publishing. http://www.oecd.org/edu/school/

Pritchard, A. (2005) *Ways of Learning: Learning Theories and Learning Styles in the Classroom.* Routledge; 3 edition (22 Nov. 2013).

Rosenshine, B (2010) *Principles of Instruction.* International Academy of Education.

Santangelo, T., Olinghouse, N. (2009) *Effective writing instruction for students who have writing difficulties.* Focus on exceptional children.

Siraj, I., Taggart, B. with Melhuish, E., Sammonds, P., Sylsa, K. (2012) *Exploring Effective Pedagogy in Primary Schools: Evidence from Research.* Pearson.

Slavin, R.E. (1996) *Education for all.* Exton, PA: Swets & Zeitlinger.

Stipek, D. (2010) *Motivation to Learn.* Preparing educators to engage families (2nd edition) Thousand Oaks CA: Sage Publications.

Sherrington, T. (2015) *Principles of Effective Teaching.* Blog: @headguruteacher.

Tierney, R. J., Pearson, P. D. (1983) Toward a composing model of reading. Washington, D.C. Distributed by ERIC Clearinghouse.

Timperley, H., Wilson, A., Barrar, H., Fung, I. (2007) *Teacher professional learning and development: Best evidence synthesis iteration.* Wellington, New Zealand: Ministry of Education.

Timperley, H. (2008). *Teacher professional learning and development.* International Academy of Education, International Bureau of Education, UNESCO.

Wells, G. (1986) *The Meaning Makers: Children Learning Language and Using Language.*

Wilcox, A. (2013) *Descriptosaurus: Supporting Creative Writing for Ages 8-14.* Routledge; 2 edition (5 Mar. 2013).

Wolf, M. (2007) Proust and the Squid. Icon Books Ltd.

Younger, M., Warrington, M. with Gray, J., Ruddock, J., McLellan, R., Bearne, E., Kershner, R., Bricheno, P. (2005) *Raising boys' achievement: a study funded by the Department for Education and Skills* (University of Cambridge, Faculty of Education). DfES RR636.

Index